TIME TO MURDER
AND CREATE

Books by JOHN W. ALDRIDGE

literary criticism

AFTER THE LOST GENERATION
IN SEARCH OF HERESY
TIME TO MURDER AND CREATE

fiction

THE PARTY AT CRANTON

edited works

CRITIQUES AND ESSAYS ON MODERN FICTION
DISCOVERY #1
SELECTED STORIES BY P. G. WODEHOUSE

TIME TO MURDER
AND CREATE

The Contemporary Novel
in Crisis

by JOHN W. ALDRIDGE

DAVID McKAY COMPANY, INC. · NEW YORK

22179

Library of Congress Catalog Card Number: 66-17353

MANUFACTURED IN THE UNITED STATES OF AMERICA

VAN REES PRESS • NEW YORK

For
Leslie
and
all my sons

I *am* damned critical—for it's the only thing
to be, and all else is damned humbug.

—Henry James

Preface

UNLIKE my previous books of criticism, this one makes no attempt to develop a thesis or advance a cause, although it does describe a dilemma out of which a cause might be made. But I am not myself carrying the banner for it. There is nothing I especially want to prove, and I have no theory that the various essays are intended to support. This to me is an altogether happy freedom, for I have found that the book containing a thesis is in some danger of being ridden by it, or bludgeoned with it, and that the reader is seldom able to resist the temptation to treat its individual parts as illustrations or exhibits of the overall scheme rather than take them on their individual merits. One sometimes imagines that the parts of a thesis book are not really read at all, since there is so much interest in the argument they may be intended to develop, and it often happens that the author's best ideas are slighted or ignored because he has been guilty of having had, at some reckless moment, an Idea.

I would hope that the essays, and the ideas, in this book will escape that fate. No Idea, at least none that I am aware of, threatens to eclipse or replace them, and since almost everything I have included was written at a different time and for a different occasion, the danger seems remote. In fact, the great advantage of the collection of essays over the integrated book is that it allows the author freedom to serve his subject and his whims without restriction, to repeat himself as much as he likes, contradict himself as much as he dares, and generally be as capricious and provisional as he pleases. It will be noticed that I have exploited this advantage to the full, and quite deliberately. I have not wanted to feel obligated to "cover" any specific topic or field in a systematic way, or to do a "survey" of the literary situation and the chief writers who comprise it. I have not wanted to be forced by some militant scheme of selection to include discussion of one writer and omit discussion of some other, or, what is far worse, feel that I had to discuss a writer who did not interest me just because my scheme required me to do so.

Yet although the book contains no governing Idea or thesis, it can be said to have a recurring preoccupation, an interest that, while nowhere fully explored or even explicitly defined, does give many of the essays a certain thematic connection with one another. In the essays devoted to the relation of the novel to its two main contemporary audiences, I am also concerned with the ways in which the novel has failed to hold the attention of those audiences. And that has led me to a preoccupation with the state of the imagination at work in the novel at this time. Anyone familiar with my criticism will have recognized that I do not, for the most part, rate the products of this imagination very high. We have obviously had a good deal of novelistic activity in recent years, and the novel has attracted to itself a great many promising writers. But the performance of these writers has seemed on the whole disappointing, and my impression is that the fault has not been primarily one of talent, intelligence, or sophistication. We have, in fact, been living in a time of enormous intelligence and sophistication about everything connected with the life of ideas and the production of serious literature. But what the novelist knows does not necessarily become a viable factor of his imagination. He may know everything except how to imagine with an intensity and complexity equal to his sophistication—and that, it seems to me, is just the trouble, his and ours and the novel's.

For there is abundant evidence that the imagination of the contemporary novel, particularly in America, has remained locked in certain stereotyped modes of perceiving and recording reality that it has inherited from the modern classic literary past, but that, as stereotypes, have now ceased to relate meaningfully to the reality of which we are, or ought to be, most intensely aware. To be sure, when we encounter them in a novel we may recognize them as having something to do with our real experience. They represent, after all, what some of the important novels of the past have told us real experience was like at least in their time, and that, in the most influential cases, was not so very long ago. But the point is that we have too often and too eagerly accepted the version of reality supplied by these novels, and that has prevented us from arriving at our own version. We may have grown comfortable with the stereotypes and be unwilling to give them up. The American theater has obviously grown comfortable with them and shows no sign of being willing to give them up. The same is true, has always been true, of Hollywood, and it is even true to some extent of the European film industry, to which we normally look for a fresh and honest confrontation of contemporary truth. All have, like the novel, been subsisting for years on visions and fantasies of experience that have nothing to do with the way we actually think or live, but that represent merely increments of style, struck attitudes, ceremonial poses of anguish, passion, perversion, hysteria, and boredom that belong to a tradition of pioneering realism that is now dead and to a convention of feeling and action derived not from life but from other plays, films, and novels.

It is possible, of course, that we have now arrived at a stage of confusion where we believe that the stereotypes *are* reality, and it may be that in a certain deranged sense they are, for modern life imitates cliché in the service of stylishness, and one can never be sure if one is witnessing a "true" event or a skillfully fabricated imitation of one. But there must come a time when our honesty, or simply our sanity, requires us to recognize that the formulations of experience with which we have grown so familiar finally bear no more relation to the real than the mannequins in the dress shops along Fifth Avenue bear to real women.

Where the novel at least is concerned, that time would appear to have arrived, for one of our most characteristic present responses to the novel is a feeling of boredom and *déjà vu*, a tired realization that we have been here before and have seen it all happen again and again and again. It is not merely that we crave something original and exciting. We crave even more intensely something true, something that represents a vital engagement of experience as it is, and that wrenches us out of our old habits of perception just because it has been conceived outside the framework of those old habits by a mind courageous enough to perceive and imagine for itself.

It is in this sense that the line from Eliot's "Prufrock" seems appropriate as the title for this book. If the novel is to survive, it must begin now to murder its dependency upon the dead literary formulations of the past and create new formulations to express its understanding of the vital present.

For the novel lives through its connection with the life of its time, and it must continually renew that connection or risk becoming an antique form, a historical document rather than a shaper of history.

JOHN W. ALDRIDGE

Acknowledgments

MANY of these essays first appeared in the following publications, and are used here with their permission: the *New York Herald Tribune Book Week*, *The New York Times Book Review*, *Playboy*, and *Life*. "The Life of Gatsby" was written for *Twelve Original Essays on Great American Novels*, edited by Charles Shapiro, and is republished here by permission of Wayne State University Press. "P. G. Wodehouse: The Lesson of the Young Master" is the introduction to the Modern Library edition of *Selected Stories by P. G. Wodehouse* and appears here by permission of Random House.

The author also wishes to thank the following for permission to use quotations: Beacon Press for *No! in Thunder* by Leslie A. Fiedler, and Farrar, Straus and Giroux, Inc. for *Classics and Commercials* by Edmund Wilson.

In addition, I would like to express my gratitude to those editors who have been generous enough to grant me space to develop my ideas beyond the length normally allowed for the standard book review. I owe a special debt to Francis Brown, editor of the *New York Times Book Review*, for the pleasure and profit of a long relationship which has provided the occasion for so many of these pieces, and to Richard Kluger, editor of the *New York Herald Tribune Book Week,* for the arrangement whereby I have been able to contribute fairly regular essay-reviews of considerable length to a new publication of high standards and large circulation. This for a critic is a rare and life-giving freedom.

Finally, I want to thank Kennett and Eleanor Rawson of the David McKay Company for their many kindnesses and their great patience and loyalty, and Professor Warner G. Rice, Chairman of the English Department at the University of Michigan, for giving me an opportunity that has become a privilege and a pleasure.

Contents

TIME TO MURDER
AND CREATE

Notes on the Novel I

Alive or Dead

UNTIL fairly recently, speculations on the health of the
novel were a morbid and monotonous feature of the American literary life. In fact, ever since Ortega y Gasset pro-
nounced the novel dead back in the twenties, and T. S. Eliot
discovered that Flaubert and James had killed it, a good
many of our critics have shown more interest in the novel
dead than alive, and have devoted more energy to conduct-
ing post-mortems than to providing resuscitation. For a
number of years in the Sunday-book-supplement world the
novel was dying as regularly as tycoons and athletes, and
of a much more interesting variety of ailments. In the main,
of course, it was the critics of that world, the middlebrow,
trend-tracking kind, who carried on the discussion over the
past two or three decades, the concern for the novel as a
whole apparently having passed from Ortega and Eliot to
Lionel Trilling and Frank O'Connor to J. Donald Adams and
Orville Prescott with steadily dwindling intensity and authority.

1

By now we are all thoroughly acquainted with the reasons why the novel is or ought to be or was supposed long ago to be dead. Every graduate student of criticism knows them, or ought to know them, by heart, if only in a remote historical way, and we do not need to be reminded by our embarrassment whenever we hear them repeated that they have no place at all in our present thinking about literature. Still, it is instructive to recall, if only for historical purposes, that at one time they did have a place and that a great many people once took them very seriously. Perhaps they took most seriously—because it sounded so unimpeachably *scientific*—the reason put forth by Ortega in his classic, forty-year-old essay, "Notes on the Novel"; namely, that the novel is played out because as a form it contained only a certain number of possibilities for development, only a certain limited supply of materials, and these have been exhausted—or, more correctly, were already exhausted as far back as Dostoevski and Proust. To illustrate his point Ortega draws the familiar analogy to mining, as does Trilling in "Art and Fortune": the novelistic vein has been heavily worked in the past and now has nothing more to yield, except perhaps in the narrow and tributary veins where the ore is thin and of inferior quality and where only the writer of the rarest distinction might still hope to find a few precious crystals of significant art.

Another reason that used to be almost as frequently given is that the cultural circumstances to which the novel originally was a response—the breakdown of the feudal order and the rise of a socially ambitious middle class—ceased many centuries ago to be dramatically operative; hence, most of the great traditional subjects for the novel, such as the conflict between money and morals, value and virtue, status and conscience, are no longer so simply and readily

2

available as they once were. Still another reason—and one that continues to have a certain currency—is that the novel has for years been on the losing end of a competition with the social sciences, which have the advantage over it of a statistical understanding of our cultural realities, and with the mass entertainment arts, which have been able to exploit to great effect their more virile understanding of our cultural fantasies. According to this view, the novel cannot hope to survive, let alone prevail, in an intellectual climate characterized, on the one hand, by the worship of empirical facts over intuitive insights and, on the other, by a lust for raw sensation as opposed to artistically comprehended emotion.

Finally, it has often been asserted, as a rule with a terrible kind of vindictive smugness, that there is nothing very much wrong with the novel that a few genuinely talented and *dedicated* novelists could not speedily cure, that when we talk about the decline or death of the novel, we are actually talking about the scarcity of talents capable of putting it to distinguished use. Ortega's reply to this is marvelously apt at the same time that it is an insult to what has become our almost religious view of the writer's independence of social forces. He says that the predicament of talent in the modern age is like the predicament of the strongest of woodsmen in the Sahara Desert. What good, he asks, are bulging muscles and a sharp axe without trees to cut? "Talent is but a subjective disposition that is brought to bear upon a certain material. The material is independent of individual gifts; and when it is lacking, genius and skill are of no avail."

As I have said, these arguments—except for Ortega's—have, for the most part, been put forward over the years by our more journalistic and middlebrow critics, and it has been an educational experience to see how much loquacity they

3

have been able to generate on an occasion clearly calling for silence and tears. In fact, it looked for a time as though, if the novel were not actually dying under its own power, it was certain very soon to be talked to death. It now appears, however, that the situation has begun in some mysterious way to reverse itself, and that it is not so much the novel as the talk about it that is dying. The middlebrow post-mortems have dwindled in number to the point where we can sometimes go for months without hearing any more baleful news of the novel than that it continues, however feebly and un-interestingly, to get written. A silence, which may or may not be tearful, seems to be settling upon this whole, formerly vociferous quarter of our hypochondria—quite as if even the neurotic claims of literary illness could not finally survive the dreariness of their own clichés.

In a sense, of course, this is exactly what has occurred. The claims have not been able to survive our recognition of their dreariness as clichés, our understanding that, as clichés, they have long ago ceased to have very much to do with reality. We have grown much too sophisticated in our thinking about literature to be willing to accept the idea that any one of its forms can so simply die, and it seems perfectly plausible that our literature has itself grown much too sophisticated to let a thing like that happen. Even though we may be convinced that such a form as the English poetic drama did in fact die, we can also tell ourselves that that sad event is just one more instance of the incomparable bungling of history, another result of our not having been born in time to point out the mistake. But when it comes to the novel, over which we at least like to think we exercise some monitory influence, we are not disposed to consider the same possibility. It is not simply because, as Trilling once said, the novel did so much for us in our youth, although it quite obviously did. The novel is, after all, the one form for which we have traditionally felt an almost filial devotion, the one form to which we have traditionally been able to turn with the assurance that it would always be there when we needed it. But what is more to the point is that we have grown suspicious now of the deterministic or programmatic Spenglerism that has made the dying of forms as indispensable a part of literary discussion as the dying of whole cultures is of historical discussion, but which, as another kind of cliché, seems to have equally little to do with reality. Ortega's approach to the novelistic problem is offensive to us for most of the same reasons that made the Marxist criticism of the thirties offensive—because it subordinates the creative event to historical law and treats the phenomenon of talent as if it were a phenomenon of social biology, the merest twitch in the slow orgasm of social process. We are by no means so sure as Ortega was, in fact we are not sure at all, that the materials for the novel are simply there or not there in the social fabric at any given historical moment. It is possible that they may be more clearly or more vigorously there at some moments than they are at others—in the eighteenth century, for example, or the early twentieth —but their presence or absence does not necessarily spell life or death for the novel. At moments when they are not there, or less apparently there, the novel may simply have to establish a different relation to the age and shift to a level of operation at which it can make use of materials that are only subtly and obliquely manifested. It must become at those moments a more delicate and sensitive instrument than it needed to be in times of greater cultural robustness, and it may even be obliged to make up out of its own artistic resources, and those of the minds behind it, the materials that are not to be found in the age. That, at any rate, is what

5

the novel, as produced by certain resourceful minds, appears to be trying to do at the present time. In short, we insist now on the right of the novel and the right of novelistic talent to be flexible, independent, capricious, and surprising; and we are perfectly willing to assume that a good woodsman can find trees to cut even in the Sahara Desert, and even if he has to grow them himself.

Finally, the whole notion of decline in the genre of the novel seems to be called into question by the continued appearance of quite healthy specimens of the genre. The novel may be dying, but novels and good novels continue to appear, and it is attracting to it a remarkably large number of talented people whose interest in it can scarcely be confined to a desire to weep at the bedside. This is perhaps to say that the evidence of our senses has forced us to discard the habit of conceiving of the novel in terms of any such pretentious abstraction as *The Novel*, whether viewed as a corpus or as a corpse. For we are aware now, if we are aware at all, of novels rather than of the novel, and we are aware of them in their particularity as well as in their diversity, as individual examples of the genre and not as the whole genre itself.

But what we are aware of and what the professional pall-bearers of the book supplements are aware of are obviously two different things. If they, with their organismal view of the novel, are growing silent on the subject of its imminent death, the reason must be either that they no longer believe it is dying or that they have simply ceased to be able to cope with the question. I would incline toward the second possibility, and I would do so because I suspect that they recognize, however unconsciously, that the question has shifted to a plane of discourse on which they cannot engage it and, therefore, cannot remain interested in it. For even if up to now they have not, like the rest of us, thought habitually in terms of novels, they must have become aware that the emphasis has changed in some important way, and that their comfortable, old-fashioned sense of the novel as an organic and moribund entity, as corpus or as corpse, does not have quite the basis in fact it once seemed to have.

The present diversity and diffuseness of the American literary life would, of course, make such a sense extremely difficult to support. In order to conceive of the novel as a dying or, for that matter, as a living organism, one has first to be able to retain an image of it as a discrete and autonomous totality, as a whole that is both something more than and something besides the sum of its particular parts. And in order to retain such an image, one has to feel on close and familiar terms with the novel and be able at least to imagine that one has as intimate a knowledge of its nature and constitution as one would have of an old friend. It is not, after all, novels that until recently were supposed to be dying, but *The Novel*, a kind of fraternal anthropomorphic abstraction with a body that presumably could sicken, expire, and be tenderly prepared for burial. But this is just the image that the book-supplement critic is no longer finding it possible to retain. Even if he persists in thinking of the novel as *The Novel*, he cannot help but be conscious that the old simplicity and cohesiveness have broken down, and that what he is actually confronted with today is not *The Novel* at all but novels, an apparently mass-produced, undifferentiated swarm of them, the majority of which are as alien to him as if they had dropped into his life from outer space.

This would seem to suggest—and I mean it to suggest—that the middlebrow critic, along with the middlebrow literary world as a whole, has suffered a profound derangement of relationship with the novel, a derangement that is typified

7

by the loss of his organismal view of it and by his seeming disinclination to talk any further about its dying. The factor chiefly responsible for this derangement is the very complex and far-reaching shift of cultural alliances, which has gradually robbed the middlebrow literary world of its former proprietorship over the novel and, therefore, of the confident feelings of intimacy that once found expression in the rather cozy idea of *The Novel*.

The Novel as News

The shift I speak of is perhaps best illustrated by the fact that thirty or forty years ago the official literary opinion in this country was fairly solidly middlebrow opinion; the official serious novel was primarily a middlebrow novel. Today the official opinion is highbrow opinion, and the serious novel, if not produced quite entirely by highbrows, appears at least to be sponsored and supported by them. Middlebrow literary opinion today is distinguished only by its abdication of critical standards and its evident inability to cope even with the flood of unserious novels that are tailored specifically to its needs, but among which it was formerly able to exercise at least a limited power of discrimination. When confronted with the serious novel, the old *Novel* now decapitalized but thoroughly recapitated, it is apparently either struck dumb or able only to choke out its feelings of frustration in the cantankerous archaisms of J. Donald Adams and Orville Prescott—both of whom stopped thinking at about the time the serious novel ceased to be middlebrow. That is, in fact, one of the several paradoxes that complicate our view of the literary life at the present time. Middlebrow literary opinion has grown increasingly ineffectual or merely

8

silly, increasingly dissociated from its former concern with *The Novel,* living or dead, while in the highbrow world there has never before been such an abundance and variety of concern, not, to be sure, with *The Novel,* but with novels and novelists. In the established literary quarterlies and the less widely circulated critical journals, the classic modern novelists are being subjected to a scrutiny almost terrifying in its tone of triumphant possessiveness, and even such serious younger writers as Saul Bellow, Bernard Malamud, and J. D. Salinger, whose careers are still, for all their prominence, very much in the developmental stage, have already had special issues of some of the smaller of these magazines devoted entirely to their work.

The principal reason for this changed state of affairs is of course not simply that middlebrow literary opinion has lost touch with the serious novel. That loss is only an effect of the more important circumstance that the serious novel is no longer the vehicle of middlebrow ideas and middlebrow experience, as it pretty largely was back in the days of Dreiser and Anderson, Lewis, Fitzgerald, and Hemingway. These writers have now nearly all been converted, by a process of academic appropriation following after deep analysis, into highbrow property, while currently active writers like Bellow and some of the others have never belonged to or written for the middlebrow world, but have from the beginning worked from assumptions about the nature of modern experience and modern fiction at least paralleling those of the highbrow world. The result is that, in sharp contrast to their predecessors and in a manner seemingly unique in our literature, these writers have been absorbed directly into the highbrow critical canon without ever having had to fight the battle for general readership and acceptance in the middlebrow world. With the exception of

9

Faulkner, they are the first writers in our recent history, certainly the first novelists, to have become critically established in their lifetime without first having been more or less widely read, and one can only suppose that this has occurred not only because of highbrow interest in their work, but also because there is no longer a ground on which the battle for middlebrow acceptance can be fought. We are admirably equipped in the apparatus of expert judgment and accommodation, but we have almost no apparatus at all for the creation of a climate of general or unprofessional receptiveness to the serious work—which is to say that we have no middlebrow criticism of seriousness.

But whatever the reason, the process by which so many of the better younger writers have been transported from obscurity to prominence while at the same time bypassing the traditional apprenticeship period in the middlebrow world is now part of the accepted routine of our literary life. The middlebrows have, consequently, been left with no established novelist of genuine high quality, and except possibly for James Gould Cozzens, John O'Hara, and the post-Nobel Hemingway, no established novelist who even approaches high quality. They furthermore have scarcely anyone at all in the younger group who is articulating emotions and experiences that are familiar and attractive to them.

This was emphatically not the case during the great period of middlebrow ownership of the novel. The established novelists of that time, although they may personally have been lowbrows or even, in one or two instances, highbrows, were not only working in the middlebrow literary world but giving voice to concerns that had a clear and concrete basis in middlebrow and middle-class life. They were able to do so because they as well as the bulk of their readership were themselves primarily middle class and provincial in background, and were therefore united by a bond of common assumption and shared experience. This made possible for a relatively short time in America what we now enviously associate with Victorian England and the France of Balzac: a novel centered in the value system of the dominant social class and able, as a consequence, to dramatize materials and themes of particular relevance to that class. While it is now obvious that the traditional themes that energized the novel in its infancy have ceased to be dramatically operative in our society, it is less obvious but no less significant that most of the themes that energized the novel in the immediate past are also no longer available to it—at least not in the condition that once gave them such massive importance in the imaginative lives of a large number of people.

Among the most important of these themes, indeed *the* most important if considered in terms of its centrality in the whole range of American imaginative experience, was the theme of first confrontation of the modern world and first initiation into the new circumstances of modern life. Undoubtedly, the powerful appeal this theme has exerted upon the American mind is connected in some intimate way with the fact that it is an analogue of the original pioneer confrontation of the New World, with its abundant suggestiveness in the vast literature related, either overtly or implicitly, to the pursuit of the American Dream. But in the many works that now form the classic body of modern American fiction, it appears as a very specific and recurrent preoccupation. Although differing greatly from one another in nearly every other respect, such novels and approximate novels as *Winesburg, Ohio, Sister Carrie, Babbitt, Manhattan Transfer, Of Time and the River, Studs Lonigan, The Sun Also Rises, This Side of Paradise,* and *The Great Gatsby* are alike in the one respect that at some point in each of them either the characters or the contemporary reader, or in most cases both, came into relationship with experience of a kind unknown to them before and markedly different from the provincial experience of their origins.

These books are all in this sense attempts to answer, either directly or indirectly, the familiar and obsessive provincial question that the European novel had begun to answer a hundred years before: what is *real* life like; what is the nature of experience in the world outside the neighborhood, town, or region? And the fact cannot fail to seem remarkable to us at the present time that this was a question for which virtually a whole American middle-class provincial culture was seeking an answer, and that the interest of that culture in the novel was largely sustained by the promise the novel held out of supplying it.

It is no accident that Scott Fitzgerald was able to refer, however jokingly, to *The Sun Also Rises* as "a Romance and a Guide Book," and to his own *This Side of Paradise* as "a Romance and a Reading List." Beneath the lightness of tone there is a perfectly serious point. Although it is hard for us to conceive today of any really literate person's turning to a novel for either romance or information, whether about books or the better bars of Paris and Pamplona, these are exactly the elements that the general reader of their time found *initially* most fascinating in these two novels. They provided him with a portrait of life at its most interesting and adventurous remove from provincial existence, yet plausible enough to be accepted by the provincial imagination, and a set of facts supposedly essential to anyone desiring entry into that life. What was important was that the reader *did* desire entry into that life. It was symbolic to him of all that his own life was not, and he wished to be informed about how he should behave if he should ever succeed in gaining entry. Hence, Hemingway's preoccupation with the rules of social form, with the etiquette of correct conduct in situations of physical and psychic test, and Fitzgerald's passion to learn the rules, to become an acceptable member of the club, made a powerful appeal to the reader's imagination as well as to his native interest in process and knowhow. It was very like the appeal made by the archetypal older brother or favorite uncle who returns to his home town after long absence to charm his relatives with tales of curious customs in far-off, exotic lands. Hemingway's role was always that of the older brother or uncle, the man to whom everything imaginable had happened; Fitzgerald's was always that of the wide-eyed younger brother or nephew, the boy to whom nothing worth imagining had ever happened. And the reader could identify equally well with both. He could identify not only because he could sense that both were themselves as enchanted and as fundamentally innocent as he, but also because they were telling him something he did not know and wished to know, and telling it in the context of moral assumptions and emotional responses that were very much like his own. The novel in their hands was, therefore, an educative form, an extension and extender of his grasp of reality, a rulebook for the conduct of the desirable life that lay beyond the limits of the undesirable life in which he felt enclosed. And it is this educative element that the novel has lost in our time and, in so doing, has lost the middle class, or what has become, by a shift from class to cultural status, from sociology to phrenology, the middlebrow.

We are all familiar with the standard reasons given for the change that has taken place in American society and, by extension, in the American novel, since Hemingway and Fitzgerald began to write. Our present population is no longer typified by a common provincial heritage or a regional and small-town mentality, but has become increasingly heterogeneous and diffuse, increasingly suburban in character and cosmopolitan in outlook. Middle-class culture has given way not merely to middlebrow but to mass culture, and while the former had some of the cohesiveness of a differentiated social institution, the latter is, as its name suggests, merely a social abstraction characterized by un-differentiated numbers. There is also some significance in the fact that it is no longer middle-class culture but minority culture that is providing the primary subject matter of the contemporary serious novel. Middle-class culture appears to have receded as a potential source of novelistic material in time with its recession as the characterizing culture of our society, while the experience of the Jew and the Negro has steadily gained in prominence and relevance, not simply as social fact but as an experience symbolic of the universal modern sense of isolation and estrangement.

This change is, of course, in large part the result of a change in the racial and ethnic character of our writers themselves. The older writers of predominately gentile ex-traction have been succeeded by a new generation composed of a large number of Jewish and Negro writers. It would appear, in fact, that throughout our literature at the present time the authority that once belonged to the Midwestern and Anglo-Saxon imagination has passed to the urban and minority intelligence, the intelligence, that is, that is just coming into the kind of self-conscious critical relationship with American society that the Anglo-Saxon imagination has exhausted and left behind. But however invigorating this de-velopment may be for our literature as a whole—and every-thing indicates that it has been immensely invigorating—it may also have served to increase still further the distance

14

now separating the novel from the general reading public. For where Hemingway and Fitzgerald were writing out of, at the same time that they were addressing, a culture racially and ethnically similar to themselves, the new minority writers are making use of a cultural experience that, while intensely real to them, is still strange and unreal to most of the people who might read their books. And regardless of how skillful these writers may be in dramatizing the full symbolic implications of that experience, there is always a point beyond which the most sympathetic non-Jewish and non-Negro reader cannot go, where the necessary suspension of disbelief can no longer be willed, and he is forced to say, "That is not and cannot be myself."

Thus, there would appear to be very little possibility today for the novel to achieve the kind of large, synthesizing sense of the whole culture that helped to give some of the older novels their outstanding range of emotional reference and public appeal. Certainly, it is no longer possible to portray experience in the novel with the old conviction that it represents the experience of a great many people besides oneself. The notion of a common humanity to which one's personal experience could automatically be assumed to have meaning, has been lost in the notion of a mass, statistical humanity to which the very idea of personal experience seems irrelevant, or a minority culture to which the relevance of the personal experience seems almost exclusively confined.

Yet over and above these sociological considerations there is the essential fact that we no longer need the novel to initiate us into the realities of the modern world. It is not merely that we have grown much too sophisticated to be willing to settle for the sort of information that the older novel provided, although there is no doubt that we have. It is also that the novel has ceased to *be* the primary source of our information about the varieties of experience that lie beyond the limits of our personal lives, and we simply cannot bring to it quite the old expectations, quite the old willingness to give ourselves up to the image of experience that it sets before us. It may be that we have lost faith in both the novel and experience, that something has gone wrong with our ability to respond not only to the imagined portrait of life but to the real possibilities of the lived life. But if it has, the fault lies as much with experience and our present relation to it as it does with the novel.

The provincial expects always to be transformed by contact with the world beyond the provinces. He may even expect to be saved by it, as though something terribly religious were bound to happen to him if only he could get out of town and on the road to his personal Damascus. Most of the characters in the older American novels believed this implicitly: Anderson's George Willard, Hemingway's Nick Adams, Fitzgerald's Amory Blaine and Nick Carraway, Wolfe's Eugene Gant, Dos Passos' Martin Howe, Farrell's Studs Lonigan were all seekers after the cosmic "it" to be found in the experience of the modern world. They were all disciples of what has come to be called the cult or mystique of experience, that innocent faith in the spiritual conversion principle of merely additive living, which has provided the American novel with so much of its basic as well as extraneous materials.

But we have come to know better—even if our knowledge is not shared by writers like Jack Kerouac who continue to practice an extinct provincialism and to exult depressingly in experience that literature and the rest of us have long since had. We are all of us very much *in* the modern world at the present time, and we cannot remember a time when we were not very much, even too much, in it. It is in fact the usual thing with us to be educated by all the secondary sources of experience to which we now have such abundant access, long before we have a chance to be educated by primary experience. We are vicariously informed about experience to the point where we do not need to *have* experience, and if we do have it, we very often feel it to be less compelling than the secondhand version of it that we already possess. This is undoubtedly the reason why the more popular entertainment media such as television and the motion pictures—media that for years have virtually done our living for us—are finding it necessary to make use of steadily more bizarre and sensational materials in their effort to maintain their hold on the public attention. Since the public knows so very much as it is and is so heavily surfeited with what it knows, it requires exposure to stronger and stronger doses of "reality" in order to be able to respond at all. And although lacking the cynicism of the more frankly commercial media, the novel has been propelled in the same direction. Because it is no longer able to discharge its older educative and generalizing function, it has been forced to concern itself with the more marginal and unusual realities —sometimes with precisely those depicted on the movie and television screens—or with kinds of experience that may have great personal meaning and importance to the author but little or none to the reader, particularly the general or middlebrow reader who is not equipped to find his satisfaction solely in the artistry with which the experience is portrayed. We cannot therefore discount the possibility that Ortega may, after all, have been partly right, and that at least one of the elements that formerly provided the novel with its basis of social fact and social relevance has disappeared, leaving the middlebrow reader with feelings of acute estrangement and causing the novel to feed increas-

17

ingly upon its own generic properties, its own technical resources as an art form, in a state of similar estrangement from cultural relationship.

The Middlebrow Reader Estranged

The middlebrow reader's estrangement from the contemporary serious novel would appear to involve a paradox of rather bewildering complexity. If we take it for granted that the serious novel does not interest him—and publishers' sales figures seem to indicate that it emphatically does not—the first explanation that comes to mind is that he does not find it relevant to his life. Yet in saying this one cannot allay the intuitive suspicion that his life is itself irrelevant to life, at least to most of those forms and manifestations of it that the novelist can get at and put to creative use. The middlebrow seems to have very little sense of a distinctive experience or a distinctive past, and such sense as he does have seems to be intermittent, fragmentary, and elusive. As I have already indicated, he lacks the advantage of involvement in some of the large cultural movements and historical changes that gave the members of the older middle class their feelings of having shared in a collective cultural past. He has had no part, for example, in the great psychological as well as physical migration from the provinces to the city; he was not on hand at the opening of the last frontier of the modern consciousness and the modern world. Hence, he cannot know the powerful response of instantaneous recognition and identification felt by those readers who discovered in some of the novels of their time an imaginative rendering of things they remembered having lived or having wished they might live. He is not, to be sure, very likely to be exposed today to novels having to do with such things, or with things of equivalent relevance to his own time and his own experience. The novelists of his time also lack the advantage of sharing in a collective cultural experience, and so tend to devote themselves to expressing experience about which they can say only that it has meaning in and relevance to their own lives. It is therefore not surprising that the middlebrow reader, having little or no sense of personal experience, should be able to make little or no sense of the experience of novelists who have a sense only of their personal experience.

It is a critical commonplace that the appeal of any novel should not depend even primarily upon its ability to deal with subject matter familiar to the reader. We have been told again and again that it is the novelist's continual responsibility to make meaningful whatever subject he may choose to write about, to treat it in such a way that it will have meaning to readers who may have no personal knowledge of the material with which he is directly concerned. Yet some basis for this generalizing function of the novel must be present in both the novelist and the reader, and when it is missing, as it seems to be today, the reader is simply unable, or finds the task too arduous, to make the initial identification he has to make if he is to enter into relationship with the novel at all.

The difficulty the middlebrow reader seems to face in engaging the serious novel at the present time stems apparently from his inability to find such a basis, his feeling that the depicted life of the novel is hermetic and fails to get out of the novel and into his own life. The novel in question may be about Jewish life in Chicago or Brooklyn, homosexual life in Manhattan or Paris, or adolescent life in one of the now dated neo-Gothic reconstructions of the South

—and if the novel is typical, it is almost certain to be about one of these things. Nevertheless, the reader ought ideally to be able to translate it into the terms of his own experience —or the novelist, even more ideally, ought to be able to do the translation for him. But since the reader has so little sense of his own experience and the novelist so little sense of any except his own, it is likely to remain simply a novel about Jewish, homosexual, or Southern life—a life foreign to the reader, even incomprehensible to him, if he does not happen to be a Jew, a homosexual, or a Southerner.

The novel may, on the other hand, be about something the reader knows or is supposed to know. It may be about suburbia, mass culture, or the advertising business, although, interestingly enough, our current serious novels are almost never about such things. It may depict a life that is virtually an exact copy of the life he leads every day. But by confronting him with that life, the novel is bound to appear to him hateful and depressing, or again simply unreal and foreign, not only because he has probably never before seen his life except in hurried glimpses through the haze of his semiconsciousness, but also because the novelist's determination to get at the truth would force him to portray realities that the reader could not accept without finding his life intolerable. Certainly, he does not want to be reminded that he is living a life that is not worth living, and the fact that in order to live it he has had to close his mind to it does not increase his ability or his desire to identify with it when he sees it depicted in a novel. Hence, it would seem that unless the novel were in other respects sufficiently unique, surprising, or salacious to amuse or titillate him, he would have little reason to read it and much reason not to read it.

Besides, the novel would very probably be written in a manner that would seem to him artificial, oblique, or deriva-

tive of cultural premises not his own, and overlaid with
nuances and discriminations that would strike him as precious, niggling, or fussy. The novelist, in short, would undoubtedly be presenting his material from the point of
view of one of the positions of alienation and disaffection
that have become habitual with novelists in our day, and
he would be trying to treat his material with a sublety and
complexity in keeping with standards set by the best literature. But the middlebrow reader, lacking such a point of
view as well as the literary knowledge required for an intelligent response to it, could hardly be expected to sympathize.
In fact, it is the presence in a novel of these very qualities
of artistic seriousness that would be most likely to antagonize him, for to the extent that he senses, but does not wish
to acknowledge, his own alienation, he is bound to mistrust
or despise the fictional portrait of alienation, particularly
when it seems in its language and form to pose an intellectual
problem that he is unable to solve. Such a problem would be
one more reason for him to find the serious novel irrelevant,
although his feeling that it is irrelevant would, of course,
be only a cover for his secret recognition of its really terrifying relevance to his own predicament.

Yet this is by no means to suggest that what the middlebrow actually wants from fiction is irrelevance of another
kind, the kind that the ordinary run of escape fiction could
be counted on to give him. The thing that makes him a middlebrow requires him to pretend to himself that he is observ-
ing the pieties of middlebrow status, that he is continuously
and consciously exercising his taste in ways that have been
approved by the cultural establishment to which he feels
affiliated. Hence, what he wants from fiction is a portrait
of experience that seems real and familiar to him, but that is
not so real and familiar as to make him uncomfortable or

21

force him to examine his life. He also wants a style of presentation that looks serious and "literary" at the same time that it too is familiar and conventional enough not to violate his preconceptions about the way good literature should sound or assault his sensibilities with the ugliness of the really new. Then, of course, along with all this, he wants the various extraliterary dividends that he could get from trash if he dared to read it. He wants sex and sensation and violence and outrage, and he wants them on the only terms on which he can be sure of a clear and powerful response, in the form of massive copulations, giant orgasms, hideous rapes, and cinemascopic murders and pillages—the bloodcurdling extremity of which is in perfect proportion to the emotional impoverishment of his life. He wants them on these terms, that is, if he can persuade himself, at whatever cost to the truth, that they are terms of serious literature.

At the moment there are not many good writers around who would be able to assist the middlebrow in this kind of self-deception. There are, to be sure, a number who could provide him with the titillation he craves, but too often the titillation would carry with it some reminder of the real world that he would find distasteful. Because of his rather gingerly orientation toward himself and toward reality, the middlebrow requires a fiction combining some of the pretensions of serious literature with some of the escapist and sensational qualities of trash; a fiction, in other words, that will feed his intellectual vanity, coddle his complacency, and enable him at the same time to drain off his more virulent frustrations—all in a context of lifelike and literature-like unreality. Certainly, there is no one writer who satisfies all these requirements, not even Faulkner, who satisfies only most of them. But it is possible to think of two who in very different ways and to very different degrees satisfy at least some of them.

John O'Hara, of course, comes immediately to mind because the large sales of his books—to say nothing of the kind of critics who praise them—are convincing proof of his overwhelming middlebrow appeal. William Styron seems at first glance to be a much less obvious possibility because he has some reputation for seriousness and is so much better a writer than O'Hara that he threatens at every moment to be mistaken for a highbrow and to disappear into the relatively readerless obscurity of highbrow status. Yet whatever their differences of talent and artistic intent, O'Hara and Styron are alike in the cne respect that both combine serious literary pretensions with an essentially middlebrow view of life. Each in his way embodies the middlebrow notion of the important novelist.

[1964]

The Pious Pornography of
John O'Hara

TO put the matter in the simplest possible terms, the middlebrows like O'Hara because his books remind them of the life they imagine themselves to be leading. Hence, he is a perfect antidote to those other writers who keep reminding them either of the life they actually *are* leading, or of a life they can imagine nobody leading. The middlebrows like Styron because his books remind them not of life but of the classic modern literature they think they are supposed to admire. Hence, he is one younger writer from whom it is possible to get the comforting impression that nothing has really changed in the novel since the golden age of middlebrow proprietorship over it.

But the matter is, of course, nowhere near that simple. O'Hara creates a familiar, seemingly respectable world—or let us say that he creates an initial illusion or facsimile of one, making use of the various social forms normally associated with respectability—that is both totally unlike the world the middlebrows live in and exactly like the world they want to see themselves as living in. The unlikeness puts a safe distance between themselves and his world, freeing them of all moral responsibility for it, at the same time that the likeness enables them to identify vicariously with it, in a state of guiltless, voyeuristic fantasy.

On the surface O'Hara's favorite locale, Gibbsville, Pennsylvania, is an American Dream community straight out of Nostalgia by way of *The Saturday Evening Post*. It is everybody's *Our Town* raised to a higher income bracket and gone sophisticated, a good, solid, red-blooded, church-going sort of place where the people seem both prosperous and nice, and the best families have been best friends of the best families for generations. There appear to be no Jews, Negroes, or homosexuals in Gibbsville, but if there are any, they would certainly be tolerated, although just as certainly not admitted to the clubs or invited to the parties. Gibbsville is, in fact, just about the only fictional community in current American literature where the middlebrow reader can escape the prevailing obsession with minority groups and perverts, and be sure that, if deviations from right conduct do occur, they will at least occur among the right sort of people. That, at any rate, is the assurance that O'Hara seems to provide. That is the sop he tosses to middlebrow snobbery and moral hypocrisy, and, as it turns out, it is absolutely vital to the success of his appeal to the middlebrow mind.

For in almost every O'Hara novel there comes a moment when the reader's conscience has to be palliated if his confidence is to be held, a moment when life in Gibbsville is revealed to be a good deal more than it appears to be on the surface. Beneath the veneer of respectability and niceness, behind the closed bedroom doors of the mansions, in the expensive convertibles parked out in back of the country club, all sorts of interesting and incredible things suddenly seem to be going on—among the right people, of course—and all of them, not so very incredibly, have to do with sex. To put the matter with typical O'Haraish directness, whatever else his characters may piously appear to be doing with their time, what they are actually doing is sleeping or trying to sleep with everybody else's wife or daughter or sister or mistress or mother. The pursuit of the Good Life, when reduced, as O'Hara persistently reduces it, to its symbiotic essence, becomes the pursuit of the Good Lay. *Our Town* is magically transformed—one might almost say, overnight—into the Kinsey Report; *The Saturday Evening Post* image fades into something with green covers out of Olympia Press; and bed emerges at last as the natural social habitat of the solid citizens of Gibbsville, a kind of fornicatory home-away-from-home where everybody sooner or later gets acquainted and settles down to the enjoyment of real togetherness.

There are even occasions when John O'Hara seems to dissolve into a pornographic Krafft-Ebing, and his fiction into a clinical recital of all the possible ways of having sex for those who feel—as even the stanchest Gibbsvilleans ultimately must—that, sexually speaking, they have already had everything. On such occasions we leave behind the world of mere work-a-day adultery and become spectators at a sort of novelistic stag-party film in which the full range of deviational activity is explored by performers as aloof and businesslike as the people who pose for French *feelthy* postcards. Lesbians make passes at little girls and soul-kiss married women. Little girls seduce older men, and older men seduce little girls. Exhibitionistic town boys seduce older girls in the backs of trucks, and older girls seduce each other in college dorms.

It all turns out to be as twisted and corrupt as the gamiest of the serious novels that the middlebrows find too ugly and distasteful to read. But there is one very important difference. Where in many of these novels the corruption exists in a context of seemingly equal distortion, in a world which the middlebrows find both forbidding and strange, in O'Hara's novels the corruption has had its sting removed through being presented within the familiar and sanctifying context of old-fashioned middle-class moral appearances. It is made acceptable not only because the right people indulge in it but because the moral machinery that conventionally condemns it is built into the setting in which it occurs. That setting is Gibbsville, and what is Gibbsville if not an idealization of our collective imaginary memory of what appears on the surface to be the perfect American town, the kind of town we like to think we have all lived in or at the very least come from? But as an idealization Gibbsville is inevitably unreal, although it is of course deeply familiar as an imaginary construct. It is removed from the reader in time by at least thirty years, and it exists out of time in a dimension of myth and nostalgia—the same dimension in which we sentimentally place *Our Town* and *The Saturday Evening Post.*

By a very human incongruity the dirty book with the green covers also occupies that dimension in our minds: sentimentality and pornography are, in psychological terms, bedfellows. Hence, O'Hara's treatment of sex, which is nothing more than bad pornography smuggled in under the thin, plain wrapper of social documentation, is finally just as unreal as his Gibbsville. It is unreal first because it is coldbloodedly enacted without love or passion by people who seem just as wooden and lifeless as the characters in pure pornography, and second because it is literary sex, book sex, having virtually nothing to do with, and therefore casting no revelatory light upon, the actual practice of sex in the living society about which O'Hara is ostensibly writing. It is merely such stuff as wet dreams are made on, sex used ritualistically and mechanically as a substitute in life for an earned emotional relationship, and in literature for an earned dramatic significance, the kind of significance that the serious novelist takes pains to find outside as well as between the sweaty sheets of his created world.

But literature's loss is, in O'Hara's case, the middlebrow reader's gain. Because of the lifelike unreality of O'Hara's setting and the impersonal nature of his pornography, the reader senses that none of it finally relates to him or engages him on the moral level. Yet he also senses that it is familiar enough and close enough to his erotic and sentimental dream of life to enable him to derive vicarious satisfaction from it. He is therefore absolved of all responsibility to judge or condemn it, and freed to lie back and enjoy the show with a clean conscience and a dirty mind. He has, in fact, been allowed to have it both ways, which is the prime requirement the middlebrows make of a novel: he has had his cheesecake and *not* eaten it too. *The Saturday Evening Post* image—the pretensions to respectability that he saw in Gibbsville and that lulled him into an it-can't-happen-here state of mind—has cancelled out the distaste he might otherwise have felt obliged to have for the pornography. The pornography has at the same time provided him with the titillation he craved; while O'Hara's seeming earnestness and detachment, above all his apparently serious commitment to the old-fashioned belief that whatever is sexy or obscene must be art ("Don't say, 'urinate,'" cried the lusty old slicer-of-life "Say, *'piss!'*") have given the reader the excuse he needs for succumbing to the capital middlebrow self-delusion, the delusion that he is reading literature while enjoying all the kicks of trash.*

[1964]

* Now that there has emerged a whole subgenre of fiction combining sex and obscenity with camouflaging pretensions to literary seriousness, it is possible for the middlebrow reader to succumb to this delusion almost constantly, and without having to undergo the stress of reading O'Hara at all.

William Styron and the Derivative Imagination

THE case with William Styron is both very similar and very different. Styron is, first of all, obviously no O'Hara. For one thing, he is an infinitely better, infinitely more intelligent writer, and for another, his place on the sliding scale of literary charlatanism is nowhere near so secure. Styron apparently writes the way he does because he honestly believes that is the way serious literature sounds—and he is right: it *does* or, at any rate, it did. His charlatanism—if it can be called that—is of the unconscious and therefore wholeheartedly sincere kind. O'Hara, on the other hand, tries to pass off as serious literature what he must know to be trash, presumably because, first, he can no longer write anything else, and, second, because he has found out by now that his particular audience is incapable of telling the difference anyway. O'Hara is an example of the once talented novelist who has sold out his original power to write well for middle-brow success. Styron is an example—and a very rare one indeed in the present younger generation—of the still talented novelist who has achieved a certain measure of middlebrow success without having to sell out at all. He is what the middlebrows want just as he is—or, to be exact, he was until the appearance of *Set This House on Fire* raised new questions concerning his status in the middlebrow club.

But that again is a simplification. Styron is better than this, and deserves better than this. Let us say that he is a victim of his age in that he happened to form himself on standards of literary seriousness that have unfortunately become too widely known and too thoroughly conventionalized to be taken very seriously any more. He formed himself, that is, on the standards set by his eminent predecessors, and now he is condemned to writing like them, to achieving his effects in the way they achieved theirs, while today seriousness can ultimately be measured only in the degree to which a writer refines upon his predecessors or goes them one better, with another kind of power and a different degree and quality of emphasis.

Yet as I suggested earlier, it is precisely this lack of primary seriousness in Styron that accounts most for such popularity as he has so far enjoyed with the middlebrow reading public. His work sounds not only to him but to them like the serious literature that they have been taught to admire—and that is of course the now classic and institutionalized literature of the twenties and thirties. For a long time this kind of assurance of continuity with the honored past has been the one element the middlebrows have sorely missed in the novels of the current younger writers. They have been confused by the fact that so many of these writers are supposed to be good, while at the same time they are obviously not good in the old familiar ways. Styron's considerable virtue is that he puts their minds at ease by satisfying the expectations that they chronically bring to new writing and vindicating their prejudices about the nature of good writing in general. He is, in short, a "literary" writer in the sense that his work resembles what is generally taken to be, or has been indemnified by previous usage as being "literary." He therefore never commits the unpardonable sin of the truly original writer: he never confronts the reader with what, disturbingly, the reader has never seen before; he never educates the consciousness by demanding that it go to work here and now, as if for the very first time, on him and his unique vision of reality. Instead, he comforts the reader, however unintentionally, with a vision of the familiar and the previously envisioned, skillfully projected through a literary manner with which the reader feels thoroughly at home. Yet Styron is a sufficiently good writer never to seem merely imitative. In everything he has done up to now he has managed to strike a fine balance between sounding familiar enough to be acceptable and not sounding so familiar as to seem entirely unoriginal.

His writing style, which has been justly praised for its evocative power and great verbal ingenuity, is an excellent example of this kind of equilibrium. It belongs to a category of literary expression that the middlebrows—and, for that matter, many highbrows—have come to identify as the "major" modern American style, the traditional language of our native form of modern literary genius. It is rich, reckless, bombastic, melodramatic, poetical, rhetorical, metaphorical, and sentimental; and in Styron's hands it clearly shows the marks of the hard usage already given it by most of our native modern literary geniuses. In fact, one can easily imagine his books as big sprawling houses of language, crammed with antiques passed down to him by beneficent forebears named Wolfe, Faulkner, Fitzgerald, and Hemingway. Yet Styron's skill at interior decoration is such that one cannot help but see at once how interesting and new the familiar old pieces look in the highly individual arrangement he has made of them. For there can be no doubt about it: the arrangement *is* individual. It at least is entirely his own, even if the materials are not. He has not therefore been altogether imitative, and neither has he been disturbingly original. He has simply exercised ingenuity in turning to his own advantage the stylistic innovations of his predecessors. But he has also inevitably done something else, something vastly more important from the point of view of his middlebrow admirers. He has managed to convey the impression that by sounding *like* his predecessors, he has earned the right to take a place in the ranks of greatness beside them. The style in his case may not be the man, but it would seem to make him. For if he writes in the certified style of geniuses, must he not be a genius too?

In very much the same way, Styron's stock situations and emotional stances are also those of serious modern literature. The anguished, possessed, drunken, demented, and tormented, the boorish, slobbish, phonily tender and sentimental—these are all the conventional materials through which modern writers have defined their sense of the forms and terms of life in the modern world. But the point is just that they *are* the conventional materials. Now at this late time of our history they seem to belong to a canon of more or less habitual arrangements of reality, and they seem valid and real no longer because of their relation to actual life and observed experience but because of their relation to past literature, which has conditioned us to the assumption that they are valid and real at the same time that it has conditioned our responses to them. Hence, in meeting them again in Styron's work, one has the feeling of having met them before, not necessarily in any specific book, but in the whole of modern literature, the feeling of being on familiar ground without the feeling of having detected a plagiarism. The intellectually ambitious reader might therefore be forgiven if he should assume that Styron must be as serious, even as original, in his handling of these materials as his predecessors were in their handling of them—if he should forget, that is, that the mark of the truly original writer is his ability to reimagine the materials of his age and necessarily to present them in ways that are uniquely his own.

Styron's first book, *Lie Down in Darkness*, which immediately established him with the middlebrow critics as the quintessential young writer of promise, is a remarkably skillful adaptation of the Faulknerian imagination to materials that have not, perforce, been reimagined at all. It is Faulknerian not only in its evocation of the familiar Southern Gothic air of evil and almost meteorological damnation (the sort that can now be had in Southern fiction simply by seeding the clouds with a little essence of sweet William), but in its heavy indebtedness to specific Faulkner novels. *The Sound and the Fury* and *As I Lay Dying* are especially prominent as original sources for the funeral setting, the idiot-child motif, and the figure of the guilt-burdened and ultimately suicidal young person who cannot escape, even in the alien North, the destructive force of Southern fatality. But as a good middlebrow novel, *Lie Down in Darkness* is required to sound generally literary rather than specifically derivative, and to scatter its indebtedness among the books of more than one important writer. It does so by sounding in its non-Faulknerian moments like the books of Fitzgerald, Hemingway, O'Hara, and even, incredibly enough, Charles Jackson. Peyton Loftis, the heroine, is a confection cooked up out of the more delectable neuroses of those beautiful, stricken, and lost girls whom Fitzgerald and O'Hara were always mooning about in their early work, at the same time that in her self-destructiveness and eager corruption she is a curious cross between Temple Drake, Quentin Compson, and Hemingway's Lady Brett. Peyton's father Milton is easily recognizable as a direct descendant of Dick Diver in *Tender Is the Night* and the drunk in *The Lost Weekend*— although *not*, it should be noticed, as he appears in the book but as he was portrayed on the screen by Ray Milland.

The use Styron makes of his borrowed materials, while evidently satisfactory to his middlebrow admirers, is finally as synthetic and fortuitous as the film one can so easily imagine the novel becoming. The Faulknerian aspect—the thick atmosphere of dissolution and ruin, the harsh tonalities of nightmare and psychic outrage—has no more than a propinquitous relationship to the dilemma of the characters. It is presumably supposed to be a dramatic projection of their overpowering sense of guilt, the modern equivalent of Shakespeare's angry heavens or the clanking chains and maundering ghosts of the old Gothic novel. But as Styron uses it, it becomes just another fruitless attempt to establish guilt by contextual association, and for all the good it does, it might as well have been sprayed around the novel with a Flit gun. It is meaningful if, and only if, the reader himself is able, by a supplementary act of the imagination, to go beyond Styron and make the connection on his own, for there is no internal evidence to indicate that the connection must be made. The reason, of course, is that the internal evidence remains in the possession of William Faulkner, the man from whom Styron borrowed but, as it turned out, could not borrow enough.

In Faulkner the atmosphere of dissolution and ruin is the logical and inevitable expression of the cultural and moral derangement of his characters. Their land is doomed, their

35

house is cursed, the spirits of their ancestors howl in anguish about the eaves, because they are people who have been wrenched out of their natural place in the communal order and have as a consequence lost the means of defining and preserving themselves as human beings. Theirs is obviously a tragedy on the grand scale, and it requires and deserves treatment in the grand manner, precisely the sort of treatment that Faulkner, with his rich rhetoric of violence and disorder, gives it. But the trouble with Styron's novel is that while the style, metaphors, and morbid temper of the characters all insist upon the presence of some transcendent evil, some Faulknerian taint of blood or soul, some unspeakable damnation that is about to overtake everything and everyone, these elements exist without relation to the thematic meaning that they are ostensibly designed to express. There is no real or felt agony to account for their implications of agony, no grand moral issue to account for the grandeur of their size. They are thick icing spread on a cake that does not exist because it has already been eaten. In fact, those of us who have fed heavily on Southern novels long ago made ourselves sick on it.

But what is most wrong with them is that they suggest a dilemma that, to change the figure, they cannot deliver because Styron never received it. It got lost in transit somewhere between Faulkner's imagination and his. They suggest a dilemma of apocalyptic importance, as important as the fall of dynasties or some doomed defiance of the wrath of God. Yet the dilemma that the novel actually records is merely psychological, merely a matter of neurosis, marital incompatibility, father fixation, and dipsomania. The only curse on the House of Loftis is, as it were, a curse of the House of Seagram's and the House of Oedipus. The style, the metaphors, and the temper of the characters are all, therefore, wasted on thin air, or rather they become a thin air of mere theatrics and rhetoric overlying a mere problem of maladjustment. The issue of the novel is, in short, not Faulknerian at all but Freudian, and Styron's effort to marry the two results in the worst sort of artistic miscegenation.

The Fitzgeraldian aspect of the novel also exhibits this curious disjuncture of theme and content, of borrowed and personal materials. Yet perhaps just because it does, it seems to be the element most responsible for the popularity the book has enjoyed over the last several years with the younger middlebrow public. College students in particular appear to have been powerfully impressed by the fact that the entire early portrait of Peyton Loftis can be seen as an adaptation of Fitzgeraldian manners, morals, and emotional patterns to the experience of their own generation. The figure of the beautiful, tragedy-haunted girl searching desperately for oblivion in a frenzy of fraternity-house drinking parties and love affairs is a seductive figure indeed to young people who have grown up in an atmosphere of extravagant nostalgia for Fitzgerald's world, but who, until Styron came along, had almost given up hope of being able to see themselves in a similarly glamorous perspective. But when Peyton reconstitutes the typical Fitzgerald heroine, she also reconstitutes Fitzgerald and makes him contemporary, and when she makes her famous remark—the one remark that all younger readers seem to remember from the book—about the Lost Generation's having not so much lost themselves as lost *us*, there seems to be no doubt but that the Great Gatsby is risen and rides again.

The remark is appealing, of course, not only because it is Fitzgeraldian, although one cannot discount the immensely pleasurable effects produced when a novel reminds the reader, regardless of his age, of emotions that he got from books earlier in his life but that he despaired of ever getting from books again. It is also appealing because it seems to offer a simple and familiar explanation for much that is opaque and confused in the motivation of the Loftis family. In fact, it seems to represent an effort, however uncalculated, to replace that motivation with a romantic reading of the old *Zeitgeist* theory of human behavior, in much the same way that the Faulknerian overtones of the style seem to represent an effort to replace it with dark intimations of ancestral blood-guilt and transcendent damnation. For the remark appears to suggest that the Loftises are tragic and lost not merely for psychological reasons but because they are victims of the moral breakdown supposedly suffered by the Lost Generation. Unfortunately, the suggestion is erroneous and misleading, exactly as misleading as the Faulknerian overtones. The *Geist* in this case as clearly belongs to another *Zeit* as the style belongs to another man. For nothing in the novel demonstrates that the Loftises are victims of any circumstances larger than their own cultural limitations and neuroses.

As Styron *portrays* them, the father and mother are not and never have been Fitzgeraldian profligates, and, if anything, their trouble is the result more of their separation from the general experience of their time than of their participation in it. They are, above all, provincial people, culturally limited people, and their tragedy, like Emma Bovary's, is a provincial tragedy, the issue of emotions overly confined by, and perversely conditioned by, the restraints of dogma and community. Take them out of that Southern town and put them down in Long Island or Manhattan, and their problems would be greatly diminished if not altogether solved—or they would become different problems open to different solutions. As it stands, the father suffers because he is trapped in that town in a marriage to a frigid wife and because he feels guilty about wanting his daughter sexually. The mother suffers because she is a neurotic Southern female who unconsciously hates herself for hating sex and consciously hates her husband and daughter for loving it. If her trouble has a history, it goes back to provincial religious fanaticism and that peculiar Southern gentlewoman form of sex fear, and not at all to the moral sickness of the modern world. Indeed, the modern world, if she had ever lived in it, would have taught her better, just as a little experience with Fitzgerald's profligates would have taught her about sex. Hence, if we were to take Peyton's word for it that her parents actually are victims of their age, we should be robbing ourselves of our only means of accounting for their tragedy—for if it is not the product precisely of their being *cut off from* the morally and sexually liberating developments of their age, it is nothing. Yet the critical problem is that we arrive at this conclusion in spite of Peyton's remark rather than because of it. Her view, and presumably Styron's view, of the meaning of the action is contradicted by the facts of the action as they are stated. If Styron's efforts to marry Freud and Faulkner resulted in artistic miscegenation, his efforts to marry Fitzgerald, Freud, modern history, and provincial tragedy can only result in artistic sodomy.

Actually, however, the two sets of efforts are basically one effort to call in some higher authority to give his book an appearance of thematic size and depth that its merely psychological and cultural materials cannot give it by themselves. In the one instance he tries to project his characters' tragedy upon the melodramatic background of Faulkner's vision of the South; in the other he tries to project it upon the historical background of the modern age as a whole. There can be no doubt that in so doing he achieves an effect of intellectual pretentiousness that is vastly appealing to readers who have become accustomed to mistaking almost any show of pretentiousness in fiction for evidence of superior artistic quality. Nor can one deny that the mélange that results is a very spicy concoction indeed. The generous portions of well-cooked Faulkner, Fitzgerald, and Freud, the big dashes of idiocy, insanity, neurosis, near incest, adultery, and suicide, even the little pinches of Pearl Harbor, Hiroshima, and Southern Negro revivalism put in just to remind us of the ironic possibilities to be found in the juxtaposition of personal and national tragedy, civilized hate and primitive love—the whole thing set before us in the certified "high" style of great writing: what could be more impressively typical of the best that can be served up in the fancy kitchens of modern literature? The answer, of course, is that absolutely nothing could be more typical *except* the genuinely best, and this Styron's book appears to be but is not. It may in fact be a typical book; it most certainly is a symptomatic book. But what it typifies is the tendency of the middlebrow novel at the highest level to emulate literature without quite becoming literature, and its symptoms are those of meretriciousness, the disease of surface "literariness" complicated by an essentially unoriginal view of life.

Styron's most recent novel, *Set This House on Fire*, is also symptomatic, although not only of Styron's further advance toward meretriciousness, but of the kind of fate that can befall a successful middlebrow writer when he tries to improve upon his former success without improving enough upon his former ideas. What happened to Styron was that he managed with this book to alienate most of the critics who admired *Lie Down in Darkness* at the same time that he failed to win the support of the highbrow critics whom he apparently intended this book to please. I say "apparently" because the book contains evidence of a sustained and self-conscious effort to make use of just about all the highbrow clichés known to the readers of *Partisan Review*—known but, unfortunately for Styron, recognized and rejected as clichés by them. The highbrow critics may have been put off by this aspect of the book or simply by the aura of middlebrow adulation that has surrounded Styron from the beginning and that may have led them to conclude that he could not be much good if he could be considered good by so many second-rate people. But in any case, they largely ignored *Set This House on Fire*, while the majority of the middlebrow critics seemed to take particular delight in attacking it. The result was that the book fell between the two bodies of critical opinion, being considered, one supposes, too highbrow for the middlebrows and too tritely highbrow for the highbrows.

On the face of it, this seems a bit peculiar, for the book contains a great many elements that ought to have assured it of instantaneous middlebrow acclaim. It has the requisite heft and garrulity, weighing in at just under two pounds and running to 507 pages. It is prefaced by a portentous and impressively unreadable quotation from John Donne (a writer whose middlebrow reputation was firmly established by Ernest Hemingway) that, when deciphered, turns out to be one of the best refutations of Styron's thesis ever written in the seventeenth century. It is organized in that loose, episodic, case-history fashion that the middlebrows have long believed to be the classic form of unbridled talent. It is set in physical circumstances as exotic and spectacular as those of any wide-screen, Vista-Vision, Cinemascope production—the same circumstances, in fact, in which a large part of *Beat the Devil* was filmed: in the town of Ravello, Italy. It is crammed full of violence, sex, drunkenness, and the various forms and styles of profanity, obscenity, and depravity. It contains not one but two particularly gruesome murders, an attempted as well as an accomplished rape, and some quite good descriptions of pornographic acts, both as witnessed in life and as depicted in books and paintings. At least two of the principal characters are sufficiently Fitzgeraldian to give the susceptible reader that wonderful old feeling that he is swimming once more in the main current of serious modern fiction. Peter Leverett (or, more cunningly, Peter Rabbit), the narrator, is a distinctly Nick Carrawayish young man who wanders through the novel taking mental notes with that morally and physically hung-over air that Fitzgerald made mandatory for young narrators, while Mason Flagg, the villain of the piece, is the very type of the Fitzgeraldian rich boy—handsome, dashing, lusty, and lovable, but corrupted beyond the wildest nightmares of poor old puritanical Scott.

But the trouble presumably is that, in spite of these seemingly sure-fire ingredients, the novel is both an insufficiently good story simply as a story and—remarkable as it may seem —much too morbid and depressing in its sensationalism to please the middlebrow critics, who must, after all, make a distinction at least in public between what they personally enjoy and what they can recommend as proper reading for our teenage sons and daughters. It is perfectly true that the novel is practically a dictionary of clichés, and that fact alone should make it attractive to the middlebrows. But as I suggested earlier, the clichés are unfortunately of the wrong sort. Where *Lie Down in Darkness* was built around the familiar and now official clichés of the serious fiction of the twenties and thirties, *Set This House on Fire* is built around the clichés of the serious fiction of the forties and fifties. And while the former novel had the great middlebrow virtue of showing the influence of Faulkner, Fitzgerald, and other safely established figures, the latter has the highbrow defect, in spite of its two Fitzgeraldian characterizations, of showing the influence of writers like Camus and Sartre—with whom the middlebrows are neither very familiar nor very friendly—and of Styron's immediate contemporaries, Norman Mailer and J. D. Salinger—with whom they are familiar enough but, in Mailer's case at least, decidedly uncomfortable.

The central character, Cass Kinsolving, for instance, is a sort of pastiche of the mannerisms and attitudes that have become standard in the highbrow fiction of the immediate present. He reminds one at times of Mathieu, the hero or antihero of *L'Age de Raison;* he is frequently as feckless and faceless as Meursault in *L'Etranger;* and he expresses himself in a style that somewhat jarringly combines the cute indignation of Salinger's Holden Caulfield with the Beat pettishness of Mailer's Sergius O'Shaughnessy. He is also fashionably slobbish, drunken, anguished, resentful, and morbidly obsessed with the problems of creative impotence and spiritual identity in a universe made absurd by the French Existentialists. But his trouble, as far as the middlebrows are concerned, is that these traits of his all belong to a fashion uncongenial to them. They are traits that connect him with the distasteful and perplexing view of reality that the highbrow fiction of the present habitually takes, and not with the view that the middlebrows find traditional and reassuring. There can be no doubt that Kinsolving is an embodiment of Styron's effort to imitate the works of his serious contemporaries and thereby improve himself critically. But as an imitation Kinsolving is merely a burlesque of the stock properties of recurrent characters in those works, rather than the expression of a view of life that just happens to be similar to theirs. He therefore does nothing whatever for Styron's critical standing except to confuse it. For recognizing him as a cliché or, even worse, as an imitation of a cliché, the highbrows can only scorn him, while mistaking him for an original creation, the middlebrows can only despise and dismiss him.

It is of course true that we live in a time when life itself seems in many of its aspects to have become such a smothering cliché that fiction might conceivably be forgiven for imitating not only the clichés of other fiction but those of the life from which they derive. The symbol of the relation of fiction to life in our day is undeniably the Chinese box, and in a sense *Set This House on Fire* is a perfect illustration of it, operating as it does consistently at the point where the clichés of fiction shade into the clichés of life, and one can no longer tell which is the imitator, art or life. But if we can forgive fiction in the abstract, on the ground that it so seldom pretends to be more than imitative, we cannot easily forgive a writer like Styron, who constantly pretends to be so very much more, for failing to make every effort to cut through to the reality that presumably still exists beneath the thick layers of cliché. That is, in fact, the special obligation imposed upon him by his pretensions to seriousness, the obligation to reconstitute the stereotyped materials of his time by informing and transforming them with his understanding, so that he will not only create order out of chaos—which at this date is no more than his routine job—but make new and unexpected arrangements of the predictable. And he must do this even though he himself, as an especially perceptive human being, may at every moment be aware of the triteness of the materials with which he is forced to work.

In order to do this a writer naturally must have a strong and certain sense of the meaning he wishes his materials to have, for it is the meaning alone, the meaning that only he can put there, that will infuse his clichés with fresh life and form them into those unique combinations that we recognize as belonging no longer to fashion but wholly to the individual genius of the writer himself. Unfortunately, there is nothing in *Set This House on Fire* to indicate that Styron had such a sense, and everything to indicate that he did not have it. His very possession of so much material and the painstaking manner in which he explores it—the piling of scene on scene, the intricate system of flashbacks, the self-obsessed excavation and examination of nuance, the sheer intensive "working" of the medium—all seem representative of a man in frantic search of his theme, driven by the hope that if he can just keep writing long enough, he will eventually track it down or it will suddenly pop up from behind some page and reveal itself.

Actually, something of the sort finally does happen, or rather Styron in his desperation finally *makes* it happen. At the very end, in the last thirty or so pages, he hurriedly fabricates an existential resolution for Kinsolving's dilemma, having him confront and purge himself of the guilt that has been hounding him throughout the novel and that becomes intolerable after he murders Mason Flagg. But the proof that Styron fabricated, and fabricated too late, lies in the fact that nothing in the action up to those last pages is selected or dramatized in terms of the meaning that is made to emerge from them. There is no evidence, in other words, that at any point until the very end he had a firm idea of what that meaning was to be. The result is that the vast material of the novel remains, for all its bulk and richness, simply material; and the clichés, untouched and unreconstituted by the meaning that Styron belatedly tried to give them, remain simply clichés—the fashionable and easy arrangements of reality to be found anywhere and everywhere in life and other people's fiction.

Without the support of a clearly understood and developed theme, *Set This House on Fire* becomes another of those rudderless works in which any move is possible because none is necessary, a novel of trumped-up and largely fortuitous circumstances having no limitation or convention of order within it to control or direct the flow of events toward a preselected dramatic objective. Lacking thematic coherence, it inevitably lacks a moral center. One is never sure, while reading it, why the characters act the way they do and not differently, why the events occur in this way rather than that, why they should have this effect rather than some other—and one feels that Styron, while writing it, was never sure.

The relationship on which the whole action depends, the relationship of the three principals, Flagg, Kinsolving, and the narrator Peter Leverett, is not held together by thematic ties or, for that matter, by convincing friendly ties. It appears to exist simply because Styron decided it had to exist so that he could write a novel around it. In the same way, the characters of the three men seem to belong only arbitrarily to the action. They could belong anywhere, to any action, and in fact they do, for they are stereotypes lifted out of the stockroom of contemporary fiction and set down in the novel without being adapted to its particular circumstances. As I previously pointed out, Flagg is the Fitzgeraldian rich boy gone sour; Leverett is a thin derivative of Nick Carraway; Kinsolving is that hardy literary perennial, the drunken sorehead and sensitive oaf—and they could *be* all these things without any help from Styron or his novel. But their introduction into his novel creates an imbalance that, in its rudderless condition, the novel cannot support, and the result

46

is a fatal disparity between their reality as stereotypes and their unreality as characters.

One sees this in a variety of instances. First, there is the fact that, although a great deal of space is devoted to Flagg, so much that the reader mistakes him most of the way through for the protagonist, he is never realized, never penetrated, never understood, either by Styron or by the reader. He is consistently seen from the outside, in terms of his money, his charm, his irresponsibility, his corruption—in short, his stereotype. Hence, his actions at Sambucco, his fiendish exploitation and debasement of Kinsolving, strike one as unprepared for and inexplicable. He becomes too suddenly, without sufficient warning and preliminary characterization, a figure of merely gratuitous evil. And the one motive that Styron gives for his conduct—the torment of repressed homosexuality—is both too trivial for the amount of space allotted him and too textbookishly trite for a novel that, by the complexity of its structure and the penetration of its style, announces that it intends a thorough and exact examination of human motive. The effect is rather like the effect *Crime and Punishment* would have had if at the end Dostoevski had suggested that the whole trouble with Raskolnikov was an Oedipus complex.

The portrait of Kinsolving shows very much the same weakness. His *experience* is developed brilliantly and at infinite length, but he himself as a *character* is not developed in such a way that one is prepared for his actions at the end. We learn that he has all his life suffered from a guilt complex, the sources of which are obscure, although Styron, again very tritely, tries to attribute it to the Negro problem. But one is emphatically not prepared for his sudden access of love for the Italian peasant girl—a touch straight out of *A Bell for Adano*—or for the almost insanely "sincere" compassion he feels for her dying father—a touch straight out of J. D. Salinger. And when one discovers that Kinsolving's whole vastly complicated difficulty is supposed to be resolved in a "conversion" and "purgation" experience triggered by a philosophical policeman, one may be forgiven for losing faith in both Styron and God. The point again is that the explanation given for a line of conduct, or, in this case, the climax reached by a line of conduct, is an inadequate justification for the large amount of space and time devoted to its development. Like Flagg's homosexuality, Kinsolving's last-minute choice of "being" over "nothingness" seems mechanical, trite, and imposed from the outside rather than prepared for by the facts as they have been given from the beginning.

Much of the problem is laid bare as soon as one realizes that beneath the documentary fat that covers the novel, the action hangs on a very slender frame indeed. All Styron essentially has is a situation in which a girl is raped, then murdered, and the rapist is in turn murdered on the false assumption that he is also the girl's murderer. All he has, in other words, is the material of a cheap tabloid thriller or at best one of those books damp-browed adolescents read on buses. Everything else is scene, anecdote, flashback, description, and digression. The novel depends, therefore, even more than normally upon the meaning that Styron is able to give to the slim situation, and that depends upon the extent to which the whole is illuminated by the meaning at every step of the way. If the whole is not so illuminated, then one asks, is forced to ask, what it is that justifies all the documentation. Certainly, it must in the end be something more than a case of repressed homosexuality confronting a case of segregation-inspired guilt feelings, regardless of the exotic nature of the setting or the fashionable nature of the psychology.

There can be no doubt that Styron as a worker in language, as a creator of scene and situation, is one of the most gifted younger writers of the present time. In everything he has written up to now there is evidence of a vigorous and sensitive talent operating under pressure of the strongest ambition to become major. *Set This House on Fire* is nothing if not a testimonial to the size and intensity of that ambition as well as to the nature of the obstacles that, to achieve its end, it will be obliged to overcome. One cannot help but recognize power everywhere in the book and some of the very best writing Styron has so far done. Such sections in particular as those describing Leverett's trip to Sambucco and his visit to Port Warwick, Kinsolving's life in Paris, and the gathering of movie people at Flagg's party are done with astounding vitality and richness of effect. But Styron is still sorely deficient in the compositional sense, in the ability to correlate and control the large masses of material with which he seems to find it necessary to work. His purely literary instincts are nearly always infallible, but when he is forced to generalize and conceptualize, to show the moral or philosophical implications of his material, he falters and falls back on something fashionable, something borrowed from the popular ideologies, something unearned by the mind and conscience of his theme.

This seems to me to be Styron's principal weakness as a novelist, and it happens also to be a middlebrow weakness. In spite of his great talent and ambition, he has still not found it possible to operate outside the system of ideological and dramatic conventions that have become the clichés of the highbrow world even as they remain the intellectual status symbols of the middlebrow world. The result is that although his books are written wonderfully well, they continue to exist in a dimension of irrelevance and unreality that is the dimension neither of life nor of literature but of something in between. They have many of the qualities of literature, just as they bear considerable resemblance to life, but they are essentially skilled adaptations of the already formulated modes of seeing and judging life and of portraying it in literature. Styron's talent seems at the present time to be imprisoned within the circle of these modes and condemned to moving round and round in a monotonous and unending routine of coming at experience over and over again from exactly the same direction and reacting to it in exactly the same way. The explanations it finds for human conduct inside the circle are always fashionable and always predictable: the motives of women are finally reducible to Oedipus complexes and the Sickness of the Age; the troubles of men can finally be traced to an inordinate fondness for the bottle, a suppressed fondness for other men, or some Topical Problem involving the "controversial" issues of race, creed, or color.

John O'Hara's talent is also imprisoned inside the circle, and that is the main reason the middlebrows like him so much. But where O'Hara continues to pander not only to middlebrow tastes in pornography but to middlebrow needs to escape from literature and life, Styron, at least in this latest book, seems to have come close to losing the middlebrows by reminding them uncomfortably of both literature and life. But he has not yet come close enough or reminded them uncomfortably enough, just as he has not yet reached the highbrows to whom this book was presumably directed. To do that he will have to subject himself to a tougher discipline even than the one that his high ambition has already imposed upon him. He will have to subject himself to the ultimate discipline of learning to see again with his own eyes and to think again with his own mind, and no longer with those of his predecessors and contemporaries. For that is the work that most urgently needs to be done by the ambitious writer today if the dead formulations of the past are ever to be put aside and the novel is ever to be freed to function again as the educator of the consciousness of its time.

[1964]

Notes on the Novel II

The Novel and the Intellectuals

IN sharp contrast to the middlebrow public, American intellectuals today give every appearance of being firmly in possession of the serious novel. They have by no means always been so, for, as I suggested earlier, the serious novel was once primarily a middlebrow property, and because of that fact, intellectuals tended to hold themselves fastidiously aloof from it, as if the smallest contact might tempt them to give in to the debasement of middlebrow success. The result was that criticism, poetry, and the rigidly noncommercial short story were for a long time considered to be the only really acceptable intellectual interests, and the novel was left to make its way largely uninstructed by the finer discriminations of mind.

But as the middlebrow influence has faded, a radical change seems to have occurred in intellectual attitudes toward fiction generally and the serious novel in particular, a change that may represent a genuine broadening of taste, a compromise of standards, or a little of both. In any case, the old snobberies have gradually given way to a new spirit of excited concern for all aspects of the current literary scene, and this has taken the form, in relation to the serious novel, of a kind of nervously benevolent intellectual paternalism, made anxious and at times overly indulgent by what may well be a guilty consciousness of former neglect.

Several factors appear to have been responsible for this change. The most obvious is that the serious novel, in losing its middlebrow character, has itself grown increasingly intellectual, not only in the assumptions that it habitually makes about reality, but in its more and more scrupulous regard for the principles of literary art. This is not exactly to say that it has become a novel of ideas or a vehicle of intellectual experiences in the sense that it was until recently a vehicle of middlebrow experiences. The American novel throughout its history has seldom been concerned with ideas except at their least explicit, where they shade off into moral and allegorical abstraction, and it has had very little to say about the experience of those for whom the drama of consciousness represents life in its most challenging and valid form.

The intellectual in American fiction has traditionally been a shadowy, rather suspect figure, more often the object of ridicule than of sympathetic examination. And what has been true of the past remains essentially true of the present. There have, to be sure, been recent novels in which the intellectual has been portrayed as protagonist, as hero or anti-hero, and there have even been others that made the heretical point that thought is not always inimical to action or brains to virility, that, in fact, the highbrow-low loins combination made famous by Aldous Huxley is fast becoming a standard, even an enviable, biological feature of our time. But we have so far had nothing like a developing trend toward the full treatment of ideas or the life of ideas in fiction, and therefore little to indicate that the interest that intellectuals now take in the serious novel has much to do with any particular capacity it has for increasing their understanding of themselves and their world. Still, there can be no doubt that at the highest level the serious novel has lately come to be written with a consciousness of craft, a technical fastidiousness, which makes it at least formally attractive to intellectual readers, and which seems to hold out the assurance that the art of fiction, in becoming more and more of an art, is at last beginning to operate from esthetic premises that have long had first importance in the intellectual world.

Another and of course closely related development has been the rise over the past several years of a new quality market for fiction at approximately the same moment that the literary interests of professional critics and scholars have spread beyond the universities to a new audience of fairly high sophistication and taste. In such publications as *Esquire, Playboy,* and the various women's fashion magazines the demand for serious writing of all kinds has reached enormous proportions. Their readership—made up, one gathers, of intellectuals, would-be intellectuals, and large numbers of other people who consider it chic to be literarily in the know—have displayed an insatiable appetite for just about anything that is or is said to be interesting and different as well as for the tidbits of gossip and scandal that circulate around the margins of literary celebrity. A general leveling or, more optimistically and perhaps more correctly, a general raising of literary standards seems to have occurred, resulting in part from the wide dissemination of cultural knowledge in recent years and in part from the increased social value now attached to the conspicuous consumption of cultural products. The lines that previously separated specialists and academicians from the large class of discriminating readers have grown arbitrary and indistinct; and this has had the effect of further diluting the snobberies of the intellectual and causing him to believe once again in the possibility of addressing the public on a basis of common interests and on subjects that until now he had assumed to be understandable only to others of his own kind.

In short, what is finally important is not the new market for fiction but the phenomenon that has made it possible: the emergence of a new audience capable of supporting it, an audience with interests closely paralleling those of the intellectual world. This is the truly significant development, and it may well be the most crucial step forward American culture has taken in our time. For the elevation in public literary taste resulting from mass university education, great-books courses, and the study of modern critical methods has dramatically changed the whole character and climate of American cultural life, and inevitably it has created as profound a change in the relation of the intellectual to it.

Within a very brief period of time, a period, I should say, of no more than five years, the traditional role of the intellectual in this country has been rendered obsolete or begun to be revealed as mere affectation. Where he once had good cause to see himself as the lone heroic defender of values that were under constant philistine siege, the intellectual is now obliged to see himself in the less flattering but ultimately more satisfying image of cultural arbiter and spokesman among vast numbers of former enemies who have suddenly taken on the appearance of friends. Where he was once secure but isolated in a position of militant entrenchment, he is now vulnerable but free to enter the public arena of open cultural debate in which his ideas may be challenged but at least understood, and he can expect to be received with unaccustomed decency and good will.

An important symptom of this change is, as I have said, the enthusiastic, although by no means always serious, interest in literary and intellectual affairs that has lately become evident in the big quality magazines. But a more striking expression of it is the appearance of such new outlets for commentary as *The New York Review of Books* and *the Herald Tribune Book Week,* both of which promise to offer opportunity for a higher-level discussion of books than was ever before thought acceptable to the general reading public in this country. Their existence is proof not only that such discussion *is* acceptable but that the general public is far less general—in the old, vaguely pejorative sense of the word —than it was only a short time ago.

Significantly enough, a great many of the contributors to these two publications are also regular contributors to the literary quarterlies (*The New York Review of Books* appears to be written almost entirely by *Partisan Review* regulars) who once would scarcely have considered publishing anywhere else, and certainly not in a mass circulation medium, because of the very real questions of loyalty and taste that that would automatically have raised. Today, however, in the face of the growing public enlightenment, these writers have been able to put aside their prejudices and function with a new sense of the possibilities of intellectual communication beyond the old set limits of in-group dialogue. In the process, they are beginning to restore to vigor and fashion the until now moribund form of serious literary journalism; and inevitably, as defensive tensions slacken, this is resulting in a much needed clarification of critical language. Jargon and abstruseness, the old trademarks of intellectual isolationism, are giving way to a critical prose of greatly increased clarity and directness, the kind of prose that testifies to the intellectual's new confidence in the public acceptability of his ideas and to his awareness that his life no longer depends upon keeping up the verbal pretense of a knowledge too precious and special to be simply expressed.

In the universities, meanwhile, there has been a parallel liberalization of intellectual interests, taking the form of a rapidly growing emphasis on the study of contemporary fiction. The massive energies of the so-called New (but now distinctly Old) Criticism, which were once concentrated upon the refinement of basic theory and the analysis of poetry, began about fifteen years ago to be redirected to the analysis of fiction, and we have just recently come to the end of a period of consolidation during which the modern classic novelists of the twenties and thirties were being closely examined and assigned to their permanent places in the critical canon. But now that that process has been largely completed, interest has shifted again, this time to the work of the still developing group of serious younger novelists—Salinger, Bellow, Bernard Malamud, James Purdy, Philip Roth, Flannery O'Connor, Herbert Gold, and others— and today it is these writers who are being subjected to a vigorous, if somewhat premature, analysis and assigned to *their* places in the critical canon.

A little more than a decade ago, when my first critical book, *After the Lost Generation*, appeared, this kind of interest in younger novelists had not yet begun to make itself felt. In fact, it seemed to be largely confined to me, and as a result I came under a good deal of fire—at least until the fashion changed, and my heresies were at last accepted as orthodoxies. The new writers whom I then took to be worth discussing, if only because they *were* new and seemed illustrative of the directions being taken by the postwar American novel, were generally considered too new, too riskily untried, to deserve the kind of detailed, full-length treatment I had given them. Even though in my young idealism I had taken so high-minded a line that I had managed to say almost nothing good about any of them, it was felt to be poor strategy for a beginning critic to commit himself so soon on a body of writing that might turn out to have no permanent literary value and force him, in ten or twenty years, to admit that he had made a mistake. Thanks to my negative position, the passage of time has not exacted that worst of penalties from me; in fact, it has only made me wish that I had had the foresight to be even more negative than I was.

But whatever my position, the point seemed to be that I should have played it safe and waited those ten or twenty years. While waiting I might, if I had insisted, have kept my hand in by doing careful little essays on Faulkner or Joyce—an enterprise that, while not even then entirely respectable, would at least not have done irreparable damage to my future prospects as a critic. But being naïve and heedless and supposing it to be one of the responsibilities of criticism to concern itself with new work and even to run the risk of being wrong, I had not waited. If I had, I should undoubtedly have been waiting still.

At any rate, all that is changed now. There soon came a time somewhere in the early fifties when it finally began to be just barely acceptable for at least an adventurous minority of younger critics to discuss immediately contemporary writers. A few of the smaller literary quarterlies started publishing studies of their work, and before long were devoting entire issues to such studies. By the middle of the decade interest in new writing had spread to some of the larger quarterlies, and in such magazines as *Harper's Bazaar* and *Mademoiselle* the image of the young writer as homosexual mannequin was soon established as a trademark of the higher New York cultural life. It had gradually become not only acceptable but almost respectable to bring out essays on McCullers, Capote, Salinger, and Bellow, and today it is not only respectable but highly fashionable. The criticism of current literature has now developed into a major industry with production centers in both the academic world and the chic world of the quality magazines.

Some of the young writers whom I had the temerity to discuss back in 1951, along with many others who have come to prominence since then, are now being examined with the care and seriousness formerly reserved for the traditional and modern classics. In fact, over the past few years in *Esquire* one has discovered some of these writers examining themselves and one another with the portentous and self-congratulatory air of men convinced that they already *are* classics. And I suppose it is possible that in a certain local and limited sense they are. They are not, after all, so very young any more. Most of them have done interesting, even important work. There is no longer very much mystery about where the talent lies, and it is now about as risky to point it out as it is to make qualitative distinctions between Faulkner and John O'Hara. With the critical tide running so heavily in their favor and in the absence of really towering competitors, it is not surprising that both the egos and the reputations of these writers should have become a little inflated. It is also not surprising in a time when the ego of criticism has become so inflated that it will have the reputations it needs to justify its existence even if it has to manufacture them itself.

The Price of Being Taken Seriously

This to my mind is the most arresting feature of the current highbrow preoccupation with these younger novelists: the fact that so many of them have been elevated to prominence almost entirely on the strength of the interest that criticism has taken in their work. I am not suggesting that this is a particularly new phenomenon. It has happened before in literary history, it is the usual thing with poets; and of course it is bound to happen in the case of certain special kinds of novelistic talent such as, for example, the Joycean variety. But where novelists generally are concerned, it has always been a rare phenomenon, and I do not recall that it has ever occurred before in relation to so many of them at one time. In this country in recent years one can think only of Faulkner as an example, the classic modern example, of an important novelist who was discovered and sustained by criticism long before his name was widely known, and who, even at that, remained to the end of his life much better known to the general public for his critical reputation than for his books—which were more admired than read. But the usual requirement is that a writer should first have achieved some sort of wide readership and produced a substantial body of work before becoming eligible for the critical accolade, and even then it is sometimes withheld until the writer is safely dead.

If this requirement with respect to the younger writers no longer seems to be in force, it is obviously not just because a wide readership in the old sense of a large middlebrow following is becoming exceedingly hard to acquire and critics are trying to make charitable allowance for the fact. There can be no doubt that such a readership *is* becoming exceedingly hard to acquire: really big reputations of the kind once enjoyed by Hemingway and Fitzgerald now seem to be a thing of the past—except apparently where J. D. Salinger is concerned—and for reasons I have already suggested. But critics cannot be accused quite yet of dispensing charity.

What seems much more plausible is that criticism has arrived by now at such an advanced stage of professionalism, has become such a sure means to academic fame and power, that it has indeed had to discover and promote certain new writers in order to guarantee its own survival and have available a fresh supply of materials on which to do its work. After all, the enormous momentum built up during the critical conquest of the classic moderns could not be allowed simply to peter out. Too large an investment was at stake; the advance had to continue; new hostages had to be taken. Something had to be done to fill the vacuum created when the important ideas about the older writers all seemed to have been expressed, and the whole complicated enterprise found itself on the verge of falling into the dreariness of perpetual reassessment and re-reassessment—that one more essay on the increasingly petty little thing in Faulkner or Joyce, stretching on and on and on into infinity. But luckily, the present group of younger novelists happened to be there to prevent this, and luckily too, they happened to be excellently suited to the kind of approach criticism was already accustomed to making. In fact, a good part of their work seemed to be tailored specifically for analysis, as if it had been produced with the critical rules of proper prose etiquette quite consciously in mind, its very finish of style and form giving the effect of a critical act already begun by the author and fairly begging for completion in *Kenyon Review*. Hence, criticism found it possible to make the transition from the classic moderns to Salinger, Bellow, Malamud, Roth, Updike, and others almost without being aware of the change. And it is not surprising that it should sometimes behave as if indeed no change had occurred at all, as if these writers had somehow *become* the classics through having invited a comparable closeness of scrutiny.

Finally, of course, there has been the influence of the highly charged and competitive literary atmosphere in which we live, an atmosphere that has conditioned us to the idea that our productive power in the arts must be at least equal to, if not indistinguishable from, our huge industrial and scientific potential, and that on all fronts we ought to be moving ahead with vigor. The embarrassing fact, however, is that on the novelistic front we have only given the appearance of moving; we have merely wished ourselves into the illusion of movement. It is true that we have had a good many talented and interesting writers and any number of solid, well-wrought novels, of which a few, a very few, might even be expected to make some difference in the way we interpret our lives. But we have generally lacked the kind of arresting largeness and intensity of vision that, in view of our high cultural pretensions and, above all, the *sincerity* of our cultural caring, we feel we deserve. And what is worse, we know, whether or not we admit it, that we have been subsisting for years very largely on the creative glamor of previous decades, taking unlawful pride in the recitation of famous names and titles that we have no right whatever to claim. With all our confidence and technical know-how, in spite of the fuss we make over every vagrant spark of originality that blows our way, we are well aware that we have still not managed to produce genuinely major talents of our own to meet the competitive standard set by the twenties and thirties.

This has been especially hard for us to take because our idea of literary success and, therefore, the extent and nature of our literary ambitions, have been very largely determined by the achievements of those two decades. For many years now we have been compulsively seeking our own image in the dream of that golden era when genius seemed to be breaking out everywhere, and the great work was done that created our understanding of what it is like to be alive in the modern world. Yet even as we have been held captive by that dream, our knowledge of literary values and methods, along with our sense of our own high creative potentialities, has been vastly increased not only by the authority that criticism has taken on in our time, but by the sheer intensity of our obsession with what the past has achieved.

As a result, our position today is frustratingly ambiguous. On the one hand, we feel jealous, resentful, and vaguely frightened of the past; on the other, we feel knowledgeable enough and dedicated enough to advance beyond it. We have managed to develop powerful institutions for the critical study of literature and the teaching of writing, institutions in which the workings of the creative mind would seem to have been shorn of their mystery and brought at last under expert control. A whole complex academic and cultural enterprise has grown up around the widespread interest in the modern classics and the desire to produce talents comparable to them. Yet the talents somehow have not proved to *be* comparable, and the very complexity of the enterprise mocks us with our failure.

Nevertheless, the competitive pressures at every level of American life have grown so severe that falling creatively behind the past has come to seem almost as damaging to the national sense of security and well-being as falling behind the Russians in the armaments race. We have begun to feel that it is dangerous, immoral, perhaps even downright un-American to be less than the best in any field of endeavor. Hence, it is obvious that something had to be done. Either we had to go out and find some major talents of our own or we had to inflate the existing talents to the desired size—and the latter is in effect what criticism has done through its close attentiveness to the younger group of novelists.

None of this is, of course, the result of dark conspiracy or calculation. Criticism has not yet given up its virtue to Madison Avenue—although it has clearly been tempted from time to time—nor has a Presidential Commission on the Development of the National Resources of American Literary Talent ever been appointed to look into the matter and take the necessary steps. It has all come about simply in natural response to the powerfully felt need of a society affluent enough to believe that it can and must have everything any other society, past or present, ever had, whether that may be intercontinental ballistics missiles or great writers. Still, there is a sense in which it can be said that if some of the younger novelists had not existed, criticism would probably have been obliged to invent them—and it is even possible that in all honesty and purity of conscience it did.

However that may be, the procedures involved in the advancement of new talent are now part of the established politics of our literary life. A young writer appears with a first novel, and if he happens to be one of the lucky few, a complicated and ultimately mysterious mechanism goes at once into operation to set him apart from the anonymous mass of his contemporaries who bring out books and then, more often than not, simply drop into the void. Perhaps he has had the good fortune to receive an unusual number of favorable reviews from people whose opinions carry weight, or it may be that his book has been enthusiastically endorsed by well-known older writers and critics in advance of publication, so that it arrives before the public already wearing on its jacket the coveted seals of expert approval. In any event, something somehow marks him out in the very beginning as a special case deserving of rescue from the usual fate of almost immediate oblivion.

After this has been accomplished, any number of things can happen to speed him on his way to eminence. Before very long his name will probably begin to be mentioned in year-end surveys of outstanding books and in popular articles on "the current crop of new talents." Women will see his photograph in *Harper's Bazaar* or *Mademoiselle* and wonder if it would be socially advantageous to have read his book. He may be mentioned again, this time more importantly, in an article by Alfred Kazin in the *Atlantic* or Irving Howe in *Partisan* or, since the status lines of literary commentary are constantly shifting, by Kazin in *The Reporter* and Howe in *The New Republic*. He may even find that his novel has been selected as a runner-up for the National Book Award, an honor that, for negative but sound reasons, is considerably more prestigious than actually winning the award. Also it is likely that by now some enterprising young academic will have happened upon him, deemed him serious, and done a carefully tentative analysis of his novel for one of the smaller critical magazines such as *Modern Fiction Studies* or *Critique*. It would not even be especially surprising—the process of academic accommodation being what it is today—if within a year or two after publication the book had begun to appear on the required reading lists of several college courses in contemporary American fiction, and eager undergraduates had already set to work trying to "place" the author in a tendency or school.

Through attention of this kind, particularly the attention of critics and scholars, the young writer will have acquired at least the small beginnings of reputation, and when that happens, it remains only for the bigtime literary promotional agencies—and they may be as various and incompatible as *Esquire* and *Life, Playboy* and *The Saturday Review*—to put a veneer of notoriety or celebrity upon him. Now his name is mentioned regularly whenever the state of the current novel is discussed. He is interviewed about his work habits, his sex life, what he thinks of his contemporaries. He engages in debates with other writers; he is invited to appear at symposia, book fairs, and summer conferences, perhaps to take part in one of those big, nationally publicized panel discussions of large, fateful topics like "Fiction in an Age of Acute Anxiety" or "Fiction in an Age of Acute Boredom" that are held periodically by *Esquire* in collaboration with various famous universities. At some point he will in all probability be asked to serve for a term or a year as a campus writer-in-residence. If not, he may decide to follow the example of other celebrated writers like himself and buy a house in Connecticut where he can settle down, entertain his New York literary friends on weekends, and get going at last on that long-awaited next book.

There may, on the other hand, be some real doubt in the young writer's mind about the necessity, or even the advisability, of settling down and doing that next book. After all, he has had ample opportunity by now to capitalize on a good many of the currently respectable ways of being a successful writer without really writing—he has lectured, debated, discussed, conferred, confessed, appeared, and resided. And having discovered that these activities have brought him as much if not more prestige than books would normally bring, and with none of the stress and hazard besides, he may very well conclude that he would be better off not writing at all.

He may in fact be entirely right about this, for a point of career can indeed be reached where it is practically inadvisable for a young writer to continue writing and far more strategic for him just to lean back and enjoy the advantages that come simply from being well known and going through the motions, putting in the appearances, necessary to keep himself in the public eye. Celebrity, after a certain amount of it has been achieved, tends to become self-perpetuating. As it grows in size, it comes to depend less and less on the specific act or gift that may initially have called it into being, and more and more on skillful public relations. Thus, for those who have it, the important thing after a while is to make sure that their names are regularly associated in print with other well-known names in a recognized context of celebrity. In that way, and that way alone, they can be certain of continuing to be celebrated without continuing to do any work.

The most available context of celebrity for the young writer is apt to be the big quality magazines that, as I have suggested, combine a taste for marginal literary seriousness with an avid curiosity about the latest thing in celebrity gossip. Within their pages the young writer can enjoy the advantages of fame by association in at least two important ways. In *Esquire* and *Playboy*, for example, he can appear in print alongside the latest reminiscence of Scott Fitzgerald or the hitherto undisclosed last words of Hemingway and derive incalculable benefit from the impression that must after a while be created that such propinquity implies equality, even fraternity, and that if he and his distinguished predecessors occupy adjacent spaces, they may very well occupy adjacent places side by side in the hierarchy of literary greatness. After all, there's old Hem and then there's old Scott and then there's old me—right there on Page 35.

Also if he is genuinely determined, the young writer can push his way into the crowded *Esquire* arena in which everybody is busy profiling everybody else and perhaps eventually get the chance to profile somebody himself. Then it may be that after Mailer on Mailer and Mailer on Baldwin and Baldwin on Mailer and Mailer on President Kennedy, Mrs. Kennedy, and Sonny Liston, and Gore Vidal on Robert Kennedy, there will come a day when it will be Mailer on *him,* or, even better, Mailer on him on *Baldwin* on Mailer— the white boy on the white boy on the black boy on the white boy, the two-toned, four-layer cake of desegregated literary incest. Such things do happen, and they have been known to make all the difference in a promising new career. For again they can create the impression that the young writer already belongs to a group of proven and accepted talents who are so securely established that all they have left to do is inspect one another's greatness.

The "Establishment" Chart

Not very long ago *Esquire* itself came forward with some excellent instruction in the art of how to have a great literary age without great books and writers. The whole effort of its famous "Literary Establishment" issue (July, 1963) was clearly to "profile" our literary life in such a way that it would seem to take on the high gloss of creative excitement and activity that we associate with the twenties and have so long wished our own time might possess. Now, through the kind offices of slanted publicity, we do possess it, or at least *Esquire* says we do—which, in an era when the prepared public image has come more and more to *be* the reality, may very well add up to the same thing. The elaborate chart of writers, agents, book publishers, and magazines, the long list of works-in-progress, the excerpts from forthcoming novels, the interviews, reminiscences, and critical commentaries—all make it appear that we are now enjoying a full-scale renaissance at least as big as the one that produced Hemingway and Fitzgerald, that, indeed, eager new Hemingways and Fitzgeralds by the dozens and dozens are already among us, simply awaiting the leg-up to eminence that the ever-alert *Esquire* editors have now given them.

This flattering picture of ourselves is supposedly authenticated first by the many excerpts from forthcoming novels, all by prominent writers, and second by the article on the founders of the *Paris Review*. In its prefatory note to the excerpted materials *Esquire* breathlessly observes that "they used to say the American novel was dead; now *Time* magazine (oxymoronically) reports 'a modest literary boom.' It takes no literary historian to recognize a vintage literary year in retrospect: in 1925, for instance, Sinclair Lewis published *Arrowsmith;* Dreiser, *An American Tragedy;* Dos Passos, *Manhattan Transfer;* Fitzgerald, *The Great Gatsby;* Faulkner had just finished *Soldier's Pay;* and Hemingway was working on *The Sun Also Rises.* But who in 1925 could have known what a great year it was? Whether 1963 is such a year we leave up to you...."

Of course it is not left up to us at all. *Esquire knows* what a great year 1963 is. But unfortunately it is obliged to prove its case with the aforementioned excerpts. After reading them one is forced to conclude that it takes no literary historian to recognize not only that 1925 is in no imminent danger of eclipse as a vintage year but that, if the books from which the excerpts were taken are all in fact published, we are entering upon one of the dullest and bleakest periods we have experienced in literature since 1925. Dreiser, Fitzgerald, and the others at least gave the impression (even in 1925) that they knew what they were doing and very much wanted to do it, while most of these pieces read like the efforts of people whom some gigantic key has set in motion and who have no choice but to go on moving until the spring runs down.

On the other hand, the article on the founders of the *Paris Review* does manage to make history—or perhaps more correctly, invent history—by providing us with a literary past we did not know and are still not really sure we had, and a group of gay and eccentric contemporaries who just a short time ago were allegedly doing the same sort of gay and eccentric things that the grand old expatriates used to do. The irony, of course, is that, as the article itself admits, the *Paris Review* people were doing these things in quite deliberate *imitation* of the expatriates, pretending as hard as they could that they were carousing in the Paris of Hemingway and Gertrude Stein instead of the Paris of Irwin Shaw and, *quel dommage!*, Gertrude Stein's *nephew*. And what is far worse, they are apparently still pretending. George Plimpton, one of the *Review* editors, is described as going to great trouble and expense to perpetuate the illusion of group spirit and creative excitement by continuing to throw large parties for the old crowd, complete with call girls, bongo players, and junkies, a local distributor of pot, a descendant of Whistler's mother, Hemingway's former boxing coach, and on at least one really swinging occasion, Jackie Kennedy.

But the saddest and most telling irony—and one that nicely underscores the fatuity of *Esquire*'s whole argument —is that the literary result of all this self-conscious effort to repeat the past was and still is simply the *Paris Review,* a perfectly conventional, quasi "little" magazine whose chief claim to fame is emphatically not the discovery and promotion of original new talent in the grand old manner of *Transition* and *Broom,* but the series of interviews that it has conducted with already established writers. That fact should tell us far more about the real nature of our literary age than *Esquire* can ever hope to contradict with its wishfully falsified picture of renaissance. It should tell us that however much we try to be otherwise, we continue to be interested more in talk about writing than in writing, more in hearing how it was done by others than in doing it ourselves.

It may just be, therefore, that in a curious way and entirely without intending it, *Esquire* actually does succeed in giving us a true picture of our time after all. For what the "Literary Establishment" issue demonstrates, while seeking to prove how fresh and original we are, is that we are really unoriginal and old. We are still trying to see ourselves in the image of the fabulous past, still trying to make the sixties look like the twenties and ourselves like our distinguished predecessors. And of course so long as we continue to do that, we will be powerless to create ourselves in our own image, and the originality of the sixties will not be created at all.

Nevertheless, the value of just about any kind of publicity being what it is today, the *Esquire* inquiry is bound to have the effect of overinflating the reputations of some of our younger writers even more grossly than they already were, while those of certain others will in a small way have been made right then and there on that chart of names alleged to compose the "Literary Establishment." It is even possible that there will be a few people whose sole distinction for years to come will be that, through clerical bungling or the benevolent intercession of friends or relatives, they managed to get on that chart. At least there are names on it I never heard of before and very much doubt if I shall ever hear of again—unless of course an *Esquire* Chartist Society is some day formed.

Then there will be those who are already well known but whose public image will, thanks to *Esquire*, take on a new bizarre and ambiguous dimension. William Styron, for example, had the honor of being referred to on at least two important occasions in the issue and both times in ways that seem certain to cause confusion. Mailer's essay on the talents of his contemporaries contains one of the most beautifully vituperative attacks on Styron's last novel, *Set This House on Fire*, (set it on fire, indeed!) that could conceivably be written. The book is called, among other things, "A bad maggoty novel. Four or five half-great short stories . . . buried like pullulating organs in a corpse of fecal matter: overblown unconceived philosophy, Technicolor melodramatics . . . the magnum opus of a fat spoiled rich boy . . . the book of a man whose soul [has] gotten fat. . . ." Then in the *Paris Review* article we learn that Styron enjoys the privilege of having Jackie Kennedy call him by his first name.

As one ponders the seemingly contradictory values of these two references, several questions come automatically to mind. Is Styron some new breed of social literary success and literary failure? Is it possible to fail so abysmally in literature—as Mailer at least claims he does—and succeed so spectacularly in the White House? Which in the end will affect Styron's public status more: Mailer's devastating attack on him or the former First Lady's prestigious gift of intimacy—and which, so far as that goes, will finally be more *damaging?* Does it really matter that he has written a bad novel if Jackie Kennedy still addresses him as Bill? Does *anything* really matter if Jackie Kennedy addresses you as Bill?

The serious point, of course, is that in the kind of world that *Esquire* represents there finally exists no clear relation between literary reputation and literary achievement or between reputation and public status. And one's perspective is constantly being deranged by the phenomenon of the young writer who may be quite widely known and gossiped about in the society of the big magazines—to say nothing of the White House—and yet whose creative work is scarcely known to, or even scarcely deserving of notice by, most of the people who find it chic to drop his name at cocktail parties.

Mailer himself, in the troubled years that have followed his first success, has, as I say, become an increasingly impressive illustration of this phenomenon, and Baldwin seems well on his way to becoming another. At this moment at least Baldwin enjoys high prominence as a public figure not because he is a writer of famous novels but because he is an extremely articulate literary Negro with explosive opinions on the race question. Almost everybody knows about Baldwin as professional Negro and Negro polemicist, just as almost everybody knows about Mailer as professional eccentric and polemicist for himself. But of those who do, one wonders how many also know about *Go Tell It on the Mountain* and *Giovanni's Room*, have really read any of Mailer's fiction since *The Naked and the Dead*, or for that matter, would consider it time well spent if they had.

Of course in Baldwin's case—and to a lesser extent in Mailer's—it is his opinions that receive the important publicity and not his novels. A socially controversial and polemical book like *The Fire Next Time* has an impact far greater than any novel of his would be likely to have; and this is bound to be so, not only because Baldwin's opinions continue to seem more interesting than his novels, but simply because we live in that kind of age. Obviously there is nothing wrong on the face of it with being best known for one's opinions, and certainly Mr. Baldwin's have the greatest social and moral significance. But opinions, to paraphrase Gertrude Stein, are not literature, nor is a polemical reputation a literary reputation. The two simply must not be confused.

Yet the point is that they are being confused, and quite openly and cynically. A writer like Baldwin or Mailer is given attention *as if* his creative work were not only widely known but widely respected, as if, in fact, his public standing actually were the logical end product of the excellence of his creative work rather than the bastard offshoot of his personal eccentricities, the color of his skin, or the distinguished company he manages to keep in or out of print.

It is therefore not so very surprising that there should be young one- or two-book writers today who seem to feel no particular obligation to settle down to their proper business of writing more books, since they already enjoy most of the advantages of having written them without having had to. It is not surprising *if* one remembers—as one persistently must remember—that what we are dealing with here is actually not a literary world at all, but a publicity and celebrity world, in which the writer simply as personality or public phenomenon can achieve, if he is lucky, a status comparable in kind, if not in scope, to that of movie stars and political figures, but in which his status may have little or nothing to do with his contribution to literature.

The fact that it is not genuine literary status he enjoys may or may not trouble his conscience. It very probably will not, for the counterfeit that he does enjoy is what passes for the real thing in the world in which he so successfully makes his way, and it would be absurd to expect him to take quixotic risks for the sake of a principle that would be certain not to pay off. The respect of his peers and contemporaries, the support of an informed and genuinely interested readership, the benefits to be derived from a criticism that senses and attempts to define the real values in his work —all these may be nice idealisms to which now and then his mind dreamily recurs. But he is far too ambitious and practical to be willing to wait for the revolution that might one day turn them into realities. Besides, if they ever became realities, who knows what might happen to his career?

Boredom with the Novel

One would expect and hope that it would be just here, in the face of the meretricious concerns of the big magazine world, that highbrow criticism would provide a corrective reminder of the form that the right sort of interest in the younger writers should properly take. That, after all, is or ought to be the function of any serious criticism of contemporary literature, and certainly it ought to be the function of one that has lately done so very much to promote these writers and even to prepare the way for their glamorization by the big magazines.

Yet when one takes sober account of the interest that up to now this criticism has shown, one cannot help but be struck by how little of it seems any more relevant to what ought to be important about these writers than is the interest shown by the big magazines. Where the magazines tend to look upon them as public phenomena, as figures of celebrity to be gossiped about, the majority of highbrow critics seem to see them almost solely as literary phenomena, as *objects* of analysis and commentary, quite apart from any really close engagement of the problem of their quality as artists and the importance of the image of experience that their novels project.

This is not, of course, to suggest that there have not been any number of perfectly sound attempts to determine just what it is that these writers are trying to do, or a great many sensitive studies of various single aspects of their work. In fact, the criticism they have received has generally been of very good quality indeed, and against it very little can be said, especially if one has grown used, as most of us have, to not holding out for any particular brilliance or originality. The bulk of it is as solid and competent, sane and well balanced, as the best of the older historical scholarship that it has slowly superseded. But while one has come to expect and allow for a certain sort of dogged averageness, the essential pedestrianism of the English-instructor-temporarily-turned-critic mentality, one most emphatically does not expect to find an air of detachment so pure that one might almost be watching biologists contemplate bugs under glass.

Yet this is just what over and over again one does find: a criticism that seems to possess all the scholarly virtues except genuine involvement with the work at hand. I do not mean that it is chary of praise or deficient in that humble tolerance of the mediocre that we so often mistake for critical generosity. There can be no doubt at all about the admiration, even the positive anxiety to admire, with which it typically approaches the work of some of the better young novelists. Nevertheless, it is clearly one thing for a critic to write an essay extolling the virtues of, say, Saul Bellow or Bernard Malamud, and quite another for him to convince

76

the reader that Bellow and Malamud really matter, that they speak really deeply to him, and that he has felt a genuine shock of recognition in reading their work, the effect and meaning of which he wants passionately to communicate. One can think of any number of critics who are highly adept at extolling the virtues of these and other writers, but very few indeed who manage to make the virtues seem really virtuous.

In short, what is truly astounding is how little excitement, how little passion, the work of the younger writers has generated among the very people who promote it most vigorously and appear to be most convinced of its excellence. In precisely what this excellence consists, just how it operates to justify their approbation, they seem curiously unable to say, and perhaps the question is finally beside the point. For, as I have said, it does look very much as though these writers in any case just *had* to be discussed, just *had* to be given the enormous amount of attention they have received, simply because they happened to be there, and criticism desperately needed materials with which to keep its highly developed techniques in working order.

Still, even where questions of professional expediency are concerned, there must come a time when the exercise of will alone proves to be inadequate and a more honest commitment of the mind and emotions is required. In this case, because such a commitment is missing, the attention cannot help but seem mechanical and contrived, willed rather than freely given, and more than one critic, in the course of discussing contemporary fiction, has expressed his boredom with what he has been doing, his sheepish recognition that the work before him may have every virtue but still lacks genuine interest to him, genuine relevance to his life. "To read a group of novels," said Leslie Fiedler, "is these days a depressing experience. At least, it is so for me; after the fourth or fifth, I find myself beginning to think about 'The Novel,' and I feel a desperate desire to sneak out to a movie. How respectable the form has become, how predictable!"

Perhaps this boredom, this curious double sense of irrelevance and predictability, accounts for the fact that, although they appear to hold the better younger writers in the highest esteem, our literary intellectuals do not customarily look to them to provide the basic terms for understanding or evaluating the experience of the present age. In view of that esteem, one would suppose that the ideological debates and cultural analyses of the time would be full of references to their work, that along with the sociologists and psychologists, the religious and political philosophers, writers such as Bellow and Malamud or Baldwin and Mailer would constantly be cited as authorities for this or that insight into the condition of American society and the place of the intellectual or the ordinary man within it.

After all, the precedent of the recent past has accustomed us to the idea that the more important imaginative literature of a period will normally provide this kind of ideological source material, and one cannot help remembering with what a profound sense of excitement the literary intellectuals of thirty and forty years ago discovered in their creative contemporaries both confirmation of and instruction for their own insights into the modern world. One remembers also that the process of discovery worked just as well the other way, that creative writers learned from their intellectual contemporaries, and made use of what they learned in novels and poems that, as a result, often read more like philosophical statements or illustrations of social and psychological theories than like imaginative works. But we know of course that that was a very special circumstance, that the discovery of the modern world was an experience that at that time intellectuals and creative writers seemed to share in common and simultaneously, and that they enjoyed a congeniality, even a startling unanimity, of vision that their successors of the present and foreseeable future will probably never know. Still, the contrast with a highly unusual historical phenomenon may serve to dramatize the extent to which today's creative writers have failed to capture the imaginations of their contemporaries and to be accepted as the moral and intellectual spokesmen for their generation.

Interestingly enough, but not at all surprisingly, the writers whose works are most often cited as authorities in contemporary intellectual discussion are still, for the most part, the traditional classic figures of the modern age. In the novel, Dostoevski, Proust, Kafka, James, Joyce, Faulkner, Fitzgerald, and Hemingway; in poetry, Yeats, Pound, Eliot, and Auden; the great creative theorists and philosophical writers, Freud, Jung, Kierkegaard, Sartre, and Camus—these are the men who continue to provide the basic terms for our essential comprehension of life. When we ask why this should be so, it is conventional to say that because some of the best of them were the first on the scene of the twentieth century, and others were products of the intense revolutionary period between the wars, they were able to proceed naturally to formulations of the most primary and vital kind about the nature of modern experience. They had, in a sense, first choice of the fundamental philosophical and imaginative materials of our time at the moment when those materials were just beginning to become available. They were the first to do what no one had been privileged to do before, and as is so often the case in philosophy and art, they were the last to do it really well.

Whether or not this is true, it seems to be a fact that the

emotional and imaginative responses of a good many American intellectuals have become arrested in the work of some of these men, particularly in the classics of the twenties and thirties. No one who has written since has touched them half so deeply; no later work has made anything like the radical difference in their lives that *The Waste Land* and *Ulysses* or *Main Street* and *The Great Gatsby*—to name only the most obvious—were able to make. It is not merely that these were among the great works of their youth, and youth is a time when, as Lionel Trilling once said, "we find the books we give up but do not get over." It is not even that they undeniably *were*—albeit in widely differing ways and to surprisingly different degrees—great works. One can think of others both before and since that have been very nearly as great or at least very nearly as original, shocking, or disturbing, but altogether lacking in the power to educate and transform that these possessed.

The point seems to be that in addition to their very considerable artistic merits, these works had the advantage of appearing at exactly the right time both to dramatize modern experience with the maximum freshness and to be read with the maximum sensitivity. They appeared at a time when modern experience had not yet become the commonplace and predictable thing it now is: they became famous during a period when the present intellectual generation first began to be consciously interested in literature, and before that interest turned self-conscious, professional, and critical, before literature ceased for them to be a passionate extension of living experience and became abstracted and depersonalized into a subject matter.

The causes of this—and it appears to involve a genuine emotional alienation from the realities of both literature and life—are familiar and obvious. They are the logical results of the institutionalization of the creative process in an age that knows persistently more than it feels and in which literature has grown increasingly isolated, often to the point of hermetically sealed irrelevance, from its natural sources in the human social scene. But because the alienation occurred, the period of their initial contact with the modern classics has inevitably taken on for many intellectuals something of the quality of a lost Edenic experience, a condition of primal, apocalyptic union having a recalled intensity rather like first sexual intercourse. Everything after has seemed, in the hot light of it, a bad dream of diminished potency and pinched climaxes, or at best a brave pretense of enthusiasms only officially felt.

It is not at all surprising that some of them—or, more correctly and honorably, some of us—should trace not merely our first but our last really vital response to literature back to that period, or that the modern classics should in effect have taken the place of experience in our minds, have seemed so powerfully right in their formulations of the basic truths of modern reality that we have unconsciously revised and even altogether reconceived such experience as we have had to fit the portraits of experience they have given us. In a very real way those great works have done our imagining as well as our living for us, and we have very little sense of being engaged with life that is not somehow connected with the profoundly moving images of life with which they first seduced and enslaved our imagination.

Enslaved would seem to be the proper word, for again as Mr. Fiedler has very correctly observed:

"What irks our age and drives us to the more shameful excesses of 'scholarship' . . . is that we feel ourselves trapped among the clichés of anti-cliché that we have inherited from the great stereotype-mongers of the twenties. . . . No one has succeeded since the age of Sinclair Lewis and Sherwood Anderson in seeing an actual American small town or a living member of the Kiwanis club. The gross pathos of Anderson or the journalistic thinness of Lewis is beside the point: for all of us, the real facts of experience have been replaced by Winesburg, Ohio, and by Babbitt; myth or platitude, we have invented nothing to replace them. . . . We have lived for thirty years in the world of someone else's dreams: a compulsive world in which Lieutenant Henry forever declares his private peace, Sherwood Anderson eternally walks out of his office, the Artist forever leaves the world of Puritanism and Respectability for the utopias of bohemia or expatriation. To be sure, we do not all relive the legendary pattern, or even believe it; but we have been unable to imagine our choices in any other image." *

That is the crucial point: we have been unable to imagine our choices in any other image. We may recognize the literary formulations of the modern classic past as the stereotypes and platitudes they have now become. We may even be convinced that they have blinded us to the changed realities of the present and forced us to plod endlessly round and round in a ring of wishful daydream and sentimental self-delusion. But because they have helped to determine the very structure and content of our consciousness, we cannot reject them without rejecting a vital part of consciousness itself. They are simply the terms in which we have been educated to see when we open our eyes, and we have not yet been able to subject ourselves to the profoundly purgative act of reimagination that would be necessary if we ever hope to see in different, fresher, and more accurate terms.

* From "The Ant on the Grasshopper," in *No! In Thunder,* by Leslie Fiedler, Beacon Press, Boston, 1960. Reprinted by permission of The Beacon Press, copyright © by Leslie A. Fiedler.

The Kilroy Effect

And this is just where the present group of younger novelists seems to have failed the intellectual most conspicuously. For whether or not he is aware of it, the intellectual looks to them, as he once looked to their predecessors, for the fresh vision of experience that he has been unable to achieve by himself. He expects them to free his imagination from its bondage to the past at the same time that he expects them to repeat the past by giving him a comparable intensity and excitement. He does not, to be sure, want reincarnations of the writers he admired in his youth, people who write *like* Hemingway, Fitzgerald, Faulkner, and the others. These have always been easy to come by, and their only effect has been to give focus to his self-disgust (for they are simply more advanced sufferers from his own disease) and send him running back to the originals. But what he does want are writers who can arouse in him the kind of response the originals aroused, who can flush out of his brain the detritis of stereotype and platitude and replace it with materials that have been mined out of a deeply personal and therefore necessarily new commitment of the imagination to the living realities of the present time. His intelligence may tell him that this is at best a very large order indeed, that even if the writers were available to fill it, he himself is no longer so receptive to literary novelty as he once was and perhaps would not be capable of responding with his old freshness and intensity if such a response were clearly indicated. Still, these are his emotional expectations, the expectations that were branded into his emotions by the heat of his first passionate involvement with the modern classics, and he will not, cannot, settle for less.

It is not merely that he fastidiously refuses to accept a substitute for the genuine article. In literature there are any number of varieties and forms of the genuine article, and there can be no question but that at least some of the current younger novelists are as genuine in their way as any of the classics were. It is more that he habitually and instinctively holds out for one kind of genuineness, the classic kind, the first-on-the-scene kind, the kind that gave him his initial overpowering shock of recognition, but translated of course into the terms of the present scene and a comparably over-powering shock. So far as he is concerned, this is the kind that any writer calling himself serious today must possess if he is to make a real claim upon the imagination.

It is perfectly true that a serious writer may be admired for his technical accomplishment—and the intellectual will be the first to concede him admiration for that—but unless he is able to bring about a purgation and renovation of consciousness, unless he is able to penetrate to the secret springs of being and reality and find there new life that we may have known was there but have never before had disclosed to us in just this way, he is doomed to be admired but not really liked, to be interesting but incapable of arousing passionate interest. This—to restate what I said earlier—has been the chief difficulty as well as the ambiguity in the intellectual's relation to the younger novelists all along. He has needed and wanted to be passionately interested in them. He has needed and wanted them to be passionately interesting. By all logic, furthermore, they *ought* to be, and for the same reason that, by all logic, this ought to be a great literary age: simply because we so clearly deserve it. But in spite of his very best intentions and the sternest promptings of his conscience, the intellectual's important feelings have not been engaged by these writers. Hence, his praise, no matter

84

how generously given, has the ring of falsehood in it. It is impersonal, ceremonial, almost at times a matter of etiquette, and in the end it is meaningless, since it acknowledges in its tone a success that is finally only the polished form of a vital kind of failure.

How then does one account for the fact that in the very process of giving these writers close critical attention and praise, the intellectual so often appears to be, and occasionally confesses to being, bored to death with them? It is true that he expects history to repeat itself through them and restore to him the lost intensities of his youth. But it is also true that he is making this presumably unfair demand at a time not only when he himself has grown so sophisticated about literature and experience that any novelist, however gifted, would be hard put to tell him anything new, but when novelists in general are finding it extremely difficult to achieve any kind of effective imaginative relationship with experience. Novelists in fact are suffering from the same smothering sense of stereotype and platitude that afflicts the intellectual. And in their efforts to break free of it, they have too often been forced to deal with materials, and to adopt methods of treating those materials, that may be original enough in themselves but are so private and idiosyncratic, evocative of so little beyond the personal experience of the author, that they can scarcely be expected to seem exciting or particularly meaningful to even the most sympathetic reader, except perhaps as displays of verbal or technical skill.

There are of course novelists, usually the less talented and intelligent, who seem to have succeeded in remaining unaware of the difficulty altogether, and who, as a result, have continued to write as if nobody, including themselves, knew very much about anything, as if life were essentially as barren of complication as it seems to have been for Dreiser

85

and Farrell. Others like William Styron seem to have tried to *make* history repeat itself by using the standard effects of the modern classics, apparently without realizing that these are precisely the stereotypes and platitudes from which their more discriminating contemporaries are struggling to escape.

But for the genuinely perceptive and talented, the burden of writing in an age of hypersophistication is heavy indeed. And for the intellectual, who reads and judges their work, the problem of imaginative ennui, the nagging little foreknowledge that wherever the work may take him he will very probably have been there already, must constantly intrude, since it is inevitable that he will know as much and often far more about literature and experience than the majority of the writers he reads, and that he will bring to them expectations that they can hardly hope to satisfy. He, after all, judges on the basis of critical standards formed by the best achievements of an exceptional past. They, on the other hand, must try to *be* best while living in the shadow of that past and fighting not only against the fear that the best has already been done, but also against the knowledge that the established ways of being best are now blinders that they must somehow throw off if they are to be any good at all.

It sometimes seems that a "Kilroy was here" sign hangs over the literary life of our age. It is a sign that flashes in the intellectual's eyes each time he opens a new novel and before he has had a chance to read a word. And of course it flashes dazzlingly in the eyes of the novelist before he has had a chance to write a word. The insolent, ubiquitous signature of the man who got there ahead of everybody else and, like Hemingway's little Indian girl, did first what no one has ever done, or may ever do, better—this is the ghost that haunts the novelist in his search for new and unclaimed territories of the imagination.

"Nothing Left to Do but Think"—Saul Bellow

Obviously, what the age demands is just what the intellectual more or less instinctively holds out for: a group of writers with minds powerful enough to recognize the stereotypes and platitudes for what they are but able to function originally in spite of them—or, even better, able to incorporate them *into* their vision of experience, so that the knowledge that, in lesser minds, has proved to be crippling, would become for them an important adjunct of vision. This is perhaps to say that our most urgent need at the moment is for a genuinely intellectual fiction, but intellectual in a new and robust sense. Certainly, there is no hope left in the various stances and poses of anti-intellectualism in which American writers of the past have found energy and comfort, and in which far too many continue to hide out today, quite deliberately confusing mindlessness with vitality, the most elementary emotions with the most significant experience, as if they had vested interests in preserving the novel as a last stronghold of freedom *from* thought.

Nevertheless, there are many people who believe that what is wrong with the novel is that it is much too intellectual already, that contemporary writers generally think too much before they feel and in the process think feeling away. It seems to me rather that the novel is not nearly intellectual enough, that contemporary writers generally think too little to be able to feel. For to think inadequately is finally to feel unvigorously; and in art, a defect in the power to communicate emotion is finally a defect in the power to understand emotion. The novel has been devitalized up to now not by consciousness but by inadequate consciousness and by self-consciousness. It has yet to discover, for the uses of our time, consciousness as a form of emotional vitality, as the very mode of passionate and original vision.

Consciousness in this form was carried to a certain point of literary development by Proust, James, Joyce, and Eliot, but no one has since been able to carry it significantly beyond that point. That in fact is one of the great perplexities: the failure of the modern artistic sensibility to build upon the foundations laid down by its pioneer minds, the curious abortion of intellectuality in art at just the time when the need for increased intellectuality has become almost a matter of artistic life or death. Fifteen years ago in his essay "Art and Fortune," Lionel Trilling made what seemed at the time the perfectly sensible prediction that "the novel of the next decades will deal in a very explicit way with ideas." Regrettably, the novel at least in America has so far given little encouragement to Mr. Trilling's powers of prophecy. Instead, it has shown itself to be essentially as inviolate to ideas as Eliot said James's mind was, although without the compensating fineness. It has remained arrested or frozen in a view of experience that is now being revealed as vastly too simple for our present sophistication, has continued to tell us perpetually less than we know, perpetually less than we have already, as educated moderns, discovered for ourselves, and immeasurably less than Proust, James, and the others had already discovered many decades ago. In fact, the distance between the level of perception to be found in the average serious novel and the level at which most of us habitually perceive has grown so wide that reading novels has become a process of willfully suspending not only our disbelief but whole functions of our intelligence.

There may, as I have suggested, be all sorts of convincing reasons why this should be so, but the fact remains that it is so. And because it is, the novel has become virtually as alien to the real interests and needs of the intellectual as it has to those of the middlebrow. For if it has ceased to be a vehicle of middlebrow experiences, it has also clearly failed to *become* a vehicle of both intellectual experiences and consciousness, and this in spite of the fact that at its best it has unquestionably grown *more* intellectual than it used to be and has captured the attention of intellectuals in a way it has never done before. But the experiences of which the intellectual is most intensely aware, the experience of ideas, the drama of consciousness in an age of almost unbelievable complexity and ambiguity, the drama, above all, of retaining one's hold on consciousness in an age in which it is becoming daily more difficult (and perhaps more futile) to retain one's hold on sanity—none of this has yet found adequate reflection in the novel. And of course it will not so long as novelists lack the courage and strength of mind to recognize it as their main hope for escape from the impasse in which they now find themselves trapped.

This is obviously not to suggest that our most serious novelists lack familiarity with the life of ideas or respect for the importance of ideas. I have said that at its best the novel has grown more intellectual than it used to be, and that can only mean that we have at least some novelists who are more intellectual than novelists of the recent past have been, however small a distinction this may seem to be. One might even go so far as to claim for some the larger distinction of being the most intellectually *aware* novelists we have had in America since the generation of Henry James, especially if by aware one means the kind of sophistication about ideas that typically expresses itself in fiction through the use of the various intellectual conventions of wit, irony, paradox, ambiguity, and symbolism. But it is one thing to be aware of and to respect ideas and quite another to have them, and it is a very different and singular thing both to have them and to be able to put them to original creative use, and so give them the quality of charged significance, of heightened dramatic force, that they possess in the minds of most intellectuals. There are many novelists today who show the influence of having done their work in an atmosphere of acute intellectual self-consciousness, just as there are many who appear to have worked in total and asinine obliviousness to it. But there are very few who write a genuinely intellectual fiction, and even fewer who write an intellectual fiction that speaks with some real urgency and intimacy to intellectuals, either because it concerns the intellectual life and intellectual characters or because it takes possession of ideas in a fresh and imaginative way. In fact, one can think of only two American writers at the present time who have come even close to producing such a fiction, and they are Saul Bellow and Mary McCarthy. Among all the writers who are praised, promoted, analysed, and gossiped about by intellectuals (and these include such special highbrow favorites as Bernard Malamud, James Baldwin, and Philip Roth), only Bellow and McCarthy seem really to have succeeded in cutting through the barrier of the intellectual's boredom with fiction and giving him a renewed sense of the possibility that a novel may after all have some meaningful relation to himself and his personal experience. Because of this, they alone have the distinction of occupying roughly the position in the intellectual world that Styron and O'Hara occupy in the middlebrow world, the position, that is, of novelistic spokesmen for their class and kind, official chroniclers in fiction of the representative interests and experiences of highbrow life. More than any other novelists now writing, they have helped to restore not only the intellectual's faith in the novel but intellectuality *to* the novel, and they have done this by taking as their principal concern the only subject matter to which the intellectual can be counted on to have a clear and dependable response, the condition of intellectuality itself, along with its social manifestations and vagaries, in the contemporary moment.

It would be altogether unfair to say that Bellow and McCarthy, in addition to occupying a comparable position, actually *are* the Styron and O'Hara of the intellectual world, and yet the thought does have a certain slight, facetious accuracy. Bellow, for example, is admired by the intellectuals in much the same way and for much the same reason that Styron is admired by the middlebrows: because he works within the standard literary conventions of his class and so conforms to the image of the important novelist officially held by that class. Both men, by virtue of this conformity, might be called Establishment or laureate writers, in the sense that their natural thematic and stylistic interests happen also to be those most in favor with their respective audience. Thus, where Styron reflects in his novels the typical middlebrow preoccupation with the anguished, possessed, drunken, and demented, the boorish, slobbish, phonily tender and sentimental, Bellow concerns himself with the anxious, skeptical, guilt-ridden, and analytical, the insulted, injured, condemning and self-condemned, the victims, dangling men, and seekers after personal salvation who most closely symbolize the intellectual's feelings of estrangement and psychic dislocation in the contemporary world.

Superficially, the styles of the two men appear to be very

much alike. Both are verbally rich, heavily metaphorical, studded with the adornments of comic extravagance. But where Styron's is bombastic, rhetorical, and melodramatic, ending most often—and often unintentionally—in a comedy of pokerfaced, rustic exaggeration and caricature, Bellow's at least in his later and more ambitious work, is witty, ironic, at times almost too coyly self-amused and derisive, overripe with literary allusions and conceits—as urbanly Jewish, even as rabbinical, in its flavor as Styron's is Southern rural Protestant. Finally and perhaps most importantly, where Styron in both his language and his subject matter recalls the modern classic tradition of the twenties and thirties, the principal clichés of which the middlebrows still mistake for original insights, Bellow seems to affirm his intellectual affiliations as well as his imaginative fastidiousness by rejecting this tradition altogether and finding his sources in Whitman and Twain and the international modernism of Dostoevski and Nietzche.

All this may be another way of saying that if Styron's work sounds to the middlebrows like the great literature they have been taught to admire, Bellow's work sounds to many intellectuals like the *intellectual* literature they have long hoped one of their number might someday produce. The particular convention or stereotype of grass-roots greatness, of the epic sweep and the "major" manner, supposedly exemplified—at least in the middlebrow view—by Styron, has never interested the majority of present-day American intellectuals very much. They have, of course, found its individual manifestations impressive, from time to time even hypnotic; they readily concede that it has in the past given rise to works of enduring significance; they may even regret that it no longer appears capable of doing so. But they have also resented the provincialism and middlebrowism, the implication of a virile but narrowly Anglo-Saxon mentality, which has always attached to it; and as a result, they have more or less unconsciously held out for something subtler, more urbane, sophisticated, provisional, and dialectical, something perhaps finally less specifically American than European, certainly less gentile than Jewish.

Bellow's early fiction in particular appeared to satisfy this requirement especially well. Not only was it obviously, almost, it seemed, deliberately, not "great" in the classic, grass-roots sense, but it embodied the intellectual-academic ideal, highly fashionable in the forties and fifties, of a fiction small in scope, tidy in form, antidramatic in content, ambiguous in meaning, which turned on the shy, sad sufferings of intellectual characters trapped in darkly internal crises of personal identity and moral responsibility. In a very real sense, it was just the sort of fiction most intellectuals would have written if they had been able to write fiction. It derived from their kind of experience and educational background; it had the staid, sedentary, vaguely pedagogical quality that they recognized, however reluctantly, to be the quality of their own lives; it was written with the same wry fastidiousness about the stereotypes and platitudes, the same distrust of cant and affectation, that their own deep commitment to literary values had given them. It quite simply expressed them in a way that the fiction of Fitzgerald, Hemingway, and Faulkner never had and never could, no matter how much they may have admired it in their youth or been entranced by the vision of experience it put forward. What, after all, had an urban Jewish intellectual, a City College English instructor and sworn upholder of *Partisan Review* and *Commentary*, to do with Fitzgerald's upper-middle-class virgins, Hemingway's Midwestern expatriates, or Faulkner's Southern primitives? It is true that they were part of the antique furniture of his mind, that they represented an important, perhaps even an especially beloved, element of his American cultural inheritance. But as projections of actual life they existed out there in the void of a world to which he had never belonged and with which he could identify only vicariously and in the abstract. With Bellow's early characters and situations, on the other hand, he had an immediate and powerfully concrete sense of identification, of moving in a world he knew intimately and among people whose predicament either was or might so easily have been his own.

[1964]

Mary McCarthy: Princess Among the Trolls

UNTIL the appearance of *The Group* in 1963, any attempt to draw a parallel between Mary McCarthy and a writer like John O'Hara would have seemed as discordant and irresponsible as the forcing of any connection between absolute opposites. Up to that time Miss McCarthy's fiction was so completely unlike O'Hara's that it appeared to stand in perpetual moral judgment upon it. It was a fiction as cleanly and heartlessly honest, as fastidiously knowing and cold of mind, as his was tumid with false heart and congested groin, emotionally sweaty and at the same time emotionally vapid, morally pretentious and at the same time eager to exploit the main chance for moral sensationalism and the cheap pornographic effect.

A parallel between Faulkner and John P. Marquand would have made much better sense. They at least would have understood each other and perhaps even have recognized that their difference was basically a difference of degree rather than kind, of talent more than essential integrity. But with Miss McCarthy and O'Hara it was not even a matter, as Fitzgerald said about himself and Hemingway, of their being unable to sit across the same table, because one spoke with the authority of failure, the other with the authority of success. Miss McCarthy could not conceivably have sat across the same table from O'Hara, and it would not have been because she saw him as a success or a failure. She would simply not have seen him as anything. He would simply not have existed for her, unless perhaps as another trophy to be added to her collection of male bores, another stuffed Brooks Brothers shirt.

It therefore came as a distinct surprise to find Miss McCarthy in *The Group* encroaching upon territory that O'Hara had long ago staked out as the province of his special and solitary vice, and resorting to methods that he has helped to make synonymous with the cheap and easy view of contemporary experience. It was particularly distressing to see her oversimplifying experience according to his formulas, reducing it to the same stock explanations that modern fiction has ordained through constant usage to be the fashionable explanations, and which he has compounded into a kind of motivational catechism to be ritually recited on any and every occasion calling for insight into human behavior.

Ask to know why a female O'Hara character is unhappy, and the answer will pop back at you with the simple-minded efficiency of a fortune told by weighing machine: either she is frigid, she is sterile, or she is insatiable. Ask to know why a male O'Hara character is unhappy, and you won't even have to put in another penny: either he is impotent or he is a repressed homosexual (unless of course he also is insatiable). Ask to know why Miss McCarthy's ex-Vassar girls, their husbands, their lovers, and seducers are unhappy, and the machine will make a great many complicated-sounding noises and take longer to respond, but when it does, the answer will be the same. Both sets of characters are victims of that classic *reductio ad absurdum* of the modern emotional predicament, the fallacy that sexual ripeness is all— or jolly well ought to be. They are characters whom the creative imagination has insufficiently created, who are insufficiently alive in the writer's mind to become anything other than inert codifications of popular psychiatric abstractions. They are also excellent examples of what must result when a writer imitates psychiatry without consulting the source material shared in common by both literature and psychiatry—the uniqueness, complexity, and ambiguity of the individual man and woman. For Miss McCarthy in *The Group* they represent a clear abdication of creative responsibility and intelligence, a perhaps fatal lapse of that fine wry fastidiousness in the face of clichés that was always vigilantly alive in her earlier work.

It is of course possible that the exact opposite is true: that beneath the stereotyped surfaces of the novel Miss McCarthy's fastidiousness is operating as powerfully as ever, that, in fact, her whole effort is precisely to expose, through a kind of dead-pan satirical exaggeration, the emptiness of her stereotypes, even that she is setting out to parody the popular psycho-sexual explanations of behavior that have become catechistic in the work of writers like O'Hara, who continue to think of them not merely as scientifically valid but as rather daringly realistic.

One wishes there were some really substantial evidence for believing this to be so, for then *The Group* might well have been a brilliant example of a rare variety of novel that we have serious need for at the present time and that one would expect a person of Miss McCarthy's intelligence to have written: a genuinely radical, antimodernist comedy of ideological manners, a burlesque of the outmoded postures of belief that obstruct our vision of reality as it actually is, with everything in it turning back on itself and commenting at every point on the triteness of its own observations, the kind of novel that Gide, with a more purely esthetic purpose, tried to write in *The Counterfeiters*. But unfortunately such an argument, while it does honor an intention that may in fact have existed in Miss McCarthy's mind, cannot show that the intention was adequately carried through in her performance.

The main problem seems to be that Miss McCarthy's point of view merges with, and finally becomes indistinguishable from, the point of view of her characters. That their point of view is frivolous and vapid is clearly indicated by the action. But it is a defect of the method Miss McCarthy has chosen to employ, the O'Hara method of objective exposition and accumulative documentation, that that point of view is allowed to go unchallenged until finally it is established as the sole vantage position from which the action can be judged. There is no other position, no other character or set of circumstances (as, for example, there is in *The Counterfeiters*), that provides a convincingly corrective or alternative point of view or that fully and dramatically incorporates Miss McCarthy's own judgment of her characters.* Instead, her judgment is confined to random touches of irony, single and isolated instances of satire, which are not

---

* There is, to be sure, one character, Polly Andrews, who is apparently intended to represent a "positive" alternative to the generally puerile value system of The Group. But her portrait is so soap-operaishly "good," her solution to the problems of her life so tritely easy, that she seems in the end as puerile as the rest. Miss McCarthy is really convincing only when she sneers. When she tries to be affirmative, she lapses into the misty-eyed sentimentalities and merely rhetorical optimisms of the secret Victorian who is so often the tough-minded satirist's bashful other self.

strong enough or frequent enough to become authoritative.

If it were not for her method, the action might serve to judge and condemn itself. But her method requires that she confine herself pretty largely to noting down the trivia of appearances, to cataloguing and documenting the look, dress, eating habits, furniture, and small talk of her characters, to creating their manners and social milieu so exhaustively that we finally have no choice but to accept this kind of evidence as representing the most real and valid truth about them. In short, the particular nature and weight of the documentation causes their values in the end to prevail and to become the values that the book as a whole seems to enforce, if only by default of all others.

One is of course sure that this could not have been Miss McCarthy's conscious intention: she is well aware that the values of her characters are false. Yet her method seems at every point to undercut her intention; in fact, its obsessive concern with material externals gives rise after a while to the suspicion that she is herself more attracted to those values than she knows, that her choice of method may perhaps be a better indication of just where her true sympathies lie than are the overt symptoms of her conscious satirical intent.

As one critic has very shrewdly observed, she pays so much attention to the furniture that one feels justified in asking why it should be a virtue in *her* to do this when paying so much attention to the furniture makes Kay Strong Petersen, one of the more prominent members of The Group, a silly girl. But the means necessary to separate the author from her characters, and to provide an answer to such a question, are simply missing. Hence, the book can be much too easily read as a silly account of mere silliness, a gossipy account of mere gossipiness, or worse, as an insufficiently ambiguous dramatization of the very stereotypes that it tries and fails to condemn.

  This may well be an important reason why *The Group* has appealed so strongly to large numbers of readers, very many of whom must have found their enjoyment in this very element of the book's failure, and why also it should have been the book that has caused Miss McCarthy to become not only, for the first time in her career, a best-selling novelist, but widely known in popular reading circles as "the foremost woman of letters in America." This is a title that, where intellectuals at least are concerned, has a sufficiently circus-side-show ring to it to be understood at once for exactly what it is: public recognition of the fact that middlebrow meretriciousness has finally overtaken Miss McCarthy, that she has succumbed at last to the ravages of *Time* and *Life*.

  Just what effect this will eventually have on the position she has so long enjoyed as the darling of American intellectuals, no one can of course say. But one can be reasonably sure that it will never again be quite what it was. I say "reasonably" because about Miss McCarthy one can never be absolutely sure. One would think that intellectuals would scarcely be likely to forgive her for the kind of treachery that consists in going over to the middlebrow enemy while posing as an intellectual high priestess who is as embarrassed as everybody else by all that dreadful publicity. Yet intellectuals have displayed an astounding capacity to forgive Miss McCarthy just about anything, no matter how treacherously she has behaved or how badly she may have treated them personally. And Miss McCarthy has displayed great cleverness in managing to stay on both sides of the fence at the same time, smiling her famous smile upon friend and foe alike, while keeping an ice-cold eye peeled for the identical little mediocrities of mind and shabbinesses of motive that made them brothers under the thick, oily skin. In particular, she has made a life work out of winning the favor and admiration of intellectuals, while she has been busily engaged in biting the hands that patted her, fed her, and even on occasion caressed her.

In short, what is surprising is not that *The Group* may cost Miss McCarthy her intellectual reputation, but that, in view of some of the novels and stories she has previously written, she should have any intellectual reputation left to lose. After all, she has been well known for years to the small highbrow public as a writer of fiction that is considered to be merciless in its treatment of various aspects of the intellectual life. She is infamous for making it a habit to include in her fiction equally merciless portraits of real people—former husbands and lovers, old friends and acquaintances, strange men who engaged her in stupid conversations or dared to make passes at her at parties and on trains, and presumably even stranger (and stupider) men who did not dare. One would have thought—human nature being what it is—that she would long ago have begun to suffer the consequences that normally follow from doing this kind of thing. By all logic people should have despised her, taken revenge upon her, perhaps even done her bodily harm, and a good many of her victims would have been quite capable of being just as merciless as she. If nothing else, one would have expected her to have been a prime candidate for that most lethal of all intellectual snubs, the carefully calculated failure ever again to mention one's name or works in print, the stuffing down the Orwellian memory hole of one's literary identity, which can be far more damaging than actual book-burning for a writer whose professional existence may very well depend on staying in the limelight of the highly competitive intellectual establishment.

Yet incredibly enough, nothing of the sort has happened to Miss McCarthy. Regardless of what she has had to say about them individually or collectively, she has gone right on being the darling of American intellectuals. They continue—with whatever mixed sensations of delight and foreboding—to read her books and discuss them seriously. They continue to mention her name as often and in as many different places as a writer of her kind can expect to be mentioned. The more deeply she wounds them, the more they appear to admire and honor her. In fact, they have been so strangely undisturbed, even so strangely pleased, by her attacks upon them that one cannot help but wonder just how deeply, after all, she *does* wound, whether indeed there may not be just a touch of dullness somewhere along that formidable cutting edge.

But of course one does not need to go this far to find reasons why Miss McCarthy's supposedly undiplomatic behavior should have earned her this curious kind of diplomatic immunity. The very fact that she writes nearly always about intellectuals has set off a series of rather ambiguous reactions, all of which have finally worked to her advantage. There is, first of all, the appeal to intellectual vanity of writing that, regardless of whether the portrait is flattering or unflattering, confers on intellectuals the dignity and importance of a subject matter, and that takes them seriously at a time when the world at large still tends to see them as irrelevant, ridiculous, or merely insignificant. Secondly, there is the appeal to intellectual masochism of the portrait that *is* unflattering and because it is, satisfies that perverse desire to be criticized that so often accompanies a professional habit of incessant *self*-criticism. Thirdly, there is the appeal to the intellectual's guilty sense of fair play (which is equally as potent as his talent, when genuinely threatened, for foul play), his liberal-progressive determination to be tolerant of opinions that may run counter to his own but that he feels have a perfect right to be expressed, *particularly* when they are unflattering to himself and everything he stands for.

Finally, there is the meliorating effect of Miss McCarthy's own intellectual allegiance, the fact that she is so patently and vigorously an intellectual herself that her opinions cannot be dismissed or ignored as they could be if she belonged to the usual run of highbrow baiters. She is very definitely "one of us," and she disarms opposition by seeming to be more completely "one of us" than most of the intellectuals she writes for and about. Her fiction sounds as a rule so knowing, subtle, and snobbishly sure of itself that the initially hostile reader tends after a while to be overawed and to hesitate to question or criticize her for fear she will show him up and prove him to be—as he already secretly suspects he is—less intellectual than herself.

"Nobody is quite so smart as Mary" is the simple, unaffected message of all her writing. In fact, her characteristic tone of voice as a writer is that of a self-righteous little girl lecturing her elders on matters that they have grown too morally soggy and mentally fatty to comprehend, and her strategy is to browbeat her readers into such a humiliating sense of their personal unworthiness that they will grant her anything, if only she will allow them to breathe the same heady air she breathes.

The very opaqueness and inconclusiveness of some of her work fortifies this impression of Miss McCarthy's sibylline powers, and so too does her enormous *reputation* for profundity. People come to her novels in very much the way that pioneer readers of the early twenties came to *Ulysses* and *The Waste Land:* in a state of prearranged bafflement, with their minds already made up that they are not going to be able to understand. They expect to plunge over their heads into deep intellectual waters, and they expect, even hope, to drown. Hence, when they discover that the work in question seems to fail in some odd fashion to cohere, that they are having trouble keeping the characters straight, or are unable to make out just what is happening and why, their best expectations are confirmed: they assume at once that the fault is in them, and they respectfully conclude that they are in the presence of "profundity." Their grave doubts about their own capacities prevent them from supposing that there might actually be something wrong with the work itself, and their vanity prevents them from admitting that they have found anything wrong. Even if they remain baffled to the end, so heavy is their reverence for what they do not understand that they will nod their heads solemnly, genuflect twice, and murmur "ah yes, ah yes" in the prescribed portentous manner of those who have got the message by direct spiritual courier from God.

Yet Miss McCarthy is supposed to be more than simply a "deep" writer. She is also supposed to be a brilliantly witty writer who is forever saying outrageous and devastating things that cut through hypocrisy like a hot scalpel through middle-aged fat. The stories about the real-life people who have been autopsied in her novels have helped to create this impression, and so have the stories about her nasty tongue, her dangerous talent for total recall, the fact that she reportedly never forgives a friend or forgets an enemy. Hence, it is not surprising that people tend to approach the satirical element in her work in much the same way that they approach the element of her highly touted profundity: with their minds already made up about how they should expect to react, already convinced that they are going to be made to giggle and squirm.

This expectation seems justified not only by Miss McCarthy's large reputation for venomous wit but her lip-smacking air of seeming always on the verge of making some kind of scandalous revelation, the promise she always seems to be holding out not only to the reader but to herself that in the very next paragraph or page the ultimate annihilating thrust about something or somebody is going to be delivered. Like a coyly inhibited Louella Parsons or Hedda Hopper of the intellectual world, she seems perpetually *just about* to descend into naughty, tabloid celebrity gossip, the spiciness of which will be enhanced by the fact that it will have to do not merely with people like you and me but with people who may very well *be* you and me.

The inevitable result is that the continual high promise of revelation after a while creates the illusion that revelation has somehow been achieved. The reader is deluded into thinking that the lethal thrust was delivered at some moment just past, and that if he missed it, it must be because he was sleeping on post or the wit was too subtle for him or he was not sufficiently in the know to appreciate the reference. Once again, because of the sheer power of the pretense to cleverness, the burden of proof falls on the reader rather than the work. Since the work cannot conceivably be at fault, he must be. He is therefore likely to decide that the only safe way to deal with Miss McCarthy is to keep himself constantly on the brink of nervous acquiescence to *whatever* she might say. He must read her as he might listen to a person famous for his brilliant but enigmatic dirty jokes, with the giggle always waiting in his throat and ready to burst out even when the person makes an apparently innocent remark about the weather. After all, who knows what layers of sexy innuendo such a remark might conceal? Who knows what would happen if it turned out that something terribly risqué had been said and one did not giggle in time or, horror of horrors, did not giggle at all?

It should be evident by now that I think the reports of Miss McCarthy's overpowering distinction as a thinker, wit, and satirist have been greatly exaggerated. I do not deny that she is an extremely intelligent writer or that her satirical treatment of the intellectual life is often highly entertaining and very much to the point. Certainly, she has written more cleverly about the comedy of intellectual manners than any other American writer of the present or any previous time. Certainly too, she may be justly regarded as the foremost woman of letters in America, and the authority of the title need not come under too much disparagement just because the competition for it happens to be slight. Yet it does seem necessary to suggest that Miss McCarthy has for a long time been widely considered to be better than she is, and that because of the cloak of immunity that has shrouded her work up to now, she has been less stringently examined than her present position would seem to warrant. It is not that she has been getting away with murder. But she has been getting away with a reputation for murder that she has not entirely earned—and that should lead us to inquire whether there are in fact real corpses buried in her garden, or whether only the garden is real and the corpses are imaginary.

I have already said that her novels tend to be more obscure than complex, more opaque than brilliantly trenchant, but that among people who attribute virtue to whatever they do not understand, to the degree that they do not understand it, these failings have been enthusiastically mistaken for the hallmarks of profundity. This seems to me true of all her fiction except the stories in *The Company She Keeps,* where there was no question of profundity as such since she was able to follow a clear reportorial, more or less autobiographical line, deal directly with her best, brightest, and most beloved heroine, herself, and thus skirt the obligation to create a developing dramatic situation, a group of characters interacting meaningfully with one another, and a theme of real depth and complication. But in the novels that follow that book, in *The Oasis, The Groves of Academe,* and *A Charmed Life,* a curious kind of vagueness and artificiality creeps in; the dramatic situation begins to seem forced and contrived, the characters become wooden, the prose stilted and mannered, and the theme so heavily refracted and distorted by the endlessly picking and peering and range-adjusting intelligence of the characters and the author that nothing finally seems clear except one's certain conviction that Miss McCarthy suffers from a fatal incompatibility with the novel form.

One bit of at least subjective proof of this is that one can never seem to *remember* anything in her novels. Characters, scenes, ideas—all drift out of the mind almost immediately after the book is closed. And while the reader is left with the distinct impression that words have been used, and frequently used well, that individual sentences and paragraphs have often made excellent sense, the overall effect tends to remain cloudy and oddly resistant to recall. This for the critic is the maddening paradox: individual sentences and paragraphs *are* so often penetrating and lucid, yet they do not form a whole of equal penetration and lucidity. Some rational principle, some principle of form or conception necessary to the attainment of real coherence, is missing. It is as if her novels were pumped up with too much intellectual helium without sufficient intellectual ballast to keep them moored down to a firm basis in idea and to prevent them from floating off into space.

Part of the trouble is, of course, that Miss McCarthy has a very defective sense of the simple mechanics of narrative. She seems incapable of following a clear narrative line and of sustaining a group of characters in a consistent development toward climax and resolution. But it is even more obvious that she is also incapable of giving intellectual coherence to her novels, and that their elusive quality is evidence not of a conception so profound that it defies easy formulation but of an uncertainty of conception for which the frequent excellence of her individual insights cannot compensate. However ironical it may seem, the plain truth appears to be that the most brilliant woman of letters in America simply cannot think very well as a novelist.

After all this, it is perhaps brutishly unchivalrous to say that Miss McCarthy's satire is neither very penetrating nor very funny. Yet in view of her reputation for ferocious wit, it seems about time some brute said it. A great deal of the satire in her novels (and again I distinguish between her novels and her relatively better work in the short story) has the exclusive, closed-circuit quality of an in-group joke, the kind of joke one might find immensely entertaining if only one knew the people involved. But since one does not know the people, it all seems rather pretentious and more than a little irritating, as any gossip about complete strangers is bound to seem.

Again, it is perfectly true that single lines and paragraphs throughout her writing may strike one as apt and clever. She is excellent at formulating hypocrisy in a phrase, particularly when the hypocrisy happens to be one that she herself shared up until last week. But so few of her phrases are really devastating. There are so few moments when one feels that she has really pinned her victim kicking and screaming to the wall or eviscerated a subject so thoroughly that nothing ever again need be said or done about it except to erect a small white marker at the scene of the catastrophe. The reader may open one of her novels with the high expectation of being made to giggle and squirm, but more often than not he simply goes on expecting to the end.

Perhaps this is why it is so hard to imagine Miss McCarthy's satire actually offending anyone, even the real people who are supposed to have served as models for some of her characters. One has heard of the indignation, the fear and trembling, provoked by her satirical portraits, but such reports are very difficult to credit. It seems much more likely that her intended victims have been more relieved than outraged by her treatment of them, since she so clearly had her chance at them and muffed it, could so easily have dropped them with a single shot but instead blazed wildly away into the foliage. In fact, in a curious way and altogether by accident, she may even have done them the service of insuring their privacy rather than violating it, of dignifying them rather than exposing them to the derision of the world. For to the extent that she failed to penetrate them in her work, she may unwittingly have created the impression that they were too complicated or intelligent or morally irreproachable to *be* penetrated. She may have aggrandized them by giving them an air of quality or inscrutability that they never possessed in life and for which they would have good reason to feel grateful. It therefore should not come as too great a surprise that Miss McCarthy has so consistently escaped censure from those whose manners and actions she has imitated in her novels. After all, such imitation in her hands may not only turn out to be harmless: it may indeed be the sincerest form of flattery.

But Miss McCarthy's satire flatters a good deal more than simply the real-life people she tries and fails to take off. It also flatters the whole body of intellectual attitudes and values that it ostensibly attacks. Above all, it gives comfort and encouragement to the intellectual at just the point where he needs reassuring most: in the queasy pit of his guilty pride in being an intellectual and possessing the superior qualities that go with that title. This is the real reason Miss McCarthy has continued to enjoy the favor of intellectuals while appearing to do everything in her power to make them look foolish. If she were the genuinely radical, genuinely subversive critic she is popularly thought to be, she would have been drummed out of the intellectual corps long ago. But it has been her special distinction—and, as it turned out, her very clever strategy—to exploit the ego drives of highbrow society by affirming in her work the supreme importance of being intellectual, not simply for its own sake or for the love of ideas, but for the status and power advantages it gives one in a world in which the only really crucial distinctions between persons are those based on superior taste and sensibility, the inner qualities of mental refinement that separate the people who count from the peasants and clods as surely as the old distinctions of breeding, accent, and inherited wealth separated the English upper classes from the lower.

Her appeal, in short, is to snobbery, and particularly to that form of snobbery characteristic of those who are intellectually on the make, who are obsessed with the styles and fads of intellectual consumership, not necessarily because they care about the life of the mind, but because they want people to *think* they care, because they know that these styles and fads have taken on real value as status symbols in society. Miss McCarthy demonstrates just how this has come about, just how intellectual values have been converted into social values, and even how they operate as a kind of secret code or abracadabra that can be used to gain admittance to the select fraternity of the culturally initiated, what Diana Trilling has called "the closed circuit of perceptivity, of elegance, of stylistic discrimination, of virtue as it is defined by taste." In doing this, Miss McCarthy confirms the intellectual in his personal sense of superiority at the same time that she flatters him by showing that while he may have thought his values were socially irrelevant or even a social handicap, they actually have as much power to win him acceptance and prestige as the fine cars, houses, clothes, and general material affluence for which he has always secretly envied his more practical, nonintellectual contemporaries.

Yet Miss McCarthy could not do any of this if she did not first take pains to neutralize the guilt that the anxiously liberal-democratic intellectual is bound to suffer whenever he catches himself feeling superior to anything or anybody, regardless of race, creed, color, or mental capacity. And this is where she makes brilliant strategic use of her satire. For having first established the primacy of intellectual values by showing how they give one the decisive upper hand in social situations, she then uses her satire to sneer at her intellectual characters *for* their snobbishness, to poke fun at their pretensions and airs, and even to suggest that in being snobbish and self-preoccupied, they are fatally cut off from those more real and basic human values that give ordinary people their wonderful warmth and directness of feeling.

Hence, she provides the intellectual with the necessary opportunity to have it both ways (and not at all incidentally, she makes it possible for ordinary people to find in her work confirmation of their worst suspicions about the coldness and inhumanity of intellectuals): she enables him to enjoy the ego satisfaction of seeing his values used to define the cultural superiority of his class at the same time that she drains off through her satire the guilt he would otherwise feel at being so snobbish. Again in a manner very much like O'Hara's, she supplies a forbidden thrill—in her case, the thrill of snobbery; in his, the thrill of pornography—in a context that appears to judge and condemn it and therefore that relieves the reader of the moral obligation to judge and condemn himself.

This effort to have it both ways, to have one's sin and expiate it too, is of course very much in keeping with the psychology, if not the spirit, of the Catholic confessional, which seems in practice to inhibit the dedicated pursuit of sin only to the extent of recognizing that one can sin more effectively if one pauses for breath now and then and puts things right with God. But there is nothing particularly surprising in the resemblance if one recalls that Miss McCarthy is a lapsed Catholic and as such may, like Joyce, be another demonstration of the truth that when Catholicism ceases to be a matter of faith, it tends to linger on like radioactivity in the bones as a secret infection of the moral life. What is surprising, however, or at least terribly ironical, is that the most dramatic illustration to be found anywhere in Miss McCarthy's work of her effort to have it both ways is to be found precisely in the one book, *Memories of a Catholic Girlhood*, in which she explicitly repudiates her early religious training, yet demonstrates in the very act and form of her repudiation just how heavily her thinking has been influenced by the psychology of the confessional, how, in fact, the innocent little tricks she learned as a child for getting around her elders and around God have become in the mature woman a not at all innocent technique of moral evasive action.

Miss McCarthy is naturally not aware of any of this, but the book, like so much of her work, tells us far more about her than she knows or would dare to admit to herself. It is composed of two kinds of material: a running account of the recalled experiences of her girlhood presented as straight autobiography, and a series of notes addressed to the reader that Miss McCarthy appends to seven of the eight auto-biographical sections. The function of these notes, she explains, is to correct errors of fact that appear in the text, to indicate exactly where and in what way the text departs from straight autobiography and, apparently uncontrollably, begins to take on some of the distortions and prevarications of an imaginative work. Thus, the reader is presented with what amounts to two versions of the same experience: the partly inaccurate, partly fictitious version provided by an autobiography with independent ambitions to be a novel, and the corrected, hence, "true" version provided by the notes.

Of course it is natural that one would be struck by the peculiarity of this arrangement and be moved to ask why, if the autobiographical version contains inaccuracies, Miss McCarthy did not simply rewrite it, incorporating her corrections, and dispense with the notes altogether. Why did she feel compelled to make use of two versions, one telling the story imaginatively but erroneously, the other setting the record straight by telling the truth?

The answer can only be that she wished once again to have it both ways: she wanted the advantage of first presenting a partially false but presumably more dramatic account of her experience and getting all the literary mileage she could get out of that; but she also wanted to square herself with her conscience or God or whomever by adding her palliating and expiating corrections. Not to put too delicate a point on it, she wanted quite simply to lie about her experience, then make things all right by confessing the lie, while at the same time capitalizing on the fact that the reader would come upon the lie first, accept it as the truth, and be impressed by it before he would come upon the notes informing him that he had been duped.

The answer, furthermore, would appear to be the same if one makes a different approach and asks a different question: why did Miss McCarthy suppose that anybody would care all this much whether or not what she says about her Uncle Myers or her Aunt Margaret (neither of whom is, at least quite yet, a major historical figure) is absolutely accurate; why did she take such pains to correct what are very often only tiny errors of fact or interpretation that could not conceivably be important to anybody but herself? Why, for that matter, did she not simply leave the autobiography uncorrected altogether and enjoy the *full* benefit of the liberties she took with the truth, since nobody would be likely to know that she had taken liberties? After all, seven of the eight autobiographical sections appeared without the accompanying notes in magazines before they were published in book form, so presumably she was not worried then about the errors they contained.

The explanation could, of course, be simple egotism, the inflated sense of the importance of every last thing that ever happened to them, solely because it happened to *them*, that so often overtakes successful authors once they start seeing their experience as potential material for future biographers. But while there is nothing whatever to indicate that Miss McCarthy is deficient in egotism, it seems much more likely in this instance that at some point between the magazine

114

and book publication of her memoirs, she began to have disturbing second thoughts: she began to be afraid somebody other than a future biographer, perhaps Somebody Up There, might have taken note of her devious behavior and be preparing a case against her that would determine not her standing with posterity but the condition of her soul throughout eternity. She knew she had done wrong, and she had been infected with the belief that wrongdoing is incomplete, even finally damning, without confession and attempted expiation. In short, the Catholic conscience went to work in her. But also at work in her was an intelligence formed on the peculiarly slippery morality of the confessional, an intelligence that had learned early in its development that if you want to lie, do so, but remember always to confess that you have lied. That makes everything all right, and provided you remember to confess afterwards, you can go right on lying as much and for as long as you like.

This inevitably simplifies what is in fact a complex and perhaps wholly unconscious effort on Miss McCarthy's part to reconcile through her work the two compelling necessities of her nature: the necessity to be herself and advance herself, and the necessity to be good and please God. Such an effort seems, as a rule, to take the form of a dramatic or narrative pattern in which these opposing necessities are placed in the relation to each other of sin to repentence: the gesture made in the name of self-interest is balanced by some gesture of conciliation or atonement, so that any given work of hers will be likely to contain evidence of both a violation of decorum and an attempt to make up for the violation, to neutralize the offense, to pay for the damage done by her destructive other self. Or, to put it a different way, Miss McCarthy seems to feel compelled to engage in some kind of propitiation of authority, be it divine or secular, whenever she has been tempted to assert her real feelings or depart from the truth or arrange reality in such a way that she will be made to look cleverer or more righteous than she really is.

In *Memories of a Catholic Girlhood* the propitiation takes the form of the notes that correct and do penance for the misstatements of the text, and in at least some of her fiction, of satire used as a cloak of ostensible self-ridicule to cover and counteract the textual affirmations of snobbery. Both notes and satire represent modes of compensation for liberties that she apparently could not help but take but about which she nevertheless felt guilty, guilty enough to seek solace in an artistic reenactment of the confessional ceremony of her childhood, a ceremony in which it would seem she has as an adult only consciously lost faith.

It may be no more than a fortunate accident that the particular use Miss McCarthy makes of satire in her fiction, whether or not it propitiates God, does in fact propitiate her intellectual readers, who have guilts very similar to her own that also must be rationalized and put to rest. But one can be certain that the process of propitiation itself is no accident where she is concerned, but is her way of coming to terms with difficulties that lie deep in her psychological nature and that can most probably be traced back to the crisis of faith that her memoirs, with understandable equivocation, not only record but exemplify.

To my mind, the best illustration of just how this process operates in Miss McCarthy's fiction is to be found in her most famous story, "The Man in the Brooks Brothers Shirt," which first appeared in book form in *The Company She Keeps* and, significantly enough, has continued to appeal more to her intellectual readers than anything else she has written. Here the encounter between the heroine—who, although unnamed in the story itself, must be the Margaret Sargent of the other stories in the collection—and the businessman Breen is handled in such a way that Margaret is shown to be both an intellectual snob and the wryly comic victim of her snobbery, a person through whom the superior importance of intellectual values and social distinctions is asserted with a vengeance, and yet who is forced in the end to *pay* for her feelings of superiority by suffering humiliation and at least temporary loss of self-esteem.

The girl's first view of Breen as he enters the club car of the train is not of a man, although she is dying to meet one, a *real* one, but of a socio-literary cliché, a vulgar philistine and updated Babbitt, who is "plainly Out of the Question" in his monogrammed green shirt and matching tie, his pale-gray háir and harmonizing trousers. Her first impulse is to snub him, perhaps even embarrass him in front of the other passengers, partly to remind him of his Place, which is emphatically not beside her, and partly to give vent to her annoyance over the fact that he is so plainly out of the question. But Breen refuses to accommodate himself to the subordinate role in which her oversimplifying and—for all her intellectual pretensions—distinctly provincial imagination has placed him. Instead of remaining true to his apparent type, he disrupts all her expectations, confuses her, and even manages to win her tentative approval by seeming to observe at least some of the rules of sophisticated conduct of which she had assumed he was completely ignorant. She is positive that he will make his approach by asking her "what-that-book-is-you're-so-interested-in," and this will give her the chance to squelch him for good and all by replying, "Why, you probably haven't heard of it. It's not out yet." Instead, he asks simply, "Can I talk to you?" and in the next few moments has astounded her by showing some familiarity with the author of the book, and then embarrassed *her* by catching her out in a bit of reflex snobbery, her "look of absolute dismay and panic" when he jokingly tells her that he is a traveling salesman.

Throughout the early part of the story Breen not only refuses to behave like a "thing," a faceless sociological statistic; he also insists upon being engaged as a person, and the particular person he is. In so doing, he neatly reverses the situation and takes command of it, shifts the burden of proof from himself to the girl, turns her contempt for him into uncertainty about her own motives, the satirical edge of the story cutting at this point more and more into her and her pretensions, as she is seen to grow increasingly ineffectual, increasingly helpless and out of depth, and he to gain in stature and assurance.

Yet the girl goes on fighting to retain her superior position and fights harder as Breen takes more and more of the initiative away from her. Even after consenting to join him for a drink in his compartment, she tries to rationalize the action by telling herself that she has been able to tolerate him only because she assumed he must really belong to one of those quaintly romantic categories of humanity that people of her sort tend to invent for the purpose of patronizing and sentimentalizing their social inferiors. She decides that he must be either "a frustrated socialist" or a "frustrated man of sensibility, a kind of Sherwood Anderson character." There must, in other words, be some logical way of accounting for her presence in his compartment, and how else if not by attributing to herself motives of scientific curiosity and a desire to see life imitate not only art but literary cliché? But once again Breen refuses to be pigeonholed and dehumanized into a classification: "... the man's own personality kept popping up, perversely, like a jack-in-the-box, to

118

confound these theories." And in spite of herself, the girl cannot help liking him, although that too she manages to rationalize in yet another theory, that he is a symbol of the American frontier and the wildcat radicalism that she sentimentally associates with her father's past. Nevertheless, there is no denying that he fascinates her simply as a man; she clearly fascinates him as a woman. Alone together in the compartment and with the help of several drinks, they begin to feel at ease in each other's company; personal histories are exchanged and intimate secrets confessed; the hours go by; the liquor flows; songs are sung; more liquor flows; the door is shut so that the other passengers will not be disturbed; the girl quotes her favorite line of poetry, from Chaucer, "I am myn owene woman, wel at ese," and she is next aware of awakening the following morning with Breen naked in bed beside her.

Before becoming conscious of his presence she enjoys a momentary sense of security and satisfaction. She imagines that she is safe in her own lower berth, and is pleased to reflect that, although she had been drunk the night before, Nothing Had in fact Happened. But then, discovering Breen, she realizes that Something very definitely Had, and she at once sets to work trying to repair the damage done, not to her virtue, but to her self-esteem, which, unlike her white Crepe-de-Chine pants, cannot be held together with a little brass pin. She begins to cast about for ways of justifying her behavior, for some explanation she can give herself that will once again put her in the right and provide defensible reasons for what apparently she could not help but do. She finds them in two fantasy projections that have the effect of conveniently reshaping reality to satisfy the demands of her egotism: she makes Breen acceptable by idealizing his qualities as a man, and she idealizes herself in the role of an exceptional female whose qualities have until now gone unappreciated because she has been languishing among inferiors. She decides that Breen is, after all, in his way superior to the other men she has known, each of whom now seems to her to have been "handicapped for American life and therefore humble in love," and that, since he is, at least by comparison, a man of the world, his attraction to her may be proof that, had she stayed on in Portland instead of coming east, she actually could have succeeded as a normal girl among other normal girls in the competition for real men. It might be that in coming east and falling in with "this fraternity of cripples," she had been unjust to herself, and that she had all along been "a sound and normal woman who had been spending her life in self-imposed exile, a princess among the trolls." "This man now—surely he came from that heavenly world, that divine position at the center of things where choice is unlimited. And he had chosen her."

This is a highly consoling rationalization and another excellent example of Margaret's talent for turning humiliation into self-flattery. But she is honest enough, at least in this instance, to admit that it is a rationalization and a pretty hollow one at that. Breen is too old (at forty-one!) to be a reliable test of her power to attract real men. "Time had made a lame duck of him. If she had met him ten years before, would he have chosen her then?" She is obliged, therefore, to find some other way of recovering her sense of superiority that will at the same time give her the chance to take revenge on him for being too old and on herself for having been such a fool.

The solution, when it comes, proves to be a brilliant stroke of sexual oneupsmanship. As he moves to take her again, she decides that she will *sacrifice* herself, quite coldly and deliberately. "*This,* she thought decidedly, *is going to be the*

*only real act of charity I have ever performed in my life;
it will be the only time I have ever given anything when it
honestly hurt me to do so."* And not at all surprisingly, the
meaning of the act is deepened for her by the thought that
it involves "the mortification of the flesh achieved through
the performance of the act of pleasure."

But we should not be misled by these pious-sounding
declarations. Self-abasement, whether accomplished through
mortification of the flesh or confession, is, as we know, a
vital part of the ritual whereby Miss McCarthy makes it
possible for herself—or, in this case, her surrogate self, Margaret—to express emotions and adopt attitudes which would
otherwise be unacceptable to her conscience. Just as it is
necessary for her to confess a lie, so it is necessary for her
to suffer either literal or vicarious humiliation as punishment
for the sin of pride, and indeed to make of her writing an
explicit satirical commentary on that sin, since satire functions in her work as both conscience and punishing priest.

Thus, when Margaret declares her intention to give when
it honestly hurts, she is acting in strict accordance with the
moral compulsions of her creator. But she is also, like her
creator, admitting that she must endure the hurt of giving
before she can feel free to enjoy the pleasure of taking. In
sleeping again with Breen she will be performing an ostensible act of charity, doing him a great favor, at the same time
that by this act she will be preparing her conscience to
accept the even greater favor which she wishes to do herself.
And that is to resume the position of snobbish superiority,
of arrogant *un*charitableness, which she occupied at the
beginning of the story, and from which she allowed herself
to be tempted away by Breen in a moment of curiosity and
emotional weakness.

So it would appear that the mortification of the flesh is on the first level a form of atonement for a sin not yet committed. But the sin is finally indistinguishable from the atonement, since Margaret makes of the act of charity an act of consummate self-aggrandizement and *droit de seigneur.*

As she has all along found ways of dramatizing herself to advantage, at whatever cost to the truth, so is she now able to see herself in the role of a great lady benevolently dispensing alms to the underprivileged, using her sex as a marvelous kind of philanthropy that she is generous enough to bestow upon this needy man. But she is also, and far more importantly, able to see herself as a suffering martyr to her sex, as the morally and intellectually superior female, the princess among trolls, who deliberately offers up her fair young body to spoliation, a "slab of white lamb on an altar" proudly sacrificed to man's constitutional grossness.

Once again both she and Miss McCarthy manage to have it both ways, and it is perfectly in keeping with the logic of her moral hypocrisy that at the end Margaret's snobbishness is fully and now quite guiltlessly reaffirmed. She has paid the price for feeling superior; she has suffered and sacrificed for it; and so is now free to relax and enjoy it. At the end she is indeed "myn owene woman, wel at ese." In fact, we can now see that she has never been anybody's woman but her own. She has long since sent Breen on his way, has recognized him for the tiresome Babbitt he was from the beginning, and the telegram he sends her on the occasion of her father's death seems to epitomize all that she despises in him. She does not file it away with the other messages, but tears it up carefully and throws it into the wastebasket. "It would have been dreadful if anyone had seen it," for it would have been considered terribly gauche and cheap by her intellectual friends, the superior people in whose company she now knows she rightfully, and self-righteously, belongs.

This closing image of Margaret happily reestablished in her snobbery is, of course, ambiguous and necessarily so, since Miss McCarthy's own view of it is itself ambiguous. On the one hand, she clearly wants to suggest that Margaret is an arrogant fool, and she is careful to make use of certain satirical effects that create this impression. On the other hand, she cannot help but sympathize with Margaret and even identify with her, for Margaret expresses attitudes for which she has all along shown a marked affinity. The balance between approval and the appearance of disapproval, between honest admiration and forced satire, is here very precisely and artfully kept. But there are moments in some of Miss McCarthy's other fiction when the coyly critical smile that she takes pains to direct upon Margaret's arrogant behavior relaxes into a quite naked smirk of self-satisfaction, when the cover and concealment of satire cannot quite disguise the note of arrogance in her own voice. There are moments, in short, when conscience, the Catholic Church, Uncle Myers —all seem to have been at least temporarily placated, and she is able to reveal herself as the woman she dared to let Margaret become: a woman compelled by an urge to dominate her subject, and through her patronizing treatment of it, to proclaim to the world, in all forthrightness and sincerity, her high sense of her own moral and intellectual superiority.

Diana Trilling, in her essay on Edward Albee, has commented brilliantly on one rather ominous aspect of this development. She suggests not only that Miss McCarthy uses intellectual values as social status symbols, but that she goes so far as to invent false or meaningless intellectual criteria in her effort to define an area of exclusiveness that she alone can inhabit, and from which she can exclude anybody she may happen not to like. Mrs. Trilling cites as an example Miss McCarthy's characterization of the actress Margaret

Sullavan as the kind of woman who at forty would love to walk in the rain without a hat. The implication here is that there is a whole category of women who more or less automatically develop an urge to walk hatless in the rain at forty, but that among the culturally initiated such behavior is recognized as being dreadfully bad form. Those in the know would never think of doing it, and since Miss Sullavan appears to be the kind who would, she obviously occupies a very low position on the scale of moral and social perceptiveness. All this is of course nonsense. No standard exists in terms of which the act of walking hatless in the rain at forty can be judged as having any significance whatever. Miss McCarthy has simply made it up for the occasion. But having made it up, she pretends that there is such a standard, and if nobody else knows about it, that merely proves that nobody else is quite so culturally initiated as she. She thus manages not only to snub Miss Sullavan for a faked breach of decorum. She manages to snub everybody else and to create the impression that she alone is in the know.

The Group is full of examples of this same calculated effort to advance oneself on the strength of largely fabricated failures of taste in others. There is all that elaborate flummery about dress, furniture, and food, about Kay's presumably damning preference for modern chairs over Hepplewhite and for Venetian blinds over drapes, about the right way to serve Welsh rarebit and salmon loaf and spaghetti (Harald prefers his with dried mushrooms and tomato sauce), about the right places to shop, and the right shoes to wear at one's wedding (Harald's shoes, brown suede, are, of course, shockingly wrong besides being symbolic of his feet of clay). Again, as happened with poor Miss Sullavan, there is everywhere the sly implication of in-group judgment. We are made to feel that we are in the presence of some quiveringly sensitive moral seismograph that is busy measuring the propriety of every last trivial thing that is being bought, worn, and eaten for dinner. But this also is finally recognizable as just another piece of clever fakery. Miss McCarthy is most careful never to tell us, except in obvious cases like Harald's shoes, precisely what the right conduct *is*, whether the various choices of furniture, clothing, and food brand the people involved as in or out. To be sure, she *appears* to tell us. The eyebrows are convincingly raised; the tone of voice is convincingly snide. Yet these are fixed responses or, more correctly, fixed poses of response. The eyebrows are raised, the voice is snide, no matter what is happening in the novel. Hence, they are expressive not so much of her attitude as of her lack of attitude, her ignorance of the very moral criteria she seems to be applying, and her determination to conceal that ignorance behind a pretense of superior judgment and taste. In short, Miss McCarthy wishes to get as much status revenue as she can out of implying that her characters are all vigorously hanging themselves every time they shop at Gristede's or Saks or put a pot on the stove to boil. But whether they are really hanging themselves, and from what cultural gibbet, she not only cannot say, she seems not to care in the least.*

Miss McCarthy is not always so subtle as this or so circumspect. There are in fact times when she leaves no doubt at all about the hanging or who is springing the trap. In *The Oasis*, for instance, one finds her employing a variation on the oneupsman technique of *The Group*, but what seems involved is not the creation of false moral criteria but the simple distortion of the facts of reality, a distortion she presumably felt was necessary to the winning of her case. Her

---

* One is reminded of Niebuhr's statement on Kant that the Radical Evil is "man's inclination to corrupt the imperatives of morality so that they may become a screen for the expression of self-love."

treatment of the intellectuals in that novel seems so nakedly and belligerently calculated to make them appear ridiculous that the illusion of credibility is violated, and one soon finds it impossible to accept them as real people, let alone as real intellectuals. Yet the loss in verisimilitude is more than compensated for by the gain to Miss McCarthy in prestige. By causing her characters to seem duller and stupider, more feckless and footless, than, as educated people, they could possibly be, she causes herself to seem brighter and generally wittier and more sophisticated than a more honest and realistic treatment would have allowed her to seem. The implication throughout is that she alone sees and understands and is able to penetrate the veneer of highbrow pretense and pomposity to the emptiness beneath. It does not matter in the slightest that this penetration is a joke and a hoax, that the veneer is so transparent a myopic child could see through it. The ease or difficulty of the achievement is not important, and neither is the degree of manipulation, simplification, or distortion required to bring it about. We are dealing here with one thing only: a determination at all costs to come out ahead of the game. Hence, the message of the novel is not the message of justice or of art. It is the message of our sponsor assuring us once again that nobody is quite so smart as Mary. The whole thing is really just another commercial after all.

It is probably not surprising that Miss McCarthy's militant egotism should ultimately take the form of a militant feminism and find its most satisfactory expression in the sexual contest between the brute male and the morally and intellectually superior female. Margaret Sargent set the pattern for this development, and there are other women such as Martha Sinnott of *A Charmed Life* and some of the girls in *The Group* who are bound together in a snobbish and self-protective sisterhood by the fact that they all prove their fineness of sensibility through suffering themselves to be sexually used by men whom they patronize as inferiors and eventually come either to pity or to loathe. Margaret Sargent, of course, was able to see herself as both a philanthropic great lady and a martyr by conferring upon Breen the priceless gift of her sex, and then using the sacrifice as a way of justifying her return to snobbery. Martha Sinnott submits to her former husband and derives gratification from the knowledge that he had fun but she didn't. He wanted merely an outlet, any outlet, for his lust, and she gave him that, while retaining her hold on her person, the abode of her proud spirit that he could neither touch nor comprehend. The girls in *The Group* also submit because they are pure and innocent enough to suppose that to make love is to love and that an affair will sooner or later be sanctified by marriage. But they too learn that men are interested only in making use of their bodies. Dottie Renfrew yields up her virginity to the worthless Dick Brown who, after winning her trust and love, sends her to be fitted for a pessary and then boorishly leaves her waiting, Manila envelope in hand, on a park bench in Washington Square. Libby MacAusland is very nearly raped by an athletic Norwegian baron who mistakes her passionate interest in necking for a passionate interest in bed. Libby is naturally horrified and revolted by the experience. Her person is much too fine to be fouled by direct physical contact with the male. In fact, it is much too fine for contact with anybody except herself, and she is careful to keep it for her own private enjoyment during those moments of masturbation on the bath mat that sometimes follow her tub.

For Miss McCarthy's women, the act of heterosexual love seems chronically to represent an act of exploitation and

127

debasement by men. A woman can only lose if she is foolish enough to credit a man with honorable intentions and yield herself up to it. This is her tragedy: that she usually does give a man the benefit of the doubt. But it is also her triumph, for it demonstrates conclusively that she is a higher order of being than the male and is capable, as he is not, of good faith and emotional responsibility. She is obviously made for better things and would go on to better things if he did not trap her with false promises and trick her into becoming the devoted and unappreciated servant of his animal appetites. It would seem, really, that her only alternative *is* masturbation. At least that way the pleasure and devotion she gives would be received and returned by a person who has her best interests at heart and has always appreciated her superior qualities. But there is another and even better alternative, one that is coyly but quite convincingly outlined in *The Group,* and that shows promise of being the only workable solution to the problem faced by the superior woman in a world dominated by an inferior, sexually destructive race of men.

This solution is admittedly a desperate one, but then, in Miss McCarthy's view, desperate measures are called for. Nearly all the husbands and lovers in *The Group* are depicted as being weak, neurotic, irresponsible, impotent, pompous, or just plain peculiar. Harald, whom Kay marries both because she has slept with him and because she thinks he is a genius, turns out to be not only not a genius but a compulsive womanizer and cold-hearted cad who has Kay confined to a psychiatric ward when there is really nothing wrong with her, and is the ultimate cause of her emotional collapse and suicide. Gus LeRoy, with whom Polly Andrews has an extended affair, is a thoroughly ineffectual character who, although seemingly sincere in his feelings for Polly, is too spineless and, she realizes, too *ordinary,* to break off his analysis, divorce his wife, and marry her. Polly finally has brains enough to break off with him and marry a good, simple, but clearly very odd man who does not exact from her the usual premarital sex payment, and is perfectly willing to share their apartment with her manic-depressive father, thus making it possible for her to live happily ever after with a husband and her father too. Dottie also manages, after recovering from her unfortunate experience with Dick, to come to her senses and marry someone of her own sort whom she does not love but who will at least protect her from the risks of passion and give her a life of comfort and security. Norine Schmittlap, after divorcing the impotent, mother-fixated Putnam Blake and surviving an affair with Harald, marries a wealthy Jewish banker and becomes his willing hostess and *Hausfrau,* although she is troubled now and then by the fact that her intellectual interests actually prove to be a hindrance to her in the efficient management of the household. Priss Hartshorn marries a pediatrician, has a baby, and turns into a neurotic victim of her husband's advanced ideas on breast-feeding and permissive child care.

The tone here is satirical often to the point of caricature. Yet the social comment is deadly serious. All these women are either destroyed by, or forced to give up their identities to, the men with whom they become involved. After having once been hurt, they drift into marriages of which the outstanding virtue seems to be that they are left alone to lick their wounds, or they seek satisfaction in motherhood only to become deranged and defrauded by all the tense idealisms that seem endemic to that state. Lacking the moral courage to hold out for higher and better things, all have settled for a way of life that provides no outlet for their capabilities and that represents a brutal compromise not only of their youthful dreams but of the educational principles of Vassar College. Hence, they are just as deserving of Miss McCarthy's ridicule as the most ineffectual of their men.

For those, on the other hand, who have had the strength to keep their integrity as well as their virginity—and the two often seem synonymous in Miss McCarthy's mind—the story is different. In fact, the only really happy and successful women in *The Group* are the unmarried women. There is Helena Davidson who has retained all the charm and sweetness of youth just because, it would seem, she has never slept with a man. There is the autoerotic Libby who makes a career-girl success as a literary agent. And finally and above all, there is Lakey, the most beautiful, most intelligent, most intact of them all, and Lakey is a Lesbian.

The sudden revelation of Lakey's sexual proclivities, coming as it does at the very end of the novel, is obviously intended to bring the reader up short and create general consternation and dismay. And of course it succeeds. The exquisite Lakey, whom the other girls have feared, envied, and secretly adored ever since college, the one member of the group whom Miss McCarthy entirely exempts from ridicule and, in fact, treats as altogether admirable, turns out to be a lover of women. How utterly surprising and devastating! What a brilliant stroke of irony! Yet how perfectly in keeping with the logic of Miss McCarthy's whole argument.

For Lakey is the embodiment of everything Miss McCarthy appears to mean by the uncompromised superior woman. In sharp contrast to her married and spiritually tacky classmates, she has had the courage to go her own way, to be herself, to side-step the trap of domesticity. Instead of repressing her contempt for men and trying dutifully to adjust to the requirements of an abhorrent sexual situation, she has acted upon her contempt and found in it the motive power for a bizarre but clearly rewarding way of life. As a result, she is not an object, a possession, a *Hausfrau,* or a slave, but triumphantly and completely a person in her own right and on her own terms. She arrives back from Europe with her trunks full of beautiful and expensive clothes, the "impressive array" making the girls "think awkwardly of schedules, formula, laundry, diapers." She has kept her figure and looks marvelous. They apparently have not kept theirs and look awful. She still wears her hair in a girlish black knot at the nape of her neck, while they have all cut theirs and had permanents. Indeed, weird as it may seem, Lakey is evidently much more feminine, much more of a *woman,* than any one of them, even though they represent everything that is normal and respectable in their sex, while she is a perverted outlaw. Even though or *just because?* Miss McCarthy does not come right out and say, but the implication is about as subtle as the *Queen Mary,* and it is not lost on the girls. As they wait for Lakey to clear her fabulous luggage through customs, they have good cause to wonder whether, in view of the embarrassing contrast between her situation and theirs, she will despise *them* for *not* being Lesbians. Lakey is naturally much too serene and secure to despise anyone. But we know that in the depths of their poor disappointed hearts they despise themselves.

Thus are we prepared for the conclusion toward which we now see the novel has evolved from its opening page: women must love one another or die—die emotionally, spiritually, intellectually, even, like Kay, physically through the treachery of the male. And again it is perfectly in keeping with Miss McCarthy's logic that it should be Lakey who at the end is appointed to deal with the most treacherous male of them all, Harald, the careless seducer, unfaithful husband, and callous destroyer of Kay, whose abiding weakness it was to try to love him when she really loved Lakey all along. Lakey does a beautiful job of insinuating to Harald that she was Kay's lover long before he got to her, that perhaps she was the lover of all the girls in the group. And having planted this poisonous seed, she lets him out of her car and watches his image fade away in the rear-view mirror. She has met and vanquished the enemy, or at least struck a blow to his manhood from which he will undoubtedly never recover. Then, her own woman well at ease, she drives on to join the other girls in the burial of Kay. Now at last they will be alone together just as they were in college, when there were no hateful men or marriages or diapers or deaths, and they were all young and beautiful and loved one another with the pure passion of girlhood.

There ought to be a satirical note rising somewhere behind this implication of a return to the lost Eden of Vassar virginity. But, alas, there is none. Satire has been left behind with Harald standing on the roadside, and Miss McCarthy gives no sign that she is not speaking in her own sincere voice—speaking not alone, it would seem, for herself, but for all the sad young women who have suffered and died, all the fairy princesses who have been lost to the trolls.

[1965]

The Complacency of *Herzog*

FOR some years now our immediate age has been under the most fantastic pressure to produce a novel we could all accept in good conscience as major. Not only have we felt we deserved such a novel. We have *needed* it to vindicate our belief that this age, with its enormous awareness of literary values, should be as creatively vital as it is sophisticated about creativity, that our intense dedication to the life of the mind ought naturally to find its corollary in the production of major works of the imagination.

Bellow's *Herzog* has lately been acclaimed by the intellectual community as such a work, and one of the chief reasons it has been is that it takes intellectual sophistication as its very subject and demonstrates that the life of the mind can in fact be as important and exciting a source of creative vitality as the life of the groin. It deals expertly with materials that most of our novelists have found immensely difficult to dramatize, the materials of consciousness itself, and it deals with them in such a way that we recognize them to be central to our experience, uniquely expressive of ourselves and our condition as intellectuals. Bellow of course sees the condition of intellectuality in *Herzog* as a mixed blessing, and it is proper that he should, since that is exactly what it is. It has given us our high cultural expertise, but it has also severely impeded us in the efficient pursuit of the practical and the amorous life. It has rendered large areas of experience unreal to us, and it has made almost impossible satisfactory relations with people who do not share our commitment to ideas. The character of Herzog embodies these contradictions and is even shown to be torn in two by them—until, that is, he achieves peace through positive thinking. Yet even as we perceive this and admire the honesty that prompted Bellow to lay before us both sides of the case, we also perceive that intellectuality, as he portrays it in *Herzog,* finally emerges as far more of a blessing than a blight. And it does so, interestingly enough, just because the blight has been *turned into* a blessing, just because Bellow makes it so clear that Herzog's suffering is right and admirable, and that suffering is not only the intellectual's occupational disease but his badge of honor, the very measure of his significance both as a person and as a dramatic figure. For it is ultimately his suffering that causes Herzog to seem worthy of major literary treatment and capable of achieving something of the largeness of reference of a major social and literary symbol.

Thus, Bellow has managed to make a virtue of what we had always supposed was our chief source of discomfort, and in very much the way that Mary McCarthy elevated Margaret Sargent to a kind of bitchy, self-indulgent martyrdom, he has made complacently suffering Christs of us all. He has done this not only through his flattering treatment of Herzog's miseries but through his highly *un*flattering treatment of the people with whom Herzog is associated, and who are hell bent on causing him misery.

Bellow has always had the habit, which in his later work has tended to become a rather facile trick, of treating his secondary characters as if they were inmates of either a zoo or a madhouse. Augie March and Herzog in particular are depicted as quiet, deferential princes set down among trolls in bedlam. Augie has to contend with the often antagonistic and at times downright berserk vitalism of Einhorn, Dingbat, the Magnuses, Mintouchian, Thea Fenchel, and Basteshaw, while Herzog is chronically badgered and exploited by Simkin, Gersbach, Shapiro, Himmelstein, Nachman, and the various other freaks and egomaniacs whom Herzog rather plaintively calls his "Reality instructors." Bellow's handling of these people constantly verges on caricature. In fact, there are moments when they seem to exist solely as verbal abstractions, creations of merely adjectival intensity. Yet their function is clearly not to suggest living people drawn from close observation of the real world. Rather, it is to provide a milieu of grotesque idiosyncrasy and self-preoccupation against which Herzog can be seen as saintly. To be sure, in comparison with them he is ineffectual, bumbling, and a fool— the very type of the silly intellectual helplessly adrift in the cutthroat world of practical affairs. But however ridiculous he may be, he is also so much more of a human being, so much more sensitive and responsible than they, that his ridiculousness becomes, like his suffering, a badge of honor, the mark of his moral superiority. For Herzog is selfless where they are selfish, loving where they are hateful, wryly comic where they are gruesomely grotesque, a wonderful, absurd, adorable Jewish Uncle Tom whose predicament is that he is finally too pure for this world. The intellectual is also too pure for this world, or so he has always secretly considered himself. But he has been obliged to assume that his purity was at best a negative virtue, one he had to settle for in place of the truly human virtues shared by those who are not intellectuals. Now, however, through the drama of Herzog, he is given abundant evidence that nonintellectuals are monsters, that if they are human, he is positively angelic, that, in fact, to be an intellectual among such people is perhaps to be the very best thing there is. For in Herzog human warmth and ideas, heart and high culture, are joined together to produce the most flattering image of the intellectual to be found in modern literature.

It would seem that Bellow could not possibly go beyond this in his effort to aggrandize Herzog and to persuade us to see him as a figure of transcendent meaning and saintliness. Yet this is actually only a modest rehearsal for the emergence of Herzog into the full glory of his ultimate incarnation in the role of the Jewish intellectual as symbol of contemporary Everyman. It would undoubtedly be even harder than it is to accept Herzog in this preposterous role if Bellow did not take care to create an atmosphere of such high fastidiousness about slick generalizations of just this kind that we almost become convinced that he hates them as much as we do and is standing guard for us against them. For example, he speaks with proper contempt of "the commonplaces of the Waste Land outlook, the cheap mental stimulants of Alienation," and that, along with his overall wariness of tone, his apparent abhorrence of obvious and easy answers, would seem to serve as effective insurance against any lapse into other commonplaces and cheap mental stimulants. But it turns out that our trust is grievously misplaced, for Bellow slyly slips Herzog into the breach left by the banished Waste Land cliché. Herzog emerges, in fact, as the Waste Land cliché irrigated and transformed into the Promised Land, while the platitude of Alienation is converted into the even hoarier platitude of Accommodation and Togetherness. For what he holds up for our inspection is a new hopeful doctrine of potato love not uncolored by righteous disdain. The trolls may be killing us, he seems to say. We may be exploited, cuckolded, hounded out of house and home, reviled, and spat upon. But we can afford to be compassionate and gracious in our torment, remembering, as Nick Carraway's father once said, that "all the people in this world haven't had the advantages" that we have had.

At the end the novel heaves a fatty sigh of middle-class intellectual contentment. "I am pretty well satisfied," muses Herzog in his lawn chair, "to be, to be just as it is willed, for as long as I may remain in occupancy." And we sense that Herzog will be a long time in occupancy. For if it has been demonstrated that intellectuals have a corner on the world's love and compassion, it is probable that they also have a corner on the world's powers of survival. And of course Herzog is finally as arrogantly complacent in his new-found affirmative position, about being stuck with his loving and erudite self, as any of Mary McCarthy's heroines. In fact, it would appear that in Herzog Miss McCarthy's princess has at last found her prince—and the many intellectuals who have long felt guilty and defensive about their role in life have found their bromide, their hero, and the justification they have long been seeking for their secret sense of superiority. The novel, in short, is as wholesome and nutritious as a dish of corn flakes, a clearly "major" Establishment work in the sense that it dramatizes a theme of considerable size with complete honesty and without once expressing an idea that could possibly give offense to anyone. On the contrary, it has brought much good cheer and glad tidings to the intellectual community, and as is so often the case, such service has not gone unrewarded.

[1965]

The War Writers Ten Years Later

JUST over a decade ago in *After the Lost Generation* I made certain cantankerous pronouncements on the work of the younger group of American novelists who began to appear immediately following the war. I felt at the time that these writers were becoming rather dangerously inflated values on the literary market, and I saw my job as essentially corrective and deflationary. What I had to say aroused considerable indignation in publishing and reviewing circles, partly because some of the writers I had hit hardest had been selected to replace Hemingway and Fitzgerald—or so their jacket blurbs said—and I seemed to be interfering with the democratic right of American literature to repeat itself. Yet the passage of time has hit most of them a good deal harder than I did, so much harder in fact that it now seems scarcely believable that they could ever have occupied the positions of prominence that they obviously did occupy in the literary life of the postwar period.

Norman Mailer, Irwin Shaw, Truman Capote, Frederick

Buechner, Alfred Hayes, Robert Lowry, Merle Miller, Calder Willingham, Gore Vidal, Paul Bowles, Vance Bourjaily, along with James Jones, whose first novel appeared after my book was written—these were some of the apparently promising younger novelists of ten years ago. Today nearly all these writers give one the impression that their best work is behind them and that they can no longer be counted on to excite or command our attention with future work that is fresh, surprising, or very much more than a haggard recapitulation of the ideas and experiences with which they began their careers. As a group they have lost the critical standing their first books won for them, and most of them seem individually to have reached a creative impasse of one kind or another. Some have dropped out of sight completely. Others have abandoned the novel for less exacting and more lucrative forms of writing. One or two others have turned their baffled search for new materials into a topic of tabloid psycho-analysis and public confession. A few have continued, as if from habit, to bring out occasional books that, in spite of good intentions, one somehow never has the impulse to read. Every last one of them has suffered by comparison with a different and, in some cases, a younger set of contemporaries whose minds were not formed on the easy simplifications of wartime, and who seem to have a firmer grasp of the enor-mously subtle and complicated realities of the immediate present.

Perhaps because they aroused such high expectations to begin with, the authors of the classic war novels appear to have stood up least well under the pressures of the last ten years. Norman Mailer of course remains the strongest potential talent of the group and the best literary mind of the war generation. Yet his personal and polemical writings continue to seem more interesting than his novels, and his prejudices more interesting than his ideas. His failure to find his line after *The Naked and the Dead* has evidently caused him to seek in sheer raw experience the intensity he cannot create in art, and in the process to mistake the quick thrills of notoriety for the solid satisfactions of earned success.

Both James Jones and Irwin Shaw seem to have suffered in recent years simply from having lived too long abroad. The result for Jones appears to be that his experience of American life stopped with the period of the war and its immediate aftermath, and having so far been unable to put his European experience to creative use, he has been obliged since *From Here to Eternity* to keep returning obsessively to that period, first for the emotional background of *Some Came Running*, then in *The Pistol*, and most recently in *The Thin Red Line*. Shaw seems to have lost touch in Europe with the way present-day Americans talk and act, and a large part of his recent fiction has been seriously flawed by his tendency to make them talk and act in patterns that have been long out of date. Yet in Shaw's case one feels that the stoppage of experience occurred even earlier than the war, that in fact he has not really been creatively engaged with American life since the thirties—and then less with its actualities than with the fashionable representations of it to be found in certain modern novels.

As for some of the other young writers who were considered so promising right after the war, Truman Capote and Frederick Buechner continue to be the most potent arguments we have against the idea that the new fiction of the period was all done by men whose sense of language came out of a Ouija board manipulated by the ghost of Theodore Dreiser. Both are highly sensitive and accomplished practitioners of the poetic "high" style, Buechner of the strain descending from Henry James, and Capote of the strain indemnified by Faulkner and then powdered and perfumed by the ladies' fashion magazines. But Buechner has done little of real interest since *A Long Day's Dying*, while Capote has become a classic example of precocity extended and professionalized into a career. In 1951, I said that as Capote grows older, he will undoubtedly have to stop writing solely about adult children and childlike adults. Apparently I was wrong, for he is still writing about them, and he has unquestionably grown older.*

One can say almost exactly the same thing in slightly different terms about Vance Bourjaily. In the novels he has done since his first book, *The End of My Life*, one finds abundant evidence of advancing years, little evidence of creative development. The world has moved on, but he has not. Calder Willingham and Gore Vidal, on the other hand, *have* moved on, straight on out of the novel into the field of its more prosperous competitors. Willingham published several abrasively funny books after *End as a Man* and for a while seemed on the point of becoming established as a kind of crackerbarrel J. D. Salinger. But some years ago he turned to screen writing and has since done only one novel, about which nothing at all need be said. Vidal, who was once notable for the large number of books he managed to produce before reaching the age of thirty, rather dramatically announced at about the same time that he had finally discovered the novel form to be unworthy of his talents. Then he, too, went off to Hollywood, later transferred to television, and for a while found success as a writer for the Broadway theater.

---

* Capote's most recent book, *In Cold Blood*, is an excellent journalistic study of a multiple murder and shows an objectivity and sophistication not to be found in his fiction. It is not, however, as Capote seems to believe, an example of a new novelistic form, but rather a skilled adaptation of fictional techniques to the old form of the tabloid horror story.

There are of course any number of plausible explanations for the failure of these writers to develop artistically or to continue with their novelistic careers. The nervous strain of creative effort is very great; the will can grow tired and become paralyzed; critics can be obtuse, unfriendly, or just indifferent once too often; the rent sooner or later must be paid. It is also entirely possible that I was right in thinking that at least some of these writers were not really so very talented to begin with, but rather were pushed into an undeserved prominence simply because they happened to be among the first younger novelists to appear after the war. Yet the group as a whole has done interesting enough work to make it clear that the problem for most of them has not been basically one of talent as such. What seems far more likely is that there was something about their initial orientation as writers, something limited or defective about their manner of first engaging life imaginatively, which seriously impaired their ability to function under the changed social and intellectual conditions of the last ten years.

The point may just be that except perhaps for Capote and Buechner these writers never really have engaged life imaginatively. From the beginning of their careers they have been singularly deficient in the power to work up their materials out of their own creative resources and, therefore, singularly dependent upon the social scene to provide them with those materials. So long as the issues of the war and the immediate aftermath seemed valid and fresh, this weakness was neither obvious nor particularly crippling. In fact, it could even masquerade as a kind of strength, for it gave to much of their work the cold realism of front-page news and the documentary film. But the war was the last large-scale socially "given" subject to which these writers had access, and to an important extent it spoiled them for what came later. It was an experience in which not only they but their entire generation were meaningfully and dramatically involved, and it was so potently *there* as experience that it could be made into a novel by almost anyone with a good memory for details, a certain indignation, and only a fair competence in the language of fiction. The war in effect stood in the same relation to them as the great collective experiences of the first war and the Depression stood to the writers of the twenties and thirties, and like those occurrences it stirred into momentary life a number of talents that might under more normal conditions have remained dormant.

But the bleak period since the war has provided these writers with nothing comparable to the experience of the war years. It has been characterized by a curious failure to jell, by a lack of distinctive form and direction, and by an inevitable retreat of the old socially oriented literary mind on all fronts. In place of a tangible and readily usable subject the period has given us the indefinite suspensions and equivocations of the Cold War against an emotional background of alternating and even at moments coexisting anxiety and apathy. The central experience of the time has had the disconcerting effect of seeming to be shut off from relationship with the individual mind, of seeming to transpire on some plane of almost mythic abstraction far beyond the reach of human understanding.

The point about the Cold War is precisely that it *is* cold and not hot. It is by definition a state of action withheld, of participation avoided, in the face of an endless recurrence of aborted crises followed by stalled negotiations followed by more aborted crises—as if the broken record of our years has become stuck forever in the groove of incipient world catastrophe. In short, there can be no question of *experiencing* the Cold War in any of the old vigorous senses of the word. One simply endures it, waits it out, and in the end gives over the mind to the protective custody of its own resources, its own power to enforce sanity and order within the closed precincts of the created work of art. But for writers in whom that power is unawakened or who have grown accustomed to having their literary materials served up to them in the form of hot wars, concrete social issues, and collective social experience, such a condition of life can be baffling indeed. It can even result in a fatal derangement of sensibility.

To deal effectively with the massive complications and ambiguities of the Cold War period, to say nothing of the present amorphous state of American society, a writer would ideally need the artistic equipment of an Orwell, a Kafka, Camus, Celine, or Dostoevski. But since such equipment is rather hard to come by these days, he ought at the very least to have an artistic orientation sufficiently similar to theirs to enable him to see that the task of the novelist in a time like ours can no longer be confined to a simple exploration of the social appearances and surfaces, but must be expanded and deepened to take into account the chaotic multiplicity of meanings that now confront us both above and beneath the surfaces. He ought, in other words, to be able to recognize that his task is something far different from what it was and needed to be in any previous time, and that he must bring to it far larger resources of mind, imagination, and technical understanding than have ever been necessary before. If the experience of the present age has failed to define itself in the form of readily usable literary material, then he must be prepared to define it imaginatively, and to make of the very difficulty of definition one of the enriching values of his art.

Yet it is just this more stringent view of the novelist's task that the majority of the war writers have shown themselves least capable of accepting and acting upon. From the beginning they have nearly all operated in accordance with the now outdated and vastly oversimplified view bequeathed them by their predecessors of the twenties and thirties. And they have remained arrested in this view even as the developments of recent history have doomed both it and them to a condition of almost quaint irrelevance to just about everything we now take to be real and true. In fact, one of the perplexing features of these writers as a group has been their apparent inability to see their experience except in terms of the literary stereotypes of the immediate past, their failure to discover new ways of seeing that would be more suited not only to their individual talents but to the changed realities of the present time.

The work of the war generation abounds in examples of this failure. There are all those novels—most of them by writers scarcely remembered today—in which Hemingway's war was fought all over again in a style so synthetically Hemingwayish that one was shocked to realize that at the time they were written, Hemingway had already ceased to sound like himself and was beginning to sound like them. Mailer, Jones, and Shaw were all indebted in their first novels to the panoramic-naturalist view of society that Dos Passos made fashionable in *USA* and *Manhattan Transfer*. This view functioned for them rather like a celluloid overlay on a military map: it got them to where somebody else had already been without requiring them to explore the uncharted and perhaps heavily mined territory of their own imaginations. As a systematic if somewhat mechanical formulation of reality, it served them well enough—so long as reality continued to fit the formulation. But in our day it evidently does not, and the writers who have failed to understand this are searching the map for an objective that no longer exists. Mailer, of course, does understand this, and one of the most encouraging things about him is that he has tried hard since *The Naked and the Dead* to break out of the naturalistic stereotype into fresh formulations of reality as he now sees it to be. Up to now none of his attempts has been quite successful, but one at least feels that wherever he is trying to get, nobody has been there before him. And one can be absolutely certain that in his case the route will be mined every step of the way.

Yet the solution for Mailer and the others does not consist simply in throwing off the influence of a specific writer or method of writing. It finally involves emancipation from the whole complex of stock responses to and literary arrangements of experience that belong to the past and have acted up to now as blinders on their vision of the present. Capote, for example, can certainly not be accused of imitating Faulkner in any sort of direct or literal way. Yet his early work represents an almost burlesque usage of the kinds of materials, and the modes of treating those materials, that have been previously patented and perfected by the official Faulknerian imagination of the South.

Jones, Shaw, and Bourjaily have been trapped in another kind of burlesque by the official literary clichés of the twenties and thirties. Their fiction is always compulsively rehearsing the shopworn melodrama of their predecessors' discovery of the facts of life, always exulting in experiences that most of us have long since had and that fiction ought by now to have long since outgrown. In Bourjaily's novels in particular, the standard characters all seem to be terribly young men who spend an inordinate amount of time thinking up elaborate practical jokes to play on one another or engaging in rather heavily witty fraternity-house repartee or drinking away their sense of the sickness of the age or naughtily smoking pot out behind the barn of conventional society or fighting down homosexual impulses for which their parents are somehow to blame or trying to get as many different girls into bed as they possibly can.

Cliché *Weltschmerz*, cliché psychology, cliché dipsomania, cliché satyriasis—these are among the counterfeit coins of the legacy left to the war writers by the twenties and thirties. At one time it was almost impossible to tell that they were counterfeit because there was so little else in circulation. But today there is a great deal else. In the last several years an altogether different group of writers have come to prominence, a group consisting of, among others, Saul Bellow, James Baldwin, Bernard Malamud, J. D. Salinger, Philip Roth, and James Purdy. And these writers are minting a fresh currency of the creative imagination, one that seems certain to remain the legal tender of the serious American novel for a long time to come.

[1962]

Norman Mailer: The Energy of New Success

FOR a good many years now Norman Mailer has been making a determined effort to exploit all the resources of literary and social outrageousness in order to impress himself in a major way on the life and thought of his time. At no point in the course of this effort has the going been easy for Mailer; in fact, it has been so difficult and personally taxing that one often supposed that his ultimate objective was not the moral reformation of his society but the annihilation of himself. The fight he has carried on has made almost superhuman demands on his will power and his courage; it has caused deep erosion of his ego, even at those moments when his ego has been most insufferably in evidence; and inevitably it has provoked him to follies and excesses that have done him and his work serious harm.

For one thing, it has led him to antagonize large sectors of the reading public and to make powerful enemies among many people who might otherwise have been disposed to help him in a literary way. For another, it has cut down on the quality of his achievement as a novelist by giving almost everything he has written since *The Naked and the Dead* a curiously strained, claustrophobic quality that seemed to speak of the existence of creative ambitions too intense for his creative grasp. One could sense in both *Barbary Shore* and *The Deer Park* that the main current of his energy was trying to go elsewhere, trying to engage certain crucial ideas that were beginning to take shape in his mind, but was being balked by some recalcitrance in his material or some limitation in his language. Deep within those books one felt the pressure of something big growing, a vision or prophecy or simply a hatred that was perhaps too radical and disturbing to find embodiment in the conventional forms of the novel, perhaps too radical and disturbing for Mailer himself, who seemed to be reaching out for reassurance and support even as he was energetically engaged in alienating just about everybody.

For a long time Mailer was driven to seek easy and sensational shortcuts to the fulfillment he appeared unable to find in his work. He tried to gain attention through self-advertisement, challenges of the law, attempts to pass himself off as a New York mayoralty candidate, as the only man with guts enough to defy Sonny Liston to his face, as the man mainly responsible for Kennedy's election to the Presidency. The essays, furthermore, in which he put forth these claims seemed to be the only writing he was able to do, and this struck many people as an open admission that he had at last decided he could not make it in an important way as a novelist and was trying to salvage what was left of his career by peddling his megalomania to *Esquire*.

It was hard to say whether prevailing opinion was right or wrong, whether these were indeed the antics of a man sick for publicity at any price, or the honestly frustrated responses of a writer who for some reason could not mediate successfully between his ambitions and the restrictive literary circumstances of his time. Undoubtedly, they were a little of both. But certain clues to be found in his random utterances and published work slowly began to give greater weight to the second interpretation. The autobiographical passages of *Advertisements for Myself,* in particular, seemed to suggest that although he was indeed sick for publicity, he was not sick for it at any price. He was much too anxious about his career to be willing to risk it by exploiting, solely for publicity reasons, his dubious roles of professional bad boy and clown. If he behaved irresponsibly, he did so for naïve but very different and wholly honorable reasons: because he suffered from a deep-lying dissatisfaction with his position as a serious novelist and was trying in all the wrong ways to break out of the impasse in which he felt himself trapped and meet what seemed to him his first responsibility to himself. It only made his dissatisfaction seem more poignant to recognize, as of course he could not, that it was based on a sadly inflated idea of the kind of position a serious novelist can expect in our day to enjoy.

Very early in his career Mailer fell victim to the notion that large popular success was the fit and natural reward for significant achievement in the novel. He appears to have arrived at this conclusion after long and jealous study of the lives and work of the important novelists of the twenties and thirties, some of whom managed to achieve popularity with the reading public at the same time that they were recognized by the people who mattered as major literary figures. Hemingway, for example, was both great and world-famous, and so, in more modest degree, were Fitzgerald, Steinbeck, and Wolfe. Mailer of course reacted powerfully and personally to the good fortune of these men and from it abstracted a formula for success with which he proceeded, characteristically, to prove himself a failure. It seemed to him that if a novelist were serious enough and good enough, he would inevitably be widely read and widely praised. If he were not widely read and widely praised, that could only mean that he was not good enough. In fact, he could consider himself a total loss unless his books made the bestseller lists and stayed on them a certain generous number of weeks.

It apparently never occurred to Mailer that his idea of literary success was perfectly suitable and applicable to the commercial novelist with his heart set on Book-of-the-Month Club adoption, or that he was drawing a false inference from historical circumstances that could only be considered extraordinary and temporary. The times in which he himself became a novelist were very different from the twenties and thirties, and the whole relationship between the novelist and the reading public had profoundly changed—and changed, according to his own logic, for much the worse. Among the writers with whom he could consider himself in direct competition, only Salinger enjoyed anything like the status of the younger Hemingway or Fitzgerald, and there was much in Salinger's work and reputation at which Mailer might legitimately have sneered. Most of his other contemporaries, furthermore, appeared to have resigned themselves to being more praised or criticized than read, and to having a certain limited status in the literary world while remaining virtually unknown to the general reading public. But Mailer was temperamentally incapable of resigning himself. He took it for granted that his really decisive competition was not with his contemporaries, for whom, on the whole, he had little respect, but with the most distinguished of his predecessors, and he continued to hold out for the kind and degree of popular success he assumed had been theirs.

Thus, one found him in *Advertisements* brooding over Hemingway's career and trying to discover the secret of the master's "strategy," or admiring, among others, Truman Capote because Capote had managed to parlay his pretty eccentricities into a campy kind of celebrity. From the beginning the emphasis was all on the image a writer might, with care and cunning, project, the impression he was able to make on the public through his personality and behavior rather than through his work. Hemingway's career had been exemplary in this regard. For years Hemingway had written nothing "which would bother an eight-year-old or one's grandmother," and yet his reputation was firm because "he knew in advance, with a fine sense of timing, that he would have to campaign for himself, that the best tactic to hide the lockjaw of his shrinking genius was to become the personality of our time." Hence, it followed with a perfect twisted consistency that the present sufferer from lockjaw had only to become a comparable personality in order to achieve a reputation of comparable firmness.

One could concede Mailer the highly debatable point that Hemingway's reputation was by that time firm, and still refute the argument he based upon it. Hemingway may have become the personality of our time, but he did not do so on the strength of his personality alone, nor was he able to use his personality to win acceptance for his poorer work. *To Have and Have Not* and *Across the River and into the Trees* were widely recognized to be inferior novels, and the only effect of the personality was to make their badness seem more pitiable than it might otherwise have seemed. There was never any question, as Mailer appeared to believe, of the public's accepting the bad work because the personality was so attractive. The truth was that the bad work hurt Hemingway so severely that he never fully recovered. He was never again so secure in reputation as he had been just after the appearance of *A Farewell to Arms.* What Mailer chose to ignore was that the original reputation, which alone made the personality possible and tolerable, was based on excellent work. Hemingway won the approval of the public in the first place by confronting them simultaneously with work they could admire and a personality with which they could closely identify. But the personality would have been meaningless and fraudulent without the work, and any firmness Hemingway's reputation might still have had was the result entirely of the respect generally felt for his early excellence, and not of any misunderstanding, willful or otherwise, about the value of his later achievement.

It is of course possible, although unprovable, that Hemingway's personality helped to do what Mailer once said Vance Bourjaily's literary politicking had done: relaxed "the bite of the snob to the point where he or she can open the mouth and sup upon the message." It is even probable that without the personality, Hemingway's reputation, or at least his celebrity, would have been nowhere near so large. An important writer can, provided he has done important work, promote his own fashion in such a way that he will win an earlier and more sympathetic reception for his work than he might have won through the more modest display of merit alone. But in trying to apply Hemingway's example to his own case, Mailer had neglected to follow the rules in two vitally important respects. He had failed to project a personality with which more than a few perverse or disgruntled souls could easily identify, and his work after *The Naked and the Dead* had simply not been good enough or appealing enough to attract a large public following. Hemingway had, after all, enlightened and entertained. He had not only been popular; he had written popularly. Mailer had, for the most part, merely baffled and irritated, at the same time that he had written with a sophistication and from moral assumptions that only a small segment of the public could be expected to share.

Nevertheless, the point seemed to be that Mailer *needed* Hemingway's kind of success and believed that he should have it. He could admit that he might not be personally attractive to a general audience. But he was also convinced that it can be "fatal to one's talent not to have a public with a clear ... recognition of one's size." Just how the public could be expected to achieve such a recognition without being provided with work of size, he did not explain. He simply had to have such a public in order to keep his talent and his confidence alive. He needed to think extremely well of himself in order to write even half well, and the trouble was that every time he would manage to begin thinking well of himself something would happen to make him think badly.

The autobiographical sections of *Advertisements* were very largely a record of the forces that conspired to deprive Mailer of his self-esteem. First *Barbary Shore*, then *The Deer Park*, failed to win the approval he so desperately required. The former did not make the bestseller lists at all; the latter made them for a tantalizing week or two, then slipped off, if not quite into oblivion, into the next worst thing: middling, lukewarm notoriety. After the failure of *Barbary Shore* he might, he said, have learned "to take [his] return ticket to the minor leagues without weeping too much in the beer"— except that he was plagued by the intuition that he was working his way toward saying something unforgivable, not something badly or opaquely said but something unforgivable. The trouble, it seemed, was not the quality of the communication but the outrageousness of the thing communicated. It was simply too powerfully and painfully honest for human consumption. Thus, he rationalized, and thus he agonized over his failure to achieve a success that, by all logic, he should have despised and probably *would* have despised if he had achieved it.

His difficulties finding a publisher for *The Deer Park* had been another blow, resulting in more serious damage to his self-esteem. He might have done so much so easily if only some publisher had accepted the book enthusiastically when it was first offered, and the reviewers had raved when it first appeared. "For the vitality of my work in the future," he said, "and yes, even the quality of my work, I needed a success and I needed it badly if I was to shed the fatigue I had been carrying since *Barbary Shore*." If *The Deer Park* had managed to be "a powerful best seller (the magical figure had become one hundred thousand copies for me) ... I would then have won. I would be the first serious writer of my generation to have a best seller twice, and so it would not matter what was said about the book ... a serious writer is certain to be considered major if he is also a best seller." And to be *considered* major by virtue of one's sales figures was not only the same as *being* major; it was essential to one's *continuing* to be major.

The implications of such statements are so appalling that one is shocked by them out of almost all understanding of the truth they conceal. Yet the truth, however ugly, is undeniable. Success, even of the most blatantly commercial kind, *can* very often make the difference between being recognized and being ignored. The fact that a writer is considered to be important or in some way appealing to large numbers of people can cause him to be singled out for special scrutiny and discovered to have qualities that may in fact *be* important and that might otherwise have been overlooked. Once again it is a matter of relaxing the bite of the snob. Bestsellerdom has often been known in our day to create a large, if temporary, reputation on the strength of very little evidence, just as it has been known to rescue from obscurity a reputation that deserved to be large. For a writer of Mailer's competitive temperament and particularly his early experience of success, it is easy to see how continued success could become a psychological necessity on which the quality of his subsequent performance might very well depend. Having once based his high opinion of himself on the public's high opinion of him, he had no choice but to think less of himself when the public's interest fell off. The fact that Mailer also happened to have become a kind of writer who could no longer please a large public no matter how hard he tried, or thought he wanted to try, did not diminish his need for the benefits to be derived from having pleased. It simply deepened his confusion and frustration.

The whole trouble was that the huge success of his first novel had infected him with the values, if not the skills, of a petty politician. He had pleased his constituents and been elected to office. Now he felt that he had to please them again in order to be reelected. And this he could not do without compromising his ambition to write outrageously and according to his changed ideas of what fiction should be. He may, as he said, have been running for President ever since 1948, but his politics had altered radically in the interval and so apparently had the character of his constituents. He could hardly expect to charm them with his bright promise of 1948. He could not go on writing *The Naked and the Dead* over and over. Yet the books he had written seemed necessarily unpleasant, and those he wanted to write seemed destined to grow more unpleasant the more he hoped

157

that by some miracle their unpleasantness would win him the election. His frustration was such that he appeared to be on the verge of doing almost anything to bring that miracle about except the thing that his needs, as he stated them, made logically imperative: to write quite cynically what the public wanted to read. Since that was unthinkable, the politician in him turned ugly and began to campaign against him. By the time he started writing the fateful *Village Voice* columns, he had acquired the suicidally belligerent habits of a man who understood his own value so little that he felt compelled to seek his image in the outrage of others (I offend; therefore, I am) and convert every public encounter into a potential occasion for challenge and test. He began to court hostility with as much vigor as he had previously courted popularity, and it was soon obvious that he did so *in order* to destroy in himself every last hope of popularity, of ever being elected President, so that he would be free to get back into some relation of honesty with his deepest and surest creative instincts. For it was only by persuading the public to hate him that he could give up the idea of trying to persuade the public to love him. And he needed to be hated in order to start loving himself once again and resume the lone, aggressively outlaw role that he sensed was his natural one.

Little by little he had left behind his dream of quick success. Now he set out quite deliberately to kill that dream and began for the first time since *The Naked and the Dead* to be honest with himself, not with his work, but with himself. For the first time he admitted that what he wanted more than success was to provoke, incite, and if possible, revolutionize—to do, in short, what he had all along been trying to do without wanting to accept the consequences. Like Henry James after his failure to find success in the theater, he felt freed by failure to write out of his profound and radical intuitions without regard for the feelings of those who had alienated him by their indifference. Ironically, it was from this time on that he began to show signs of becoming the major writer he had been asking the public to take him for. And it was a deeper irony as well as perfectly logical that those signs were most evident in the sections of *Advertisements* in which he lamented most bitterly his lost battle to be accepted as major.

There and in the essays he soon began to publish in *Esquire* and later collected in *The Presidential Papers*—the essays that so many people saw as evidence of his creative failure—he produced by far the best writing he had ever done. In particular, it seemed that at some point in that troubled journey back to himself, at some moment in that bleak period of foiled prospects and compensatory bluster and brag, he had discovered a style, his true style, one entirely unlike any to be found in his earlier novels. Both *Barbary Shore* and *The Deer Park* had suffered badly from verbal constipation. The clean, hard, yet flexible language of *The Naked and The Dead* had given way in those books to something choked and flat, without flexibility or ease. Everything in them came out sounding like a metallic voice announcing the arrival and departure of aircraft—heavy, toneless, and very dead. There was a loin-wrung, post-masturbatory quality about the style of *Barbary Shore*, and *The Deer Park* bore the marks of an act of sheer will working against an enormous inertia of imaginative fatigue and lost hopes. It was not clear at the time why this should be so, but it is clear now in the light of Mailer's subsequent stylistic breakthrough. He was quite simply never a novelist in the true sense after *The Naked and The Dead*, and that book, like most war novels by young men, was as much an accident of experience as it was a creative achievement. But after it Mailer began to have real difficulty projecting his feelings and ideas into an objective dramatic situation. The necessity to create characters and relate them meaningfully to one another obviously forced him to be concerned with problems that did not really interest him and that, therefore, impeded the development of his talent in the direction it appeared naturally to be trying to take. His natural subject was not, it seemed, other people but himself. He did not want to invent; he wanted to confess, to display himself as the sole recorder and protagonist of significant contemporary experience.

So it was that when he came to write *Advertisements* and the *Esquire* essays, Mailer experienced an immense release of inhibitions and was able for the first time to confront his feelings and ideas in their full complexity. He found it possible to make complete use of his resources not only as a highly skilled worker in language but as an intuitive thinker of an at times almost superhuman sensitivity to the psychic realities of his time. And he expressed this sensitivity in a style that combined the mean talk of the hipster and the edgy rhetoric of psychiatry into a prose instrument as lethal as a switchblade. Hence, it would appear that, far from being a symptom of failure, Mailer's excursion into the essay was actually a vital preparation for the moment when his language would at last be adequate to his ambitions, and he would be ready to undertake the major creative breakthrough that his latest novel, *An American Dream*, so clearly represented, a novel in which Mailer for the first time made sustained use of his new style in fiction.

There were, of course, many readers and critics who felt that the book represented not a breakthrough but the final stage of breakdown. It was severely criticized by some very respectable and responsible people, and one could certainly understand why. By conventional standards it was an unpardonably ugly book and, taken in terms of its story, a profoundly silly book, full of grotesque and implausible occurrences and characters who appeared to be uniformly insane. But what the critics failed to comprehend was that it could not be properly judged by standards normally applied to the novel and that, for all its ugliness, it was essentially a work of humor and self-satire, most humorous in those places where it treated derisively some of its most serious-seeming effects. It was a burlesque treatment of the obscene version of the American Dream that possesses the unconscious mind of America at the present time, and what appeared to be, and patently were, excesses and absurdities were also an integral part of the humorous intent, and perfectly in keeping not only with the psychotic quality of the dream but with the tradition to which the book seemed most clearly to belong, the tradition of the prose romance, in which fantasy and fact, witchcraft and melodrama, myth, allegory, and realism combine to produce what Richard Chase has called "a profound poetry of disorder." The book's antecedents were not the novels of Henry James or Jane Austen but the romances of Cooper, Melville, and Hawthorne, and one of Mailer's contributions was to rehabilitate the form of the romance and adapt it to the literary needs of the immediate present. The book, in short, was an examination not of human and social surfaces but of our fantasy life, a vastly hallucinated yet deeply real account of the American dream become in our day the American nightmare.

In it Mailer explored the possibilities for both damnation and salvation to be found in some of the most reprehensible acts known to our society—murder, suicide, incest, fornication, and physical violence. He attempted to dramatize, and always with a clear sense of their comic implications, the various ways a man may sin in order to be saved, consort with Satan in order to attain to God, become holy as well as whole by restoring the primitive psychic circuits that enable him to live in harmony with himself and find his courage, regardless of whether his courage seeks its test in the challenges of love or the temptation to murder, whether he ends by becoming saint or psychopath. He wrote, in short, a radically moral book about radically immoral subjects, a religious book that transcends the conventional limits of blasphemy to expose the struggle toward psychic redemption that is the daily warfare of our secret outlaw selves.

As a piece of fiction the book had, to be sure, outrageous flaws. Mailer committed every sin known to literature, but like his hero he somehow succeeded in getting away with murder. For the book's defects could do nothing to alter one's impression that it was the product of a devastatingly alive and original creative mind at work in a language capable of responding with seismographic sensitivity to an enormously wide range of impressions. There seemed to be no limit to what Mailer was now able to do with words, particularly in recording the physical and psychological realities of people as they impinged upon the mind of a man constantly flagellating himself to new heights of awareness. In fact, it is possible to say that in it Mailer brought to full development a prose idiom of higher sensitivity to the exact condition of contemporary consciousness than any we have had in fiction since the best work of Faulkner, and that he managed through that idiom to create an image of our time that will undoubtedly be recognized as authoritative for this generation.

Mailer stands alone among his contemporaries in possessing a coherent metaphysics of the human condition as it now exists. He also stands alone in possessing an intellectual force that is at the same time a dynamic and uniquely personal imaginative vision. He alone, therefore, seems likely to possess the power to shift us out of our old comfortable modes of seeing and feeling and cause us to experience the shock of recognition we always experience when we have placed before us realities seen for the first time with the honesty of a truly original talent. If Mailer has not yet become the great novelist he has so long fought to become, he has clearly become a major creative consciousness and conscience, the most annoying, destructive, hateful, but altogether remarkable writer of these undistinguished years.

[1965]

The Private Vice of
John Updike

JOHN UPDIKE is one of those writers around whom we have generated a flamboyance of celebrity quite out of keeping with the value of anything they have so far written. In any reasonably discriminating age a young man of Mr. Updike's charming but limited gifts might expect to make his way in time to a position of some security in the second or just possibly the third rank of serious American novelists. But this is not a discriminating age. Hence, Mr. Updike has been able to arrive with ease at the very gates of first-rank status, and considering the size and fervor of his following, he should have no trouble at all getting in.

Just why this should be so it is extremely difficult to say, and the appearance of his new novel, *Of the Farm*, does not make it any easier. Mr. Updike has none of the attributes we conventionally associate with major literary talent. He does not have an interesting mind. He does not possess remarkable narrative gifts or a distinguished style. He does not create dynamic or colorful or deeply meaningful characters.

He does not confront the reader with dramatic situations that bear the mark of an original or unique manner of seeing and responding to experience. He does not challenge the imagination or stimulate, shock, or educate it. In fact, one of the problems he poses for the critic is that he engages the imagination so little that one has real difficulty remembering his work long enough to think clearly about it. It has an annoying way of slipping out of the mind before one has had time to take hold of it, and of blending back into the commonplace and banal surfaces of reality, which are so monotonous a part of our daily awareness that the mind instinctively rejects them as not worth remembering.

Yet there can be no doubt that Mr. Updike does on occasion write well, although often with a kind of fussiness that makes one feel that the mere act of finding words that look attractive together on the page occupies entirely too much of his time and energy. There are, nonetheless, passages here and there in his novels of excellent description, mostly of landscapes, such as the long account in *The Centaur* of Peter Caldwell's early morning drive with his father into town, and Rabbit Angstrom's abortive flight down the highways in *Rabbit, Run.* There are also moments when Mr. Updike seems on the verge of becoming profound on the subject of the larger issues of life, love, death, and God. But then as a rule one senses that he does not, after all, know quite what he means to say and is hoping that sheer style will carry him over the difficulty. It is true, as Norman Mailer once remarked, that Mr. Updike tends to become confused when the action lapses, and so he cultivates his private vice: he *writes*. And the conviction grows on one that he *writes* a great deal too much of the time, and is too frequently ridden by the necessity to distract the reader's attention from the lapse by planting in his path yet another exquisitely described tree, shack, or billboard.

In his first three novels Mr. Updike should have been able to avoid these problems because he appeared to take great pains never to treat a subject for which a safe and secure precedent in literature did not exist. This, in fact, may well account for the high esteem in which he is currently held by so many people. For what he essentially accomplished in those novels was a skilled adaptation of the standard mannerisms and styles that have come over the years to be identified as belonging to the official serious modern mode of treating experience in fiction, and with which, therefore, many people felt comfortable, since they were relieved of the obligation to accommodate themselves to the new and unfamiliar and could sit back and enjoy being informed once again of what they already knew. Mr. Updike, in turn, was relieved of the obligation to think creatively and free to indulge his considerable talent for mimicking to perfection the best effects of other writers' originality.

It became apparent, however, that Mr. Updike shared with his admirers the handicap of being a good many years behind the times in his literary tastes. For example, his first novel, *The Poorhouse Fair,* was exactly the sort of book that back in the twenties and thirties would have represented an honest and rather radical confrontation of reality, but which by the middle fifties had become so respectably and fashionably "modern" that schools of writing were proudly turning it out by the dozens. It was a book essentially of style and terribly oblique and opaque and tinily inward observations of people, in which nothing discernible *happened,* but everything went on with dark throttled meaningfulness just beneath the surfaces, and faint ectoplasmic wisps of sensibility floated spookily about the page. In it

Mr. Updike proved not only that he could work well in an outmoded convention, but that he could, if the need arose, *write* to cover a lapse of book-length duration.

Rabbit, Run, although brilliant in many of its superficial effects, was a botched attempt to explore certain important disorders of the modern will and spirit. It raised vital questions of freedom and responsibility that it answered vapidly. At just the point where it should have crystallized into meaning, it collapsed into a shambles of platitudes and stereotypes of alternative—rebellion versus conformity, the loving, passionate prostitute versus the dull, drunken, respectable wife —which nicely dramatized Mr. Updike's failure to come to fresh imaginative grips with his materials. *Rabbit, Run* might have been a deeply subversive book. Instead, it merely recapitulated subversive elements that had ceased with time and repeated literary usage to be subversive. It was spiced with a stale, High-Camp brand of *Angst* and a sexuality that had become merely a form of *writing* done with a different instrument, and, perhaps appropriately, the most viable possibility it appeared to hold out was that Rabbit probably ought to try very hard to make his peace with society, family, and God.

At the time he wrote *The Centaur,* Mr. Updike must have been alone among living writers in supposing that there could still be anything interesting or original to be done with the device of juxtaposing ancient myth and contemporary fact in fiction. Although T. S. Eliot did say after *Ulysses* was published that "Mr. Joyce is pursuing a method which others must pursue after him," one had assumed that the serious imitators of Joyce had all by now died of old age. But Mr. Updike, with his infallible instinct for the dated, apparently decided that there might be some kind of intellectual chic or status value to be found in carrying on the pursuit. He seems accordingly to have set out equipped only with the idea that all one needed to do was bring together some mythological figures and some contemporary characters and say that they were parallels, without troubling to create a dramatic situation in which they actually *became* parallels and therefore meaningful. Thus, he indicated in a thoughtfully provided epigraph and index that his story was a modern-dress reenactment of the legend of Chiron and Prometheus. But there was no reason to suppose that his protagonist, George Caldwell, was Chiron or anybody else but George Caldwell. His actions did not relate significantly or even coherently to those of the noblest of centaurs, and Chiron's shadow behind him contributed none of the comic irony that Odysseus contributed to Joyce's Bloom. It only served to muddle more completely a story that had no structure or point, and that Mr. Updike was clearly attempting to trick out in a bogus and antiquated literariness.

Of the Farm, although physically a small book, affords Mr. Updike a large opportunity to exercise his considerable powers of description. Never before has his private vice been so eloquently publicized. In fact, since he now has no rabbits or centaurs running for him, Mr. Updike is forced to describe pretty much all the time. There are descriptions of houses, barns, fields, flowers, trees, farm equipment, garden produce, and dogs. There is also a very good description of a tractor mowing a hay field.

The story itself is slight enough to have served as the basis for one of Mr. Updike's *New Yorker* stories, but even in the *New Yorker* it probably would have had to crescendo just a little, and this it does not do. It simply stops. It concerns the tensions that develop between a son and his ailing mother and the son's second wife when they all come together during a weekend down on the mother's farm. The mother, it seems, really preferred the first wife, although she appears not to care very much for either wife, and she certainly does not care for her son, who is full of bitterness toward her. At any rate, this drama, which develops at about the speed of creeping crab grass, is interrupted at intervals to give Mr. Updike an opportunity to make sure that the reader has the scene firmly in mind. And just to make doubly sure, he inserts some further descriptions of details he failed to mention earlier, such as the appearance of a church where the mother and son attend service, a supermarket where they go to buy groceries, and the new wife's excellent thighs in a bikini.

But these digressions come to seem more and more pleasant and necessary as the novel proceeds. Indeed, one begins to feel almost grateful to the action for lapsing, for at least the interludes of scenic commercials introduce subjects about whose reality there can be no question. They have what Henry James would have called "density of specification," and finally they justify their existence in the novel by creating a happy heterogeneity of clutter into which the domestic tensions sink and finally disappear. It seems after a while that all the difficulties we have watched developing among the characters become assimilated into the bucolic setting, that a satisfactory mediation has been achieved between the petty troubles of men and women and the eternal harmonies of nature, so that what at first promised to be a disturbing book turns out to be an essentially placid and contented book.

The effect of the book is finally so agreeable and reassuring that one feels that it would be almost offensive to speak of its possible meaning. Yet meaning it most assuredly has. In fact, one can even say that it has a message, although as is the case with all Mr. Updike's books, it does not yield up this message easily. Every effort is made to keep it subtle, and the reader is constantly being put off its track by various cagey covering movements of Mr. Updike's. But one can, after some searching, ferret it out from its hiding place behind the rich, beautiful scenery of the descriptive prose. I suppose there is no harm in revealing it, since it is bound to become common knowledge very soon. Mr. Updike has nothing to say.

[1965]

John Cheever and the Soft Sell of Disaster

IF you have searched as I have for critical discussion of John Cheever that goes beyond the mere review and treats of his special gifts with some real thoroughness and force, you will probably already share my conviction that Cheever is one of the most grievously underdiscussed important writers we have at the present time. It is perfectly true that his first novel, *The Wapshot Chronicle,* won a National Book Award in 1958, and that he was the subject of a cover story in *Time.* But this scarcely constitutes critical attention. In fact, the receipt of either of these honors may be the best conceivable reason for withholding it.

Still, every now and then and perhaps altogether by accident, good writers, even distinguished writers, have been chosen to receive one or both, and however cheaply they may be valued in the intellectual world, they do represent a kind of good housekeeping seal of middlebrow literary approval; they signify that somebody up there, or down there, in the mass power complex likes you or at any rate finds you innocuous; and one would have thought that, if nothing else, the very wholesomeness of it all would have provoked some nasty young critic into coming forward before this with a blistering denunciation of Cheever as a paid moralist of the button-down collar Establishment, or at the very least, into finding out what the ballyhoo was all about. But thus far no critic has, to the best of my knowledge, been so provoked, with the result that Cheever remains secure in his position of official celebrity curiously unsupported by real reputation, a writer whom a great many people have obviously heard of and a good number must surely have read, yet in whom nobody who genuinely matters seems to take very much interest.

Cheever has, of course, all along been unfortunate in the company his work has kept. His lengthy association with the *New Yorker,* in which ever since the early thirties the bulk of his fiction has appeared, has not helped to attract serious critics to his work, and as his image has come over the years to be more and more closely identified with that of the magazine, he must long ago have resigned himself to the fact that if recognition should one day come, it would very probably take the form of some such damning encomium as the *Time* profile. For the *New Yorker* air of blasé superciliousness and the *Time* air of blasé sanctimoniousness are both generated by the same wind machine, and a writer can hardly expect to be buoyed up on the one without sooner or later being borne off on the other. It was no accident that *Time* should have offered Cheever to the world as a kind of crew-cut, Ivy League Faulkner of the New York exurbs, who could be both artistically sincere and piously right-thinking about the eternal verities, and who was somehow so stalwartly imaginative that he could parlay even the eternal banalities into a disturbing yet comforting, whimsical yet tragic fable of immense significance for the present age.

But the question is not whether the *Time* profile was an accident, but whether it was altogether mistaken, and one is compelled to admit that it was not. There are moments, to be sure, when Cheever does indeed seem to resemble Faulkner—in his distinguished story-telling gifts, his obsession with, and creative mastery of, a cultural territory of which he has made himself the sole owner and proprietor, even in his essential integrity and toughness of mind, which have enabled him to be consistently better than the medium he writes for and more serious than his middlebrow admirers would be able to recognize. There are also moments when he seems extraordinary in his power to infuse the commonplace and often merely dyspeptic metaphysical crises of modern life with something of the generalizing significance of myth, particularly at a time when it is precisely the ability to deal with the modern social experience in terms of any principle of imaginative coherence that seems to be missing in so many of our most important writers.

Certainly, more thoroughly than anyone else now at work in the field of the American short story, Cheever has explored the troubled surfaces of the new affluent society in which so many of us now live and cannot quite find our being; and as the best of the stories in *The Brigadier and the Golf Widow* make clear, he has also penetrated beneath the surfaces into the special conditions of psychic purgatory that we have been able to afford to create for ourselves. He understands just what happens when a man making too much money awakens to the fact that there is nothing left to spend it on except some form of anesthesia against the knowledge that there is nothing left to spend it on. His people are all exempt, at least in his later stories, from the problems of economic insufficiency; hence they are open to all the torments of economic surfeit. They drink too much, fornicate when they can, and then with all guilt and no pleasure, and the men ride commuter trains with the feeling that they are being borne along on fur-lined conveyor belts from somebody else's fabrication of Happiness to somebody else's merchandising image of Success, with no chance that anything ever again will happen to them. So they are obliged to take refuge in small arbitrary or merely ceremonial rebellions, in nostalgia for a past that they may not particularly have liked but in which they at least had something to feel, and in daydreams, not of Walter Mittyish grandiosity, but of almost girlish modesty and poignance.

Yet on the rare occasions when they do open their eyes to the real world, they tend to find themselves in another dream in which the most incredible things are likely to happen or *appear* to be happening. A beautiful woman without any clothes on combs her long golden hair in the window of a passing Pullman car; a husband and wife, also naked, chase each other around the terrace of the house across the street; the teenage baby-sitter suddenly turns into a siren of unspeakable loveliness, awakening in them quaint, implacable longings to flee with her across the Atlantic on the old *Mauretania* and settle down in some sex-smelling Bohemian garret. Or just as incredibly, they feel their identities slipping away, and *others* notice: the elevator operator mistakes them for deliverymen; the train conductor thinks they are waiters; when they arrive home, they are attacked in the driveway by their own dogs. Or they decide it would be fun to swim home from a party by way of various friends' pools, until they discover that everything they had always taken for granted is beginning to seem untrue, that they have all along been swimming from some crazy illusion of the real into some horrible hallucination that just happens to *be* the real,

174

and in which the reassuring image of the four beautiful daughters safely at home playing tennis, the popularity enjoyed in the community, the affluence and the martini parties, are all revealed to be a lie, part of some fantastic and unnamable hoax perpetrated, oddly enough, on themselves by themselves.

These are some of the typical projections of Cheever's sense of the contemporary world, and I hope I will not seem unfaithful to my own sense of their importance if I say that showing through them are the qualities that have made Cheever likable to the *New Yorker* and *Time,* and which have helped to obstruct his breakthrough into genuine excellence and serious reputation. Somehow the nightmare tonalities of his work come to seem after a while a little too coy and cloying, the postures of psychic torment a little too much like the smartly macabre decor of some Fifth Avenue shop window in which creepy mannequins stand around draped in the latest creations by Charles Addams. For Cheever's vision of all the exactly right contemporary horrors comes perilously close to expressing itself in the stereotypes and platitudes, rather than in the perceived actualities, of experience, and one wonders if he is any longer capable of dealing with his materials in any other way, so that his characters and situations, his Proxmire Manors, Shady Hills, and Bullet Parks, will cease to seem interchangeable, and his resolutions predictable and harmless because stylish.

One also notices, particularly in his novels, and more particularly in *The Wapshot Scandal,* that his most aberrant effects are not only represented in the clichés of aberration—in nymphomania, dipsomania, paranoia, and sexual narcissism—but are often neutralized by some last-minute withdrawal from the full implication of their meaning, some abrupt whimsical detour into palliating fantasy. And while less obvious in his stories, the same tendency is discernible in them. All discordant extremes of conduct and perception are finally absorbed into a fundamentally equable view of life, in much the same way that the *New Yorker* tends to substitute for the distasteful realities a kind of gloss or meringuey confection of the real, which provides us with a faint sickening flavor without actually disturbing our psychic digestion.

It may be that Cheever is temperamentally the sort of writer who prefers to give comfort rather than to educate and transform consciousness. After all, he has been quoted as saying that "one has the impulse to bring glad tidings to someone." Sometimes he even seems to be registering certain grotesqueries simply because he thinks he ought to, or that they are expected of a writer who wishes to be taken seriously, or quite blatantly because he imagines them to be the going literary thing this season. Certainly, his work always seem on the verge of escaping from under its weight of nightmare into an almost Dionysian celebration of the joys of clean living and positive thinking, and of course this is the quality that *Time,* with its stethoscopic sensitivity to the uplifting rhythms of the heart, was able to make serve its pietistic ends.

In any case, it is obvious that Cheever needs both to strengthen and to expand his imaginative grasp, and there is some evidence in this new collection that he has at least tried to do the latter. The stories here are more varied in situation and locale than those in his previous two volumes. Several have to do with expatriate life, and there are some experimental pieces and character sketches that show that he has become aware of a world that is not entirely regulated by the arrival and departure every weekday morning of the 9:14. But they are also more uneven in quality, and the touch is very often unsure, even rather mechanical, as if Cheever were writing at times from habit or falling back on certain effects that he knows by now will do because they served him well in the past. He also seems to be experiencing some difficulty in telling his good work from his bad. A really fine story like "The Swimmer" is followed by the group of vignettes in "Metamorphoses," some of which are vapid beyond belief, and the last and best story in the book, "The Ocean," is forced to work hard to overcome the pointlessness of "A Vision of the World," which immediately precedes it. Perhaps three or four of the stories at most come up to the level of the best in *The Enormous Radio* and *The Housebreaker of Shady Hill*.

There is, in short, still very little to convince one that Cheever is moving on. He still needs to find something more and, above all, something different to say about his subject. In fact, he needs to be more drastic than that. He needs to break out of his present mode and rearrange or retool his imaginative responses, not only so that he will be able to confront squarely the full implications of his vision, but so that his vision can become in fact a vision and not simply a congeries of shy and whimsical glances through a glass darkened by a pessimism not quite his own, not quite earned by his imagination. One wishes to say to him now what Gertrude Stein once said to Hemingway: begin over again and concentrate. For he does not yet disturb us enough. He does not yet rouse enough fear. And until he does, he seems destined to remain a writer best known and most admired by all the wrong people for his comforting limitations.

[1964]

Art and Passion in
Katherine Anne Porter

EVER since the publication of *Flowering Judas,* her first
volume of stories, in 1930, Katherine Anne Porter has enjoyed a reputation for excellence that criticism has done
little to confirm or deny. This is not to say that criticism has
neglected her. Over the years a small but respectable amount
of commentary has grown up around her work, and individual stories of hers have so long been the standard subjects
of undergraduate explication that it is now possible to mistake them for hieroglyphs belonging to the archaeology department. Yet the bulk of this criticism has failed to establish
for Miss Porter the clear claim to distinction that everyone
seems to agree she possesses. It has nearly always approached
her with the highest admiration, yet been singularly unable
to say exactly what is admirable about her. It has sounded
her symbols, plumbed her metaphors, prodded and poked
among her ironies and ambiguities, and come up with very
little that would distinguish her writing from a newly ex-
cavated Babylonian grocery list.

As a result, Miss Porter occupies today a most peculiar

position. She is widely recognized as a creative artist of almost awesome fastidiousness, whose very paucity of production has come to be regarded as the mark of a talent so fine that it can scarcely bring itself to function. Her stories are considered to be distinguished examples of their type and have undoubtedly had enormous influence on the contemporary development of the form. Yet the precise nature of her artistic qualities continues to be one of the great unsolved mysteries of modern literature. She remains the symbol and custodian of an excellence that is almost everywhere appreciated but almost nowhere clearly understood.

In his review of her third volume of stories, *The Leaning Tower*, in 1944, Edmund Wilson described some of the problems that Miss Porter poses for the critic. "Miss Porter is baffling," he said, "because one cannot take hold of her work in any of the obvious ways. She makes none of the melodramatic or ironic points that are the stock in trade of ordinary short story writers; she falls into none of the usual patterns and she does not show anyone's influence. She does not exploit her personality either inside or outside her work, and her writing itself makes a surface so smooth that the critic has little opportunity to point out peculiarities of color or weave. If he is tempted to say that the effect is pale, he is prevented by the realization that Miss Porter writes English of a purity and precision almost unique in contemporary American fiction. If he tries to demur that some given piece fails to mount with the accelerating pace or arrive at the final intensity that he is in the habit of expecting in short stories, he is deterred by a nibbling suspicion that he may not have grasped its meaning and have it hit him with a sudden impact some minutes after he has closed the book." *

* From *Classics and Commercials* by Edmund Wilson, Farrar, Straus, New York, 1950. By permission of the publisher.

The appearance of Miss Porter's *Collected Stories* would seem, on the face of it, to do nothing to simplify these problems. It merely confronts the critic with more material to puzzle over and be baffled by, and the initial effect of reading it is rather like having to eat through a large plateful of hors d'oeuvres while wondering if dinner will ever come or whether perhaps this *is* dinner. The book brings together all the shorter fiction Miss Porter has ever published: the entire contents of the three previous collections—*Flowering Judas; Pale Horse, Pale Rider;* and *The Leaning Tower*—as well as four stories never before published in book form. It is thus, with the necessary omission of her one book of essays, *The Days Before,* and her one novel, *Ship of Fools,* a complete representation of the literary achievement of her long lifetime. And what strikes one with dismaying force is how much less impressive this achievement seems than, given her reputation and obvious stature, it ought to seem.

The scope of the volume enables one to recognize and appreciate the variety of Miss Porter's imaginative interests and the range of her technical skills, but it also throws into rather harsh perspective certain qualities of hers that were less noticeable in the various earlier volumes when one read them separately. The effect, for example, of a good deal of her writing does indeed seem pale. At times it seems downright colorless. And the explanation is scarcely that she writes such a pure English, but rather that all contradictions and discords appear to have been sacrificed to the purity of the English. If Miss Porter ever faced a choice between creating colorfully and dangerously and preserving the fine veneer of her style, she obviously decided in favor of her style. She has been most careful to take no imaginative risks that she could not easily and gracefully put into words. As a result, the purity of her English—and there can be no doubt that it *is* pure—is at once a tribute to her verbal fastidiousness and testimony to the existence within her of psychic and artistic limitations that have prevented her from producing work of the first magnitude.

These same limitations have also, to my mind, been responsible for the failure of certain of Miss Porter's stories to arrive at the final intensity that Mr. Wilson was deterred by his nibbling suspicion from expecting, but which I see no reason not to insist upon. But then Mr. Wilson was much too eager to give Miss Porter the benefit of every doubt, presumably because he took it for granted that she is too good not to know at all times exactly what she is doing. I incline toward the opposite view. I think she is not quite good enough always to know, that she is frequently uncertain of her meanings, and that at times she is even downright baffled by the direction in which her work is taking her. It simply does not seem to me true that one is justified in withholding criticism of her lapses from intensity on the ground that the meaning of the stories in which they occur will very probably hit one some minutes after closing the book. This, to be sure, can happen, and when it does, the sensation is most agreeable. But one would be foolish to live in hope of this kind of tardy revelation, for too often one is not hit at all, after no matter how long a wait.

Of course this may indicate only that one is stupid. But it may also indicate that the meaning is too obscure or ambiguous to be apprehended. Certainly, there are moments when such seems to be the case, when inspiration evidently failed and the original idea was not conceived with sufficient force to be fully embodied in materials best suited to its expression. In fact, one often has the sense of a low creative vitality at work in Miss Porter's stories, a vitality capable of only intermittent flashes of real intensity and coherence, even though the pressure of discipline, of sheer will power and craft, may be enormous behind it. The discipline frequently gives to even her most uninspired productions a surface effect of elegance and stylistic finish, but it cannot compensate for the lack of true imaginative strength and originality of vision.

Yet however true this may seem to be, one is forced to admit that it is a fair judgment of only certain of Miss Porter's stories. About others one's judgment is necessarily very different. Actually, a good many of both her admirers and her detractors have made the mistake of looking in the wrong place for evidence of her most characteristic achievement. They have too often focused their attention on those of her stories that are popularly supposed to be her best, and have either been baffled by much that they found in them and said so as Mr. Wilson did, or they have adopted the less courageous course of praising the profundity of what they did not always understand. The virtue of *The Collected Stories* is that, in addition to providing insight into Miss Porter's limitations, it enables one to see that she does not stand or fall on the basis of her best known or merely fashionable work, but that there is an abundance of much more interesting material that is rarely given the attention it deserves. The book also makes clear what Mr. Wilson by the end of his review had come to suspect: that although Miss Porter is known chiefly for her stories of delicate and oftentime overly subtle psychological complication, in which everything is tightly packed in the manner of a symbolist poem, her best work has not been done in this form at all, but in the form of the loosely organized, leisurely developed, semifictional reminiscence, in which people and places are more meditated upon than evoked, the meaning is simple and plain, and there is no overt attempt to create an effect of art.

This is to say that Miss Porter's important achievement appears to be represented not by such a story as her famous "Flowering Judas" or any of her other stories about Mexico that have attracted and merited so much attention, but by her longer stories and short novels about childhood, wartime romance, and family life such as "Old Mortality," "Pale Horse, Pale Rider," and "The Old Order." In comparison with these works, "Flowering Judas," though beautifully formed, seems self-conscious and coldly, effortfully inward, full of straining for symbolic effect, while they have about them an air of relaxation and warmth, as well as a seemingly natural richness of texture, which gives them such a very different quality one might almost suppose them to have been written by another person altogether.

The difference makes two things clear about Miss Porter: first, that she is at her best in the short novel rather than in the short story, and second, that although she is usually considered to be an international writer who is equally at home in Mexico, Germany, and the various other places that have provided settings for her fiction, she is actually a regionalist writer who is truly at home in only one place, the American Southwest of her childhood. The Southwest, along with her ancestral Old South, is the source of her most potent imaginative material, and it is significant that she seems obliged to imagine it least of all her materials. It is simply part of her personal and cultural inheritance, as Faulkner's Mississippi was part of his, and she writes about it so well and with such apparent ease because she remembers it both as experience she lived through and in the form of stories about her family's history that she grew up learning by heart. Miss Porter tells some of these stories in her essay, "Portrait: Old South," and reveals not only the depth of her emotional involvement with Southern culture but how extensively and literally she has used her own and her family's experience in her fiction.

It seems to be a particular pity that she has not chosen to make even more extensive use of it than she has. But this has all along been her problem. More than anything else, she appears by talent and emotional inclination to be a Southern story-teller and memoirist in the Faulknerian or even the Wolfean tradition. And these materials dealing with her native region suggest the vitality she has occasionally allowed herself to bring to this tradition. Yet some perverse fastidiousness or shyness has always compelled her to turn away in the main body of her work from the Southern experience, to repress her feelings of intense personal connection with it, and to try to serve an ideal of complete artistic objectivity. In the process she has written many flawlessly executed stories about other people and places, stories that so often seem to possess all the admirable virtues except the warm responsiveness to life that distinguishes her Southern writings, and that final intensity of meaning to which Mr. Wilson referred. There exists, in short, a great distance between the work in which Miss Porter's art seems purest and the imaginative materials about which she evidently feels most passionately. Somewhere along that distance lies a possible point of reconciliation, where art and passion might have joined to produce a great writer and did not.

[1965]

A Last Look at the Old Man

IT is now thirteen years since Hemingway's last published novel, *The Old Man and the Sea*, appeared, and in that time a great deal of dross has been burned out of our conception of Hemingway. We have had to make our peace as best we could with the deeply unsettling fact of his suicide (an event as traumatic for many of us as the death of a father), and with the somber knowledge that followed from it: that he was a sick man for a large part of the time we had been supposing him to be robustly well and judging him, perhaps in a manner hurtful to him, by the standards of the well. He suffered from a debilitude that most of us wrongly understood to be altogether creative, and his behavior at the end had behind it none of the controlled and usable compulsions that had once served him so well in his art, but a morbidity of mind and body that his art could do nothing to relieve, since he could no longer serve it well.

We have also had, in the light of this and more recent knowledge, to revise our assumptions about just how effectively productive Hemingway was able to be during the final period of his life. It had for years been widely taken for granted that he was engaged upon a very big book, the biggest of his career, which was to deal on an epic scale with the second world war on land and sea and in the air. He was frequently reported to be at work on such a book; he frequently reported himself to be at work on it; and as far back as 1949 he told Malcolm Cowley that he had completed more than a thousand pages. Apparently, work was interrupted while he wrote *Across the River and into the Trees* (a book he rushed to finish because, ironically, he was afraid he was going to die) and again while he wrote *The Old Man and the Sea*, which was once rumored to be a sort of prologue to the big book. But he later announced that he had resumed work, the manuscript having now grown to three volumes but shrunk to 667 pages, and was within three chapters of the end.

Although reports issued since his death have been peculiarly contradictory, there seems at present to be no firm evidence for supposing that the big book was ever finished or, for that matter, that it exists. At least one knows of no one who has actually seen it, or any part of it, and Hemingway's publishers, who have been sifting through the materials he left, seem uncertain as to whether a connected book can be put together from them. Of course a miracle just may occur. The big book may one day be found, and there may be other manuscripts hidden away in bank vaults and the back rooms of bars, as well as fragments among his available papers, that will deserve to be put into shape and published. But it seems highly doubtful that anything very startling will be discovered that is not at least twenty years old. I myself would be greatly surprised if the big book, when and if found, turned out to be much more than a mélange of disconnected impressions, notes toward a masterpiece he no longer had the strength to envision coherently. For it now seems clear that Hemingway was in a state of progressive creative decline for at least the last two decades of his life. And this decline is attested to not only by the notoriously bad *Across the River and into the Trees* but by the notoriously good *The Old Man and the Sea,* the book that, perhaps not at all surprisingly, won him the Nobel Prize and continues to be widely regarded as marking the triumphant climax of his career.

Rereading it on the occasion of the new Scribner Library paperback edition is not a very happy experience, particularly when one recalls the high hopes one had for it when it first appeared, and considers how nice it would be if one could now feel that it is really terribly good. But one cannot feel this, not even in deference to the memory of a much loved and great writer. It is, of course, nowhere near so bad a book as *Across the River,* a disaster no writer, however great, could conceivably perpetrate twice. In fact, when compared with that book, *The Old Man* appears to represent one of those wholly remarkable recoveries that occurred regularly in Hemingway's career, and that were so spectacular they almost persuaded us to forget that each time they occurred, the recovery was a little less complete. Yet in the case of *The Old Man* the recovery is not only less complete than it was, say, when *For Whom the Bell Tolls* followed *To Have and Have Not,* but it also has a distinctly synthetic quality as though brought about by the massive injection of drugs.

The trouble with *Across the River* was that the emotion it dealt with was both of an inferior, self-pitying kind and exactly suited to the requirements of burlesque. But the book, regrettably, was written not to be funny but to be serious. Hence, it succeeded in being merely embarrassing.

There was nothing in it or behind it to restrain Hemingway from expressing his personal feelings through his hero, and the temptation to be maudlin turned out, as it always did for him, to be irresistible and fatal.

The trouble with *The Old Man* seems to be something else altogether, actually an opposite kind of trouble. Now the emotion is neither inferior nor maudlin: it simply seems to be missing. There is no lack of restraint or, at any rate, of the appearance of restraint. On the contrary, everything in the book gives the effect of having been pared down to the bone, and nothing comes through that is not carefully monitored and meditated and made to appear terribly *chosen*. But the difficulty is that one has no sense of what temptations were withstood, what incoherences and violences of feeling were brought under control, in order to achieve this effect. That whole vital Hemingway dimension of simplicity forced under enormous pressure out of complexity is absent from it.

In the best of the early Hemingway it always seemed that if exactly the right words in exactly the right order were not chosen, something monstrous would occur, an unimaginably delicate internal warning system would be thrown out of adjustment, and some principle of personal and artistic integrity would be fatally compromised. But by the time he came to write *The Old Man* there seems to have been nothing at stake except the professional obligation to sound as much like Hemingway as possible. The man had disappeared behind the mannerism, the artist behind the artifice, and all that was left was a coldly flawless façade of words.

The action of the novel is also, to my mind, a façade, a classic parable in stone, terribly picturesque and *meaningful*, but quite dead. One must question the vitality of a story that becomes a myth too quickly, that is accepted as universal before it has been felt as particular. It is perfectly true that in old Santiago's contest with the big fish we seem to be back once again on the safe ground of a familiar and creatively dependable Hemingway obsession, the obsession with physical procedure, with the proper forms one follows in order to accomplish artfully a difficult and dangerous task. But standing alone and constituting the whole show as it does in *The Old Man,* Santiago's contest can have only a limited significance and a low-grade dramatic impact. For according to the artistic formula that served Hemingway so well in his fine early novels, such a contest was never meant to stand alone, any more than the bullfight scenes in *The Sun Also Rises* were meant to stand alone. Not only was it not the whole show. It was not even the main show. In fact, that entire class of physically contesting artists in whom he always displayed such intense interest—the bull fighters, big-game hunters, and fishermen—were never given more than secondary importance in his best work. They were significant only as they had metaphorical relation to another and darker drama, which was and remains Hemingway's great subject, a drama played out on the psychic rather than the physical level, within the tormented consciousness of the utterly unheroic hero.

The contest for the hero was not with a giant marlin or a bull, but with the terrors that haunted the darkness of his mind and soul. His fear was not of physical death or defeat but of nervous breakdown and moral collapse. He was obsessed with the possibility that he might under pressure lose control of himself and go berserk, cease, in effect, to be the disciplined master of his fears, the artful matador, and become the raging bull. Hence, the skill and courage of the matador, the care and patience required to land a big fish or track big game, held a special fascination for him.

189

The contest of sport was an analogue of the contest of nerve he himself was carrying on, but it was a ritualized and highly disciplined analogue in which real rather than phantom perils were confronted and vanquished, and therefore through which the hero could purge his fears and achieve a vicarious victory over his weakness. This ended, of course, in a whole unique style of living and writing, in a vocabulary that was the precise verbal equivalent of the disciplined restraints of the sportsman, and that was meaningful just because it dramatized the vital connection between the world of artful physical action and the world of modern dislocated sensibility.

It seems apparent that with *The Old Man* the emotional compulsion behind this dramatic design had faded in Hemingway to the point where only a vaguely remembered but now quite lifeless pattern of responses remained. There are no more fears of nervous breakdown, no more terrors to haunt the hero and charge the language with all the taut apprehensiveness of a nighttime passage through a minefield. What was always secondary and illustrative before has become primary and illustrative of nothing beyond itself. The physical combat now is simply a physical contest. It is Santiago trying to land a big fish. And Santiago is no artful matador. Like his creator he is too old and tired to obey the rules. He only remembers that he should have obeyed them and did not. In fact, in his brutish endurance and simple perceptions he is rather like a bull, but a bull who has lost his rage and his power and so has become a victim. Perhaps that is why he feels such brotherhood with the fish: because brute man and brute fish have changed their relation of victor and victim and become not only brothers but doubles. "Is he bringing me in or am I bringing him in?" Santiago wonders, and no one can be sure.

At the end, exhausted and beaten by the sharks, the old man sleeps. The struggle has been too much for a man of his age, and there is no more fight left in him. One senses he will die soon, if not this day, then some other day, after some other struggle. But death may come any time now. There is no longer anything to lose, since he can no longer pursue his craft with honor and success. As he sleeps, the old man dreams once again of the lions he saw long ago. They are not savage beasts in the jungle. There is no danger that they will spring out at him and disturb his sleep. They are happy lions. They are playing on an African beach. They remind him of his youth when he was strong and confident and the champion of them all.

[1965]

The Life of Gatsby

IT is probably about time we stopped writing essays on *The Great Gatsby*, just at the moment, this is to say, when a really proper criticism seems threatening to begin.* Certainly, it has been a saving paradox of criticism up to now that it has taken very little precise note of *Gatsby* while appearing to take vast general note of it. If we are not going to disturb that happy state of affairs, we had perhaps better call a halt before we yield up the book altogether to the dignifying but always transforming fire of criticism, and risk finding, after we have done so, that we are left not with the cleansed bones of the novel itself but with the ashes of one or more of its several meanings. I ask simply that we hold onto the living object in hand: the well-wrought urn on the mantelpiece can remain empty a while longer. Posterity, if it is to get at *Gatsby* at all, will most assuredly have to breathe back into it the life we take out, and we should take care to see that posterity does not waste its breath on a corpse. For *Gatsby* is above all a novel to be directly

---

* Since this essay was written, it has, alas, not only begun but reached the proportions of an industry. Luckily, however, the life of *Gatsby* has proved remarkably hard to snuff out.

experienced and responded to; it is a fragile novel, to be sure, in some ways imperfect, in some ways deeply unsatisfactory, but it is clearly alive because produced by a directly experiencing, living imagination, one that habitually and with great innocence so perfectly confused its own longings, fears, defeats, and chimeras with those of a certain portion of American society, that a certain portion of American society ever since has confused its own image with it and made its plans for itself on the vision of an accessible future which, as a skeptical imagination, it tooks pains to condemn. *Gatsby*, therefore, is a work of art particularly prone to being confused with its meanings, just as its meanings, if we are not careful, can be made to substitute for its life as a work of art.

Such a cautionary approach to *Gatsby* should count for something with us, although it probably counts for less than it would have at one time. We are accustomed now to having our experience of life abstracted for us by fiction, and our experience of fiction abstracted for us by criticism, both life and literature projected into a construct twice removed from the original and signed, sealed, and delivered over to our captive imaginations. We no longer want to do the imaginative job ourselves: we cannot quite afford the time; the code governing the division of imaginative labor would not permit it, nor do we really believe it can or need be done. Undoubtedly one of the reasons *Gatsby* continues to seem alive to us is that it represents one of the last attempts made by an American writer to come directly at the reality of the modern American experience while its outlines were still visible and before the social sciences convinced us that they could do the job and do it better. I assume that those outlines have not since been so visible and that we no longer have the sense of a distinctive American experience or even much of a certainty that there is one. After Fitzgerald, one feels, the door onto the native scene banged shut for American writers; the process of creation ceased to be a matter of opening the eyes and letting the sensibility take moral readings; the forms of social conduct, the traditional modes of action in which the drama of the will in crisis had formerly been displayed, no longer seemed directly accessible to the novel; suddenly no one appeared to know how anyone else behaved. Among the newer writers, certainly, who aspire to something more than journalism, there has been a sort of retreat of consciousness from the nearly insupportable task of dealing creatively with the fluid social situation and with the immense complication of status values and drives that the sociologists have discovered to be typical of the present age, and in comparison with which Fitzgerald's reality seems almost banally primitive. But Fitzgerald came to the novel at a time when the patterns of our present society were just being laid down; he had the inestimable advantage of the primal view, and so we return to him, particularly in *Gatsby*, with the feeling that we are seeing ourselves as we were in the light of an intensity that we are unable to direct upon ourselves as we are. If *Gatsby* is one of the very few books left from the twenties that we are still able to read with any kind of enduring pleasure and without always having to suffer a reminder of emotions we no longer care to feel, I suspect it is so because it dramatizes for us those basic assumptions and modes of assumption about the nature of American experience that belong to the antique furniture of our minds but that our experience of the present age and its literature has not been able to renew or replace. In this sense *Gatsby* constitutes not only a primal view but, at least to date, a final view; it crystallizes an image of life beyond which neither our books nor our own perceptions seem able to take us; for two generations in fact, in that turgid area of consciousness where life and literature seem interchangeable, it has pretty largely done our perceiving for us. It therefore has about it some of that particular poignancy that we reserve for the lost moments of the past when we felt the emotions we would like still to feel, if we were able to and had again those exactly right opportunities. In this sense too *Gatsby* is mythopoeic: it has created our legend of the twenties, which at the present time is our common legend, and like *Moby Dick* and *Huckleberry Finn* it has helped to create, by endowing with significant form, a national unconscious; its materials are those of the collective American mind at its closest approach to the primary source of native frontier symbols. As a result, we must all feel on reading it a little as Nick Carraway felt on hearing Gatsby's words—"reminded of something—an elusive rhythm, a fragment of lost words, that I had heard somewhere a long time ago." I do not mean that I much hold to the more obvious and popular mythological view of *Gatsby:* carried too far, as it usually is, it threatens always to smother the novel within the strictures of meaning. But I can understand its attraction and its relevance: Fitzgerald's technique of pictorial generalization, along with what Lionel Trilling has called his "ideographic" method of character portrayal, insists on far more than the novel primarily signifies. Yet at this late stage in Fitzgerald criticism one can hope to escape cliché only by refusing to rest content with meaning and by inducing some contemplation of *Gatsby's* life as fiction.

A prime feature of that life is of course the marvelous style that shows it forth, and while it is now commonplace to say that in *Gatsby* Fitzgerald found, certainly for the first time and probably for the last, his proper form, it is less so to say that he could not have found the form had he not experienced an immense deepening as well as a marked shift of his relation both to himself and to language. The essentially expressive form of the earlier novels had indulged Fitzgerald in all his younger, easier, and more sentimental mannerisms; it encouraged him to describe emotion rather than to embody it, and whenever he could not find emotion, to fake it; it put up no resistance whatever to his habit of seeking, and then descending to, the lowest level of feeling his characters could sustain, or of making use, whenever he thought he could get away with it, of the cheapest rhetorical devices cribbed from Compton Mackenzie and the gothic novel. It is also evident, particularly now, that the subjects of his first novels were not suitable vehicles for his real emotions, and if they were bad, it is partly because they never allowed him to discover what his real emotions were. Fitzgerald never believed with anything like his full heart in the life he was describing; his deeper sensibilities were not only not engaged but offended, and the necessity to appear to believe, to try to pass off childish infatuation as adult devotion, only served to make him seem frivolous and girlishly Beardsleyan. In this sense, of course, Fitzgerald's first subjects kept him young: they arrested him for the time at a level of emotional development precisely adequate to their capacity for receiving emotion, and they asked nothing more of him than that he disguise the deficiency behind effusion and rhetoric.

It is not clear from his biography exactly what happened in the time between *The Beautiful and Damned* and *Gatsby* to mature Fitzgerald, nor is it very likely that his biography knows. Obviously he found a way of untangling his moral imagination from the gothic bric-a-brac of ghosts, mysterious medieval gentlemen, and wispy lurking presences, among which it had searched for an object through the earlier novels, and under the sponsorship of that imagination he was able to achieve a sufficient penetration of his subject to engage for the first time his real emotions and his best talents. In *This Side of Paradise* "the problem of evil had solidified" for Amory Blaine "into the problem of sex," and one felt that this had behind it some affront to Fitzgerald's romanticism stemming from the discovery that a physical act could be imagined for nice girls beyond the kiss. By the time he wrote *The Beautiful and Damned* the problem appeared to have risen on the anatomical scale and lodged somewhere near the heart, although one could never be certain whether it really belonged there or in Wall Street. But with *Gatsby* there was no longer any doubt: the problem of evil had by then solidified into a problem of responsibility and spiritual condition in those rich enough to be able to choose their morals; Fitzgerald's opposing selves, the giddy, bibulous boy and the morose, hung-over tallier of emotional chits, had struck a bargain and a balance.

This deepened understanding of his subject inevitably brought Fitzgerald to an awareness of the need for a narrative form far stricter and at the same time far subtler than that demanded by his earlier novels. It is doubtful if up to *Gatsby* he had given any serious thought at all to matters of form, and considering the limited conception he had of his subject at the time, he probably felt little necessity to. By Jamesean standards *This Side of Paradise* was abominably constructed, and *The Beautiful and Damned* was only slightly less so. But the loosely episodic, rather spongy form of the juvenile *bildungsroman* borrowed from Mackenzie and Wells was not hopelessly unsuited to the situation of the young man only faintly disenchanted with the life of glamor, particularly so long as in Fitzgerald's mind the difference between the rich and you and me could still be equated with the possession of more money, better looks, looser morals, and greater daring. All that was required was an involved, naïve consciousness capable of moving more or less horizontally through a series of episodes, the function of which was slow instruction in a kind of eager irony, and for this the one-dimensional mock-heroes, Amory Blaine and Anthony Patch, were perfectly competent pupils. But with *Gatsby* Fitzgerald's talent took a dramatic turn; his sense of his subject and his involvement with it became too complex and ambivalent to be portrayed through the limited single consciousness; he needed a narrative form at once firm enough to correct his tendency toward emotional bloat and supple enough to allow full range for the development of a set of individual characters who would display his theme and at the same time serve as suitable dramatic equivalents for his contradictory feelings toward it. He had suddenly and without quite knowing it arrived at a point where he was ready to put to use his mature understanding of his material within the framework of his advanced knowledge of the formal art of fiction.

The pictorial method of Conrad, James, and Wharton, combining the "single window" technique of the engaged narrator with that of the scenic tableau, made it possible for Fitzgerald to overcome in *Gatsby* the severe limitations of the merely expressive form and to achieve the kind of distance between himself and his subject that must be achieved before the job of true fictional creation can properly begin. In Nick Carraway he found the protagonist of his own most central ambivalence, a median consciousness and conscience vacillating between admiration and judgment, a "first-rate intelligence" able "to hold two opposed ideas in the mind at the same time, and still retain the ability to function." The foil-figures of Gatsby and Tom Buchanan serve him as devices for breaking down into contrasting parts and recombining in even more ambiguous relation his twin senses of the physical glamor of the rich and their spiritual corruption, their force of character and their moral weakness, the ideal nature of romantic vision and the baseness of the methods employed in its service, the essential shabbiness of romantic vision in a society that can measure vision only in money. Daisy Buchanan and Jordan Baker function on a somewhat simpler level to complete the symbolism of identity and contrast—Daisy standing initially as an embodiment of the purity of the vision, finally of the corruption and the baseness of method; Jordan holding up to the world a mask of sophisticated, though precarious, self-composure, but concealing behind it, like Nicole Diver, an awful secret of interior derangement. George and Myrtle Wilson alone remain almost untouched by the process of imaginative revision through which Fitzgerald transformed, by immensely complicating, his typical thematic effects in the novel: Wilson carries forward and for the first time fully characterizes Fitzgerald's earlier horror of poverty and illness, while Myrtle dramatizes his formerly incoherent, at moments hysterical, aversion to direct sexuality when unaccompanied by beauty and wealth.

Lionel Trilling is undoubtedly right in calling this method of characterization "ideographic" and in applying the term as well to the method of the novel as a whole. Nothing and no one in the course of the narrative is really developed; everything is seen in tableau, in a state of permanent pictorial rest. The characters are little more than a collection of struck attitudes, frieze figures carved on the entablature of a moral abstraction, a greatly generalized intuitive view of the nature of American experience. Their individual identities are subordinated to the central idea they are meant to signify, perfectly embodying the "platonic conception" behind the remark made by Gatsby when he admits the possibility that Daisy may perhaps have once loved her husband: "In any case it was just personal." The secret of the entire technique of the novel may in a sense be said to lie hidden in this remark, for its effect is to divert attention from the personal and particular to the abstract conception, the allegorized whole.

In achieving this effect Fitzgerald carried the pictorial method considerably beyond James; in fact, the closest parallel to its use in *Gatsby* is the Joycean "signature" or "epiphany" technique where character is broken down into its separate parts, and one or two of the parts are made to stand for the whole. The result for Joyce, in both *A Portrait of the Artist* and *Ulysses,* was the establishment of a virtual iconography of character, a system of extravagantly distilled symbolic essences, usually suggested by a gesture or an article of clothing, through which the soul of being was shown forth. The result for Fitzgerald is not nearly so elaborate, but it is very similar in kind. Nick Carraway is revealed to us through his signature of honesty; Gatsby is identified by his pink suits, Tom Buchanan by his rippling pack of muscle, Daisy by her voice, Jordan by her balancing act, Myrtle by her fleshy vitality, Wilson by his hollow-eyed stare, Wolfshiem by his hairy nostrils, the butler by his nose. In the case of each of the major characters these attributes take on metaphorical significance in the thematic design of the novel. Nick's honesty is called into ironic question by Jordan in an effort to shift the blame for her own dishonesty; Gatsby's pink suits suggest the meretriciousness of his role, Tom's muscle the brutal strength of his; Jordan's balancing act is indicative of her precarious control over herself and her need for a stabilizing moral convention, while Daisy's voice serves as the gauge of her "basic insincerity," which it is the principal business of the novel to penetrate. Initially full of warm excitement and promise, it is finally shown to be "full of money," and in the long interval between the two observations the pathetic futility of Gatsby's dream is gradually made clear.

To create an effect of involvement and movement while retaining the advantage of the pictorial method, Fitzgerald made constant use of ironic parallelisms of both character and event, still very much in the manner of Joyce. Both Gatsby and Daisy are "insincere," Gatsby about his past, Daisy about her present feelings; Tom's unfaithfulness to Daisy is balanced by Gatsby's faithfulness to her; yet Tom and Daisy belong to a "secret society" of ultimately deeper faithfulness. Nick keeps faith with Gatsby to the end, but not with Jordan. Jordan's dishonesty is revealed in time with the Buchanans' and Gatsby's; Jordan like Daisy is a "careless driver," and the episode in which this fact is first made clear to Nick prefigures the moment when Daisy's carelessness results in Myrtle's death; both, furthermore, are anticipated by the comic accident scene in Gatsby's driveway and are finally commented upon during Nick's last meeting with Jordan when, to conceal her own dishonesty, she insists that she met in Nick another bad driver. Just before the showdown scene with Gatsby in the Plaza Hotel Tom feels that he has lost in one afternoon both his wife and his mistress; during the scene he wins back his wife, and Gatsby loses his mistress and is symbolically murdered by Tom—all to the accompaniment of Mendelssohn's Wedding March being played in the ballroom below. As Gatsby the dreamer dies, Nick remembers that it is his own thirtieth birthday, the time of life when, in his and Fitzgerald's romantically limited chronology, all dreams must end. On the way back to East Egg Daisy kills Tom's mistress, Wilson loses a wife, and a while later Tom arranges through Wilson to murder Gatsby in fact, Wilson believing that Gatsby has been Myrtle's lover as well as her murderer. All the principal male characters lose the women they love, and in each case through some act of faithlessness on the part of one or more of the women.

This system of carefully plotted interior parallels and cross-references serves greatly to enhance the thematic "size" of the novel and to give back to it some of the quality of dramatic specification that the method of static character portrayal takes away. The same can be said for the reflexive relationship of the parts in the narrative design as a whole. Each of the nine chapters is composed of one, or very occasionally more than one, dramatic scene presented pictorially and surrounded by skillfully foreshortened panoramic material, and each achieves significance not through the standard depth-wise plumbing of character, but through its contribution of fresh facts to the linearly developing sequence of facts that gradually illuminate Gatsby's central dilemma and mystery. Each functions, furthermore, in reciprocal relation to every other, at times ironically, at times by simple contrast, so that an effect of counterpointed motifs comes ultimately to stand, very much as it does in *The Waste Land,* in place of the more conventional and predictable effect of events arranged chronologically and naturalistically.

The opening and closing pages of the novel frame Gatsby's story within the parentheses of an elegiacally retrospective vision of time, history, and moral conduct. The first two pages state the terms of the ambivalent attitude that Nick is to take toward the subsequent action and which it is to be the task of that action to resolve. Presented initially as a young man taught by his father to "reserve all judgments" in the knowledge that "all the people in this world haven't had the advantages that you've had," Nick describes himself immediately afterward as one who has since been taught better by first-hand contact with some of the people who have had even more of the advantages than he, and who have left him with the feeling of wanting "the world to be in uniform and at a sort of moral attention forever." He then goes on to substitute a new and much more complex ambivalence for the one that, on looking back over his experience, he feels has now been resolved: he has been educated in the power of condemnatory judgment, but he is still unable to condemn Gatsby—"Only Gatsby . . . was exempt from my reaction—Gatsby who represented everything for which I have an unaffected scorn." It is to be Nick's fate in the course of the novel, as unquestionably it was Fitzgerald's, that while he is to learn intolerance and finally moral indignation, he is never to come to terms with his contradictory feelings toward Gatsby: his moral indignation remains to the end the slave of his moral idealism. After Gatsby's death it is simple enough for Nick to recognize the Buchanans as "careless people," for he has accumulated more than sufficient evidence of their irresponsibility to cancel out his earlier admiration of them. But of Gatsby the poseur, racketeer, and liar he can only speak in the name of Gatsby the dreamer, and eulogize him only in the name of the founding of America itself, for Gatsby is one who escapes the monitory conscience of the "spoiled priest" by being himself priestlike, with a priest's passionate and self-sacrificing dedication to an ideal, a religion, of romantic transcendence. Nick's point of view, which we see in the process of gradually becoming reeducated with regard to the Buchanans, is incapable of reeducation with regard to Gatsby, for Gatsby is both a suitable object for the fascination that Nick earlier felt for the Buchanans and an embodiment of the ideal against which he measures and condemns them. It is an inadequate ideal, and Nick—or at least Fitzgerald—is entirely aware of the fact, but within the limits of his given experience it is the only one he has to set against the world of Buchanan values, the only one he has, therefore, to exalt into triumph over those values at the end.

But the image of Nick that dominates the opening chapters is of another, as yet uneducated idealism, the kind indigenous to his Middle West, a rural frontier fascination with the appearance of culture and worldly manners. In fact, the first chapter centered in the scene depicting the dinner party at the Buchanan estate is clearly intended to dramatize Nick in his primal condition of reserved judgment juxtaposed with the gradually emerging facts of spiritual corruption and deceit that finally cause him to arrive at condemnatory judgment and become morally initiated. Firmly established amid the grandeur of his physical setting, Tom Buchanan first appears to Nick as an heroic figure, but almost at once Nick is struck by the change in him since their New Haven years.

> Now he was a sturdy straw-haired man of thirty with a rather hard mouth and a supercilious manner. Two shining arrogant eyes had established dominance over his face and gave him the appearance of always leaning aggressively forward. Not even the effeminate swank of his riding clothes could hide the enormous power of that body.... It was a body capable of enormous leverage— a cruel body. His speaking voice, a gruff husky tenor, added to the impression of fractiousness he conveyed. There was a touch of paternal contempt in it, even toward people he liked—and there were men at New Haven who had hated his guts.*

* From *The Great Gatsby*, by F. Scott Fitzgerald, Charles Scribner's Sons, New York. By permission of the publisher.

This swift appraisal of Tom establishes him in the role he is later to play and constitutes the first element in the developing contrast between appearance and reality on which the chapter turns.

A moment later Nick is taken in to see Daisy and Jordan, and the picture of glamorous buoyancy and charm that they present temporarily restores his powers of admiration. In fact, the quality of physical inflation, suggested entirely in tableau, that pervades the scene stands as an exact equivalent for the emotion the sight of the women arouses in him.

> The only completely stationary object in the room was an enormous couch on which two young women were buoyed up as though upon an anchored balloon. They were both in white, and their dresses were rippling and fluttering as if they has just been blown back in after a short flight around the house.... Then there was a boom as Tom Buchanan shut the rear windows and the caught wind died out about the room, and the curtains and the rugs and the two young women ballooned slowly to the floor.[*]

But the effect is only temporary. As the scene deflates itself, so subsequent events deflate Nick's illusion and impel him toward condemnatory judgment. At the dinner table he learns that "Tom's got some woman in New York." Gatsby's name is brought into the conversation and hastily dropped. Nick dimly remembers having seen Jordan, or a picture of her, somewhere before. Sitting on the porch with Daisy after dinner and listening to her tell about the birth of her child and her feelings about life in general, he is suddenly struck by "the basic insincerity of what she had to say" and begins

[*] Ibid.

to feel that "the whole evening had been a trick of some sort to exact a contributory emotion" from him. A moment later Daisy smirks "as if she had asserted her membership in a rather distinguished secret society to which she and Tom belonged." Nick leaves East Egg that night sufficiently disturbed to want Daisy to "rush out of the house, child in arms," and upon returning home he catches sight of Gatsby standing in the darkness of his lawn and looking across the water to the green light at the end of the Buchanans' dock. Thus, by the end of the first chapter the basic dramatic situation has been established; all the principal characters have been introduced or alluded to; and the destructive element in the Buchanans has been brought into fatal juxtaposition with both Nick's naïve admiration and Gatsby's naïve aspiration. The contest now will be between the force of the secret society, epitomized by Daisy's insincerity and Tom's cruel selfishness, and the persuasive power of Gatsby's illusion. But we already know the outcome: it has been ordained by the quality and content of the action itself.

The second chapter develops the destructive statement of the first in two ways: through the contextual symbolism of the "valley of ashes" image dominated by the gigantic eyes of the oculist Dr. T. J. Eckleburg, and through the pictorial scene of the drunken party at Tom's New York apartment. The valley of ashes establishes the situation of evil that is conventionally, and in Fitzgerald habitually, associated with hopeless poverty, and it projects that evil into literal contrast with the kind that wealth and privilege induce in the Buchanans. Theirs is at once a more serious and reprehensible kind because it involves the possibility of moral choice and an identical kind because it has behind it an equivalent impoverishment of soul. The eyes of Dr. Eckleburg can be variously and, if one is not careful to preserve a sense of humor, fatuously interpreted. They are reminiscent of some of Fitzgerald's earlier gothic figures of evil—the ghostly apparitions and "somber palls" of *This Side of Paradise* and *The Beautiful and Damned*—but they have the virtue of thematic relevance that these lacked, as well as the dramatic advantage of association with a developed physical milieu. They are, of course, suggestive of Nick's monitory conscience and are related to the image of "the casual watcher in the darkening streets" that is evoked during the party scene by his sense of being "within and without, simultaneously enchanted and repelled by the inexhaustible variety of life." They are also specifically associated by George Wilson in the eighth chapter with the eyes of God and, since Gatsby is represented as a son of God, we are probably justified in associating them in turn with the holiness of his romantic aspiration. More generally, they operate as an open symbol of transcendence and judgment set down in an opposing environment of defeat and subhuman amorality, or, to put it differently, they serve as a terminal point for the two principal thematic lines of the novel: the evil of the human condition overseen and modified by conscience.

The party episode pictorializes in scenic form the evil implicit in the valley of ashes, and since it stands in ironic contrast with the earlier scene at the Buchanans', it shows up that evil to be merely the nether side of theirs: the moral debasement of the party is the Buchanans' moral hypocrisy with its clothes off, the ugly truth beneath the veneer of social elegance that first charmed Nick, the corruption behind Daisy's enchanting voice and Jordan's delicate balancing act—in effect, the vulgar barroom scene in *The Waste Land* in comparison with the sterile "game of chess" episode.

The third through the sixth chapters perform for Gatsby

the same service that the first two chapters performed for the Buchanans: they present him in the alternating conditions of illusion and reality, mystery and fact, successively as genial host, shady character, and romantic visionary. In the third chapter he is dramatized in his public role of host, but like Conrad's Heyst he is seen by various observers in the roles created for him by his legend, and this has the effect of endowing him with the mythic generality and largeness that his thematic role requires. It also gives concrete endorsement to the premise that he is the product of his "Platonic conception of himself." Nick is himself momentarily taken in by the "Oggsford man" role, but quickly recognizes its absurdity, especially after the luncheon with Wolfshiem when he becomes acquainted with the underworld role. He shortly discovers, however, that the truth about Gatsby, as it is gradually revealed to him, first by Jordan, then by Gatsby himself, is far more remarkable than any of the stories circulated about him, and ultimately far more compelling. By the end of the sixth chapter he has become convinced of the high quality of Gatsby's aspiration, but he has also gathered fresh evidence in the form of the Buchanans' high-handed behavior at one of the parties that that aspiration will eventually be defeated. Daisy has initially been hypnotized by Gatsby's display of wealth and ardor and for the moment is attracted by the prospect of an affair, but during the party she reveals her snobbish inability to participate wholly in any form of life outside herself.

She was appalled by West Egg, this unprecedented 'place' that Broadway had begotten upon a Long Island fishing village—appalled by its raw vigor that chafed under the old euphemisms and by the too obtrusive fate that herded its inhabitants along a short-cut from nothing

to nothing. She saw something awful in the very simplicity she failed to understand.*

Like Daisy's first show of "basic insincerity," this reaction
is proof that she will never finally join Gatsby in his efforts
to "repeat the past."

It is interesting to see how these chapters devoted to
Gatsby exactly reverse the revelatory processes of those
devoted to the Buchanans. The illusion of sophisticated
elegance was penetrated in their case to reveal a basic sickness and poverty of spirit. Gatsby, on the other hand, is
seen initially against a veneer of fraudulent finery, is then
revealed as actually fraudulent as well as lawless, and finally
as morally innocent in the midst of the lawless. Superficially,
he is as bad as the Buchanans, but only superficially. Theirs
is a fundamental lawlessness of the heart: they are "careless
people" in the worst and deepest sense. His is the lawlessness
of the merely illegal and is excusable on the ground of the
service it renders in enforcing the highest laws of the heart.

The seventh and climactic chapter brings into dramatic
conflict the opposing elements of destruction and aspiration,
the morally lawless and the morally innocent within the
illegal, which have been separately developed in the chapters alternately devoted to the Buchanans and Gatsby. The
occasion is a gathering at the Buchanan estate, precisely like
that of the first chapter, but the tonal differences between
the two are obviously intended to unite them in ironic contrast. Again Daisy and Jordan are seen in tableau, but where
formerly they had about them a quality of inflation and
buoyancy suggestive of the emotion they first aroused in
Nick, they now appear in a state of fatigued deflation, as if
the intervening events had drained away their vitality along

* Ibid.

209

with their charm. "The room, shadowed well with awnings, was dark and cool. Daisy and Jordan lay upon an enormous couch, like silver idols weighing down their own white dresses against the singing breeze of the fans." The whole situation, furthermore, seems to Nick to be touched with nightmare. He imagines he overhears the butler replying to a telephone request for "the master's body." Daisy impulsively kisses Gatsby the moment Tom leaves the room. Daisy's child is led in by a nurse and introduced to Gatsby who, Nick is certain, had never "really believed in its existence before." Finally, as the party prepares to leave for New York, Gatsby has his first insight into the quality of Daisy's that is to prevent him from winning her.

'Her voice is full of money,' he said suddenly.... That was it. I'd never understood before. It was full of money —that was the inexhaustible charm that rose and fell on it, the jingle of it, the cymbal's song of it.... High in a white palace the king's daughter, the golden girl....*

This is the quality that indemnifies Daisy's commitment to Tom's world, but it finally involves much more than just money: it is a whole philosophy and tradition of life belonging to those who have always had money and marking them as a separate breed superior to those who have not. And in the chapter's closing scene, following on Gatsby's defeat and Myrtle's death, the difference is epiphanized:

Daisy and Tom were sitting opposite each other at the kitchen table, with a plate of cold fried chicken between them, and two bottles of ale.... They weren't happy, and neither of them had touched the chicken or the ale— and yet they weren't unhappy either. There was an unmis-

* Ibid.

takable air of natural intimacy about the picture, and anybody would have said that they were conspiring together.*

The "secret society" has at last won out over romantic illusion, and Gatsby, standing outside in the dark just as he was at the end of Chapter I, is now "watching over nothing."

The movement of the novel, then, is from illusion to reality, innocence to knowledge, aspiration to defeat, and of course suffusing them all, tolerance to judgment. It is Gatsby who pays the price for the learning, who functions by turns as the hapless Mme. de Vionnet and the finally unteachable Chad, but it is Nick who does his learning for him and through whose experience—as through Strether's in the case of Chad—it is made dramatically concrete. Gatsby's dream is dramatically unspecific because it is unspecific to him. That is, symbolically, its limitation and meaning: it is based not on things as they are, but on things as they might become. It is real only to the extent that one can imagine for it some successful embodiment in action, and this the logic of the novel never permits. Nick's sensibility, therefore, serves as a surrogate for Gatsby's, making external all that the dream, because it lacks concrete basis in fact and action, cannot make external by itself. In doing this, Nick's sensibility fleshes Gatsby out to very nearly epic size, endowing him with the character of heroism seen against a broadly generalized conception of national life and history.

This is accomplished in the novel in two ways: through Nick's direct participation in the life of the Buchanans, which educates him in the folly of innocence, and through the larger symbolism of place against which Nick measures the meaning of both his own and Gatsby's experience. In practice, how-

* Ibid.

ever, the two function as one: Nick records the experience as well as the meaning almost entirely in terms of place. Place affords him his basis of vision and evaluation, and the change that occurs in his vision and evaluation results in a change in his evaluation of place.

At the beginning of the novel the East appears to Nick— as by implication it does to Gatsby—as a land of wealth and future glittering with the promise of "shining secrets." But as the action proceeds, the "shining secrets" tarnish, and it becomes clear that the wealth and quality of purposeful movement into the future are illusory virtues imposed upon the East by the innocence of the beholder. Like Gatsby's isolated dream, the wealth feeds on itself; the Easterners are imprisoned by it to the point of spiritual stagnation; the "flow of life" moves in a purposeless circle. "The rich grow richer" because they have no other way to grow; "the poor get—children" as well as poorer and end ultimately in a "valley of ashes." But the Middle West too is stagnant. There "dwellings are still called through decades by a family's name"; one is oppressed by the "interminable inquisitions" and by a moral code that demands that life survive as a tradition rather than flow dynamically into the future. It follows, therefore, that West Egg, the Eastern analogue of the Middle West, should also end in a "valley of ashes," and that *both* East and West Egg should be imperfect ovals "crushed flat at the contact end," equally defective in their reception to life.

Fundamentally *Gatsby* is, as Nick says, "a story of the West, after all." It begins in the Middle West, makes a "riotous excursion" into the heart of Eastern promise, and returns to the Middle West in what at first appears to be disillusionment. Actually, of course, it is an affirmation of the true values following on disillusionment: the initial image of Middle Western stolidity resolves itself into a closing image of Middle Western solidity. Upon Nick's return from war the Middle West, "instead of being the warm centre of the world . . . seemed like the ragged edge of the universe." Coming East to learn the bond business he settles down in West Egg in a "small eyesore" of a house to enjoy "the consoling proximity of millionaires" and to plumb if he can "the shining secrets that only Midas and Morgan and Maecenas knew." Having just left the restrictive environment of the Middle West, he is at first especially aware of the free flow of life in the East, although he is also aware that it is intimately associated with the free flow of wealth. He speaks of Tom and Daisy as drifting "here and there . . . wherever people were rich together." But they "drift unrestfully," and he sees that Tom "would drift on forever seeking, a little wistfully, for the dramatic turbulence of some irrecoverable football game." Like Gatsby's dream, the Buchanans' drifting is an effort to recover in the present some of the lost sensations of the past as well as the sensibilities of youth that, in Americans, alone seem capable of deep response.

But Nick's first impression of the East is one of exciting, restless movement, and throughout the scene of his visit with the Buchanans his enchantment with their kinetic radiance alternates with moments of insight into their superficiality. Their lawn "started at the beach and ran toward the front door for a quarter of a mile, jumping over sundials and brick walls and burning gardens—finally when it reached the house drifting up the side in bright vines as though from the momentum of its run." Tom appears to be "leaning aggressively forward," filling his "glistening boots until he strained the top lacing, and you could see a great pack of muscle shifting when his shoulder moved under his thin coat." Inside the house as well everything seems to be flow-ing, but only because of a momentary breeze. "A breeze blew through the room, blew curtains in at one end and out the other like pale flags, twisting them up toward the frosted wedding-cake of the ceiling, and then rippled over the wine-colored rug, making a shadow on it as wind does on the sea." On the "only completely stationary object in the room" Daisy and Jordan appear to be "buoyed up as though upon an anchored balloon." But as soon as Tom shuts the window, the wind dies, and the floating effect proves to have been only an appearance. Nick is charmed and enchanted by the appearances, but soon begins to recognize them for what they are. Tom and Daisy make only a "polite, pleasant effort to entertain and be entertained. They knew that presently dinner would be over and casually put away." There is little meaning or sincerity in what is going on. Daisy suddenly declares that Nick is an "absolute rose," but he realizes that she is only "extemporizing." Daisy and Jordan converse in language that "was as cool as their white dresses and their impersonal eyes in the absence of all desire." Inevitably Nick compares the scene with similar occasions in the West "where an evening was hurried from phase to phase toward its close, in a continually disappointed anticipation, or else in sheer nervous dread of the moment itself." But here in the East among expatriated Middle Westerners even anticipation has been lost; all desire is dead; the Buchanans are the spent shadows of action. "You make me feel uncivilized, Daisy," Nick says. "Can't you talk about crops or something," and the "or something substantial" is implied.

In the second chapter culminating in the party at Tom's New York apartment the contrast of place motifs is reinforced by an implicit symbolism relating place to dream and ultimately to Gatsby. The natives of West Egg are depicted as a race of the living dead, "ash grey men . . . who move dimly and already crumbling through the powdery air." Only Myrtle Wilson is alive: "There was an immediately perceptible vitality about her as if the nerves of her body were continually smouldering." She alone is free of the "white ashen dust" that veiled her husband's "dark suit and pale hair as it veiled everything in the vicinity," and we learn later that she has remained alive and uncontaminated because she is nourished by her dream of an eventually legal life with Tom in the West.

During the party a change occurs in Myrtle that pictorializes a crucial fact about the nature of her own dream and, by implication, Gatsby's. Although the dream has kept her alive, now that she is surrounded by circumstances approaching those of its fulfillment she undergoes an ugly transformation: "The intense vitality that had been so remarkable in the garage was converted into impressive hauteur." She now presents a pathetic, ridiculous figure dressed in expensive clothes that contrast sharply with her commonness and her "violent and obscene language." Apparently the dream, by the very fact of its existence, can be lifegiving, but as it approaches realization it invests life with inconsistency and vulgarity: it is doomed to remain a "Platonic conception," an ideal incapable of embodiment in fact, particularly when the fact can only be material. But Myrtle's dream is a long way from realization. It is confined, as it turns out permanently, to illegality and the East.

For Nick the party represents a vulgarization of what he previously experienced at the Buchanans. The "flow" of the East has become confusion. "People disappeared, reappeared, made plans to go somewhere and then lost each other, searched for each other, found each other a few feet away." There is a photograph on the wall apparently of "a hen sitting on a blurred rock. Looked at from a distance, however, the hen resolved itself into a bonnet, and the countenance of a stout old lady beamed down into the room." It seems to him that there is a "blurred air" to the faces in the room, and in a fatuous effort to restore order he wipes from McKee's cheek "the spot of dried lather that had worried [him] all afternoon." But he is still "simultaneously within and without, simultaneously enchanted and repelled by the inexhaustible variety of life." Tom has told Myrtle that he cannot get a divorce because his wife is a Catholic, and although Nick is "a little shocked at the elaborateness of the lie," he has not yet learned to relate the lie, in all its elaborateness, to the false promise of the East or to the larger lie on which his whole experience rests.

But we cannot help but see the relation, just as we cannot help but see Nick, Myrtle, and the Buchanans as actors in a dumb show caricaturing Gatsby's tragedy. Like Nick, Gatsby is enchanted by the "shining secrets" of the East and mistakes the purposeless movement for the free flow of life into the future; like Myrtle he is given vitality by a dream that is far larger than any possibility of fulfillment; and like the Buchanans he is thwarted in his efforts to "repeat the past." He shares with them all the deficiency that makes them "subtly unadaptable to Eastern life," but he also shares their fate of inhabiting a culture in which dreams along with most demands of the spirit have no place. He aspires to the good life as though it were a thing of the spirit, while the culture can afford him the means only for a life of material achievement—a material woman or a woman corrupted by materialism. In his aloofness from his own material possessions he dramatizes his uncompromising faith that life can and will yield more, if only he can manipulate circumstances properly. And it is no more than the justice of irony that he should finally be thwarted by an utterly faithless but infinitely more powerful materialism than his own. For the Buchanans, wealth is not a means to the fulfillment of any dream: it is the hard fact of life against which the hard fact of Gatsby's manipulations can have no effect. It is also ironic that the illusions of Gatsby's party guests are seen in conjunction with his cold and aloof factualness, and that this factualness is the product of an illusion far more romantic than theirs. The guests come to his parties in pursuit of some final ecstasy, some ultimate good time that the American Dream has always promised them. Gatsby is the self-appointed agent of that dream, but they can never get close to him or discover his true identity, just as neither he nor they can hope to discover an identity for the dream.

It is dramatically just, therefore, that at the close of the novel Nick should relate Gatsby's aspiration to the feelings aroused in the early Dutch voyagers to America by their first glimpse of the "fresh, green breast of the new world."

> For a transitory enchanted moment man must have held his breath in the presence of this continent, compelled into an aesthetic contemplation he neither understood nor desired, face to face for the last time in history with something commensurate to his capacity for wonder.... And as I sat there brooding on the old, unknown world, I thought of Gatsby's wonder when he first picked out the green light at the end of Daisy's dock. He had come a long way to this blue lawn, and his dream must have seemed so close that he could hardly fail to grasp it. He did not know that it was already behind him, somewhere back in that vast obscurity beyond the city, where the dark fields of the republic rolled on under the night.[*]

[*] Ibid.

But it is also logically just that he should go on to say that those voyagers were face to face "for the last time in history with something commensurate to" their capacity for wonder. For it may well be that the moment when America was first settled was the last moment when America was able to embody the dream that the settlers brought to its shores, and that ever since the wonder and the dream have lacked a suitable object, or have had to languish and die in pursuit of an unworthy object—mere money or mere surface display—just as Gatsby's dream had to die in part because Daisy was, and could not help but be, unworthy of it.

It is perhaps too much to say, as at least one critic has, that Gatsby is a symbol of America itself. But he is a major figure in the legend created by the complex fate of being American, and he is the hero of the tragic limitations of that fate in a world that, as the eclipsing myth of the twenties recedes, seems more contemporary than we knew.

[1958]

The Man from Main Street

SINCLAIR LEWIS had, at the time of his death in 1951, an extremely insecure reputation as a writer of serious fiction and practically no reputation at all as an essayist and critic. Of the twenty-two novels he had produced in the thirty-seven years of his active career, five had been forgotten before the publication of *Main Street* in 1920; perhaps four had had genuine literary merit; six were readable; three were nearly unreadable; and the remaining four, of which the posthumously published *World So Wide* was regrettably one, were the sheerest trash. As for nonfiction, one scarcely imagined he had the time or inclination for it or, if he did, that it could be of a very high order. There had of course been the famous and penetrating literary essay he had read before the Swedish Academy in Stockholm shortly after receiving the Nobel Prize in 1930; and one had heard of the furor occasioned by his brilliant exposé of labor conditions in Marion, North Carolina, during the mill strikes of 1929. But it was generally assumed that, in the main, what ideas he had he had used in his novels, and that outside his novels he had no ideas.

That this was as gross an underestimation of Lewis as it was an overestimation of his fiction is made clear in the range and depth of the writings that Harry Maule and Melville Cane have brought together in *The Man from Main Street* from nearly a million words of nonfiction that we now learn Lewis wrote during his lifetime. Many of the pieces are occasional essays, fragmentary, inconclusive, and deliberately limited to the short view. Others are meandering reminiscences of boyhood days in Sauk Centre, of the years of struggle as a young house editor and writer in New York, of the leisurely later years of European travel and gentleman farming in Vermont. Still others are remarkably astute critical studies and portraits of writers he admired—Thoreau, H. G. Wells, William Lyon Phelps, his close friend Carl Van Doren—and of critics he quarreled with or despised, like Bernard DeVoto, who once made the mistake of attacking Van Wyck Brooks. All of them suggest the surprising breadth of his intellectual interests, the generosity of his mind, his passionate concern—amounting at times to a mother-hen fussiness—with every manifestation of the creative spirit of his age. But they also suggest, in their very richness and vitality, the reason for the startling failure of his novelistic career.

Lewis had, it is now plain, a first-rate practical mind coupled with an arrested and largely third-rate sensibility. His mind was continually expending in controversy and journalism what his sensibility could not express in art. It was the defect of his fiction, as well as the source of its popular appeal, that it was always dominated by an extravagant sense of the actual, always threatening to spill over the bounds of artifice into the banality of life. If this sense had been less strong in Lewis and his creative power had been greater, he might have succumbed to that necessary befuddlement, that elision of the practical intelligence and memory, which Henry James once defined as the "holy stupidity" of the artist, and as the result of which many lesser minds than Lewis's have blundered into greatness. But it was his abiding misfortune to be always intelligent, to be always under the control of a sense of reality so keen that, once established, it could never be shaken.

In the end this betrayed him; for when the world he knew in his youth, with its expanding social frontiers, its village chauvinism, and its cult of business success, ceased after 1930 to be quite real, he continued for years to write of it as if its conventions were still intact, exposing stupidities and injustices that were dead and pointing an angry finger at an emperor who had long since put his clothes back on.

[1953]

The Critic's Novel

I Thought of Daisy

EDMUND WILSON'S literary intelligence is no longer a matter we need question. By degrees over the past thirty years we have come to recognize it as one of the five or six finest to appear in this country in modern times, and one of the last to remain oriented in the great tradition of the humanist man of letters, the line of Boileau, Sainte-Beuve, and Taine. But we need to be reminded once again, as the reappearance of *I Thought of Daisy* does remind us, that the situation of the man of letters in our day cannot be maintained without cost, either to his dignity or his art.

It is his fate to be continually the victim of his humanistic intelligence, his passion for ideas, in a dehumanized and dispassionate world, and to discover, once he deserts criticism for the novel, that it is precisely his ideas that he can turn to least account imaginatively, since his experience in his society affords him no sustaining subject, no scheme of manners, through which his ideas can be effectively portrayed. Properly speaking, Edmund Wilson is a nineteenth-

222

century Jamesean sensibility adrift in the world of Scott Fitzgerald and John O'Hara. All his instincts and interests compel him toward the novel of political and esthetic speculation, a *Princess Casamassima* or a *l'Education sentimentale*. All his experience compels him toward the shoddy material of a *Butterfield-8*. All his imagination can make out of the split is *I Thought of Daisy* and *Memoirs of Hecate County*.

The material of *I Thought of Daisy* is drawn from the impoverished manners of Greenwich Village in the twenties. The theme is a dramatization of one of Wilson's favorite ideas: that the common life of a country can be entered through the formulation of the proper intellectual attitude toward it. For the young narrator of the novel, it is American life that must be entered; and it is Daisy, a chorus girl, who represents that life to him. Daisy is seen in a different perspective—so that she is constantly appearing as a new person —each time the narrator tries to fit her into one of a series of different intellectual systems—successively, social revolution, romanticism, animalism, materialism, metaphysical idealism, and, finally, democratic realism, at which stage the common life is attained. The story thus arranges itself into the traditional pattern of the novel of the developing consciousness or *Bildungsroman*.

It is essential in such a novel that there be something for the consciousness to develop through, some tangible medium of persons and events that can be made meaningful enough to dramatize the various changes in its ideas. But here the gap between the consciousness and its medium remains hazardously wide. The narrator moves among the characters like a shred of ectoplasm at a seance. He is all disembodied mentality; they are all stupidity made flesh. Daisy, the intended image of the narrator's shifting point of view, is vitiated dramatically by the very role Wilson requires her to play. She changes shape so often, is seen from so many different directions, that finally she is wiped out of existence altogether. What is worse, she comes through, in the brief moments when we do see her, as one of the emptiest young women to appear in literature since Moll Flanders.

Perhaps because he sensed Daisy's inadequacy as a character, Wilson unconsciously inflated the terms in which he describes her. The result is some of the most embarrassingly bad writing he has ever done, reminding us that even as a young man he had a defective ear and no sense of humor, and that the peculiarly frigid passion one feels behind the language of *Memoirs of Hecate County* was no mere defect of old age. Here we have the narrator on the subject of Daisy's feet: "I held her firm little insteps for a moment in my hands: in pale stockings, her tired and sweaty feet were like two little moist cream cheeses encased in covers of cloth: her body, which seemed now so slight in its pale blue dress, lay as limp as a lettuce leaf soaked by the summer rain."

In an essay called "A Preface to Persius," written at about the same time as this novel, Wilson describes himself as he sat alone one evening in an Italian restaurant before an excellent antipasto. A bottle of yellow wine and a goblet of pale green glass are on the table, and a volume of Persius lies open at his elbow. Across the room but an immense psychic distance away, a party of men and women are being vulgarly loud, and one rather pretty girl "of an obviously simple nature" is showing "some sort of professional interest ... in a rather defective-looking man." Wilson observes all this for a moment, and then, in faint distaste, turns back to his Persius. I can think of no clearer illustration of the problem that *I Thought of Daisy* represents.

[1953]

The Second Stone

The novel about the sex life of intellectuals, in or out of the universities, is fast becoming such a hackneyed subgenre of American fiction that just about the only thing left to do with it is turn it into a parody of itself and make it serve as a laughing critical commentary on its own clichés. Nothing else would seem to suffice, for played straight and intended seriously, the intellectual sex novel has a subversive way of taking the matter out of the author's hands and falling naturally and in spite of him into self-parody. When that happens, it is the author who is laughed at rather than the form.

Leslie A. Fiedler of all people should know this, and know it well. In the last fifteen years he has established a solid reputation for astringent criticism and has exercised the sternest kind of monitory intelligence upon the clichés to be found in other people's novels. In fact, he suggested not very long ago in one of his essays that the treatment of sex in contemporary fiction has become a tissue of outworn literary conventions and truisms, and that nothing is to be gained by making "a second-hand protest" against the prevailing sexual taboos or in carrying on "a long, more and more pointless quarrel with grandma."

It comes as a distinct embarrassment, therefore, to find Mr. Fiedler producing a first novel of his own that seems exactly to prove his case. It is a book that vigorously compounds the conventions and truisms of which he speaks, that is unrelentingly secondhand in its protest against the taboos, and that manages to sound in its thrilled insistence upon the nasty as if grandma with her poor old fluttering indignation were the principal reader in view. The worst of it is that there is no sure way of telling whether Mr. Fiedler is laughing at his material or his material is laughing at him. The distance between the author and the point of view of his characters is hazardously narrow. But since his tone is so grim and his material so absurd, one is finally forced to conclude that the joke is all on Mr. Fiedler.

This seems a particular pity because the novel contains elements of what might, with more sophisticated handling, have become a fine, free-wheeling sexual comedy. The action is played out against the background of an International Congress of Love held in Rome under the joint sponsorship of the United States Information Service and a rich manufacturer of vaginal jelly. The spiritual leader of the Congress, a sort of rabbinical Dr. Kinsey named Mark Stone, preaches a new gospel of the orgasm to a high-browed, low-loined collection of disciples that include British spinster philosophers, Hindu mystics, young American writers, assorted Communists, and the rabbi's boyhood friend and namesake Clem Stone, a not-so-young American writer who, having packed his family off to the States, has settled down in Rome to work impotently on a war novel. But there is nothing impotent about his lust for the rabbi's beautiful, neglected, yet somehow four months pregnant wife. And while the Congress grinds vapidly on toward *interruptus*, Clem conducts an excruciatingly anguished but finally successful campaign to get Mrs. Stone so worn out visiting ruins and churches that she will collapse without protest into the nearest bed.

All this is, of course, good dirty fun and reveals nice possibilities for caricature. But the distinction between caricature and stereotype is enormously hard to preserve, and unfortunately Mr. Fiedler does not preserve it. His characters have a habit of collapsing into cliché with as much ease as they collapse into bed—which is to say they become literary in the sense that they seem to derive from books rather than from the close observation of life. The young writers talk the way one has read about young writers talking. Mrs. Stone is one more projection of that adolescent erotic dream of infinitely compliant womanhood that is fast turning the American novel into an instruction manual for voyeurs. Clem Stone is a cardboard representative of all failed, soured, smelly ex-young men whose creative talents have been short-circuited to the groin. Even the Italian setting, which supplies the inevitable ironic contrast between rich, robust Latin sensuality and the pinched, dry lust of the Anglo-Saxons, takes on the staged quality of *La Dolce Vita* and Tennessee Williams' sad little story of that other Mrs. Stone.

But the most obtrusive cliché of all is the cliché of sex as a Dirty Little Secret, that curiously inverted sentimentality of those who have never got over the shock of their childhood discovery that love is not entirely a thing of the spirit but is inextricably connected with a bodily function. The whole treatment of Clem's affair with Mrs. Stone is distorted by the felt implication that what is being revealed is deliciously unclean, even deeply hateful, and that physical relations between men and women are somehow so monstrous that they amount to perversion. The result is a series of scenes that for sheer grisliness must be unparalleled in contemporary literature. In one, the unquenchable Clem grows dizzy with

227

desire over the spectacle of poor pregnant Mrs. Stone vomiting over monks' skeletons in the underground cemetery of the Capuchins. In another, while shuddering with cold and terror in the depths of the San Clemente Church, Mrs. Stone is herself suddenly overcome by passion and tries to drag *him* to the clammy floor. In still another, Clem in a moment of tenderness squeezes her body "hard, hard, to hurt" and feels the urge to "pluck away bleeding the whole gluteus maximus." Then there is the unforgettable scene in which, after the end of a cocktail party, the lovers come crashing together, fall to the floor, roll from wall to wall, "across the unswept floor, damp napkins, crushed olives, toothpicks, butts—their mouths engaged, each slobbering with the other's spit."

All these repulsive acrobatics are indicative of one very evident fact: that Clem has a sadistic hatred of women and sex. Just why he has, the novel never quite manages to make clear, although there are hints, of which Mr. Fiedler may or may not have been fully conscious, that Clem is a repressed homosexual whose true interest is not at all in Mrs. Stone but in her husband, the rabbi. There does not seem to be very much thematic point to this. Yet one remembers that in another of his essays called "Come Back to the Raft Ag'in, Huck Honey!" Mr. Fiedler argued that chaste homosexual love is actually the great hidden theme of American fiction from the Leatherstocking Tales of Cooper through *Moby Dick, Huckleberry Finn,* and the novels of Hemingway. It may just be, therefore, that he created the character of Clem to prove the truth of his critical theory, thus making him a rare instance of art imitating not nature but literary criticism. In any case, Clem and Mark Stone have now joined the distinguished company of Natty Bumppo and Chingachgook,

Ishmael and Queequeg, and Huck and Jim to show that love between man and woman is a snare and delusion, and that the real thing is reserved for us boys all alone together out there on that raft.

[1963]

The Brief, Stale Anger
of the English

Declaration

IT would be terribly courteous but false to pretend with
the publishers that *Declaration* is in fact the book it should
have been—a collection of credos by the real leaders of the
literary group that has come to be known, to the profound
regret of its members, as Britain's Angry Young Men. But
of the writers whose names are, at least in this country,
conventionally associated with the group, only three—John
Osborne, John Wain, and Colin Wilson—are represented by
statements, and even of these only Osborne seems really
angry; Wain is merely irritated when he is not actually complacent; while Wilson simply arouses anger. The others—
Kingsley Amis, John Braine, Peter Towry, and Thomas Hinde
—are missing, although, in all fairness to the editor, Tom
Maschler, it should be said that Amis at least was invited
to contribute and rather vociferously refused. The rest of the
contributors—Kenneth Tynan, Bill Hopkins, Lindsay Ander-

son, Stuart Holroyd, and Doris Lessing—are not, with the exception of Holroyd, members of the group at all, and Holroyd is only by virtue of having written one angry play. In other respects he seems, like Hopkins, to be a disciple in Wilson's religionist cult. Tynan is of course well known for his drama criticism, and Anderson is an excellent film critic and director, but they and the others seem to have been brought into the volume simply because they share certain of the attitudes of the group and happen to be more or less young writers.

Perhaps this is the reason why the essays do not constitute the sort of blasting manifesto of group principles and solidarity that all the publicity may have led one to expect. Most of them, in fact, are no more than curiously mild, rather bemused, and frequently confused discussions of the British social and political scene, the world situation, and the place of the writer within it. John Osborne, to be sure, fires off some wonderful invective at the royal family, whom he calls "the gold filling in a mouthful of decay," and Lindsay Anderson's essay is a brilliant statement of the writer's responsibility to be fully committed to the realities of our time. But Colin Wilson merely rehashes the religious argument of his last book *Religion and the Rebel;* Stuart Holroyd follows obediently along by rehashing the religious argument of his first book *Emergence From Chaos* (both essays sounding so much alike that one can only suppose them to have been divinely inspired); Bill Hopkins writes about the future of literature with the exhortative zeal of a college sophomore founding a magazine; and John Wain, that Tory in borrowed Cheapside clothing, adjures us to keep a cool head and a firm hand on the tiller in this time of crisis.

The critical refrain of the volume, insofar as there can be said to be one, is that the British people must break off their middle-class love affair with the illustrious British past, put aside the cant and hypocrisy of royalism, and face up squarely to the grim facts of the world in which they live. All the contributors are, in one way or another, deeply dissatisfied with the existing order, particularly with the still existing old order, some for esthetic and metaphysical reasons and others because they are Socialists and themselves members of the newly articulate working classes. But they are either oddly inspecific or naïvely Utopian in their suggestions for reform. Most of them face the world with a sort of derisive diffidence, and, like so many of the characters in the plays and novels of Osborne, Wain, and Amis, they seem to prefer the lightly comic to the boldly revolutionary stance.

In view of the alternating innocuousness and very young brashness of this volume, one cannot help but wonder why it is that the group for which the contributors are acting as spokesmen has been so seriously taken up in England and in this country. It would seem that at this stage of our developing sophistication we would require newer and sterner stuff. To be sure, the more vigorous members of the group have been saying things that in England at least have never been said in quite that way in literature before. They have opened a full-scale attack on the status quo from the viewpoint both of the working classes and of the younger intellectual generation, and have given expression to feelings that ever since the war have badly needed an outlet. But in this country, where we have almost always had a literary tradition of social protest, the infatuation is harder to account for. One supposes it is partly a result of our disappointment with our own younger writers for having failed to take a stand or launch a new movement, and partly an effect of our having ourselves so little sense of the issues on which such

232

a movement could be based. It is also undoubtedly due to the fact that these writers give us an excited feeling that something rather outrageous is happening in literature, but at the same time not happening directly to us. Hence, we get from them the vicarious pleasure of outrage without having to suffer the pain of actually being outraged. Finally, the Angry Young Men perhaps remind us of our own lost literary youth, when the issues were so much simpler and clearer cut, and one did not have to be self-analytical or precise or polite, but just joyously and mindlessly on the attack. Sooner or later, however, our chilly sense of critical proportion will reassert itself and bring us back down to business, and when that happens, we will be obliged to ask the really crucial question that must be asked about the group as a whole: not why they are angry, but whether they can write.

[1958]

Colin Wilson

Ever since the publication of *The Outsider* it has been a fashion among certain American intellectuals to accuse its author, Colin Wilson, of having opened his career by attempting to palm off as literature the interminable reading lists of his adolescence. During the same period in England some quite distinguished compatriots of Mr. Wilson's have made public pronouncements suggesting that they regard him as Francis Bacon's worthiest successor in the modern age. Both extremes of opinion serve less to define Mr. Wilson's position than to point up basic differences between the literary attitudes prevailing in the countries in which they have been expressed.

Here in America we tend to mistrust the maverick intellectual mind, particularly when it appears in so young a man as Mr. Wilson and in so advanced a stage of bibliographical elephantiasis. Our sense of the lean rigor and scrupulosity of humane culture is now classical in precept and middle-aged in sentiment, and nothing less than middle-aged performance—trussed up by scholarship and braced by footnotes—is likely to satisfy it, and then only grudgingly. But the English, gazing across the vista of low eminences that, with few exceptions, distinguish their present literary generation, look to the gifted young man for salvation from the doldrums of their Welfare Stasis. They are not in the least disturbed by Mr. Wilson's lack of the proper academic credentials, for most of his great predecessors lacked them also, and through their example, have elevated the lack into very nearly a badge of incipient literary distinction. By English standards Mr. Wilson belongs to the recognized and respected European tradition of the unaffiliated lower-middle-class man of letters and ideas, the tradition of Wells, Shaw, and Orwell. His defects can for the moment be excused on the ground of his youth and the high hopes held out for his promise. By less charitable American standards Mr. Wilson is quite simply brash, conceited, pretentious, presumptuous, prolix, boring, unsound, unoriginal, and totally without intellectual subtlety, wit, and literary style. But then if Mr. Wilson were living by American standards, he would undoubtedly be grubbing for a Ph.D. instead of writing books.

Yet it cannot be said that Mr. Wilson lacks a thesis, or that, after the manner of the doctoral inquisition, he fails to find proof of its veracity in everything his remarkable talent for wide reading brings to light. His new volume, *Religion and the Rebel*, is an extension of *The Outsider* in the sense that in it he sets out to explore the religious and mystical implications of the Outsider predicament and enlists in his cause a new group of great figures in the history of Western and Oriental thought. It seems to Mr. Wilson that the Outsider's problem is basically existential, in that, unlike other men to whom the physical world is more or less adequate, the Outsider can find fulfillment only through the resolute pursuit of freedom from the physical and the extension of the limits of personal consciousness. Mysticism and religion, since they are based on the idea of self-knowledge and the achievement of special states of awareness, are, therefore, logical Outsider goals. "Existentialism," says Mr. Wilson, "is the revolt against mere logic and reason. It is a plea for intuition and vision. It is a plea for recognizing oneself as being *involved* in the problems of existence as a participant, not just as a spectator." And finally: "The Outsider's ultimate problem is to become a visionary."

Unfortunately, Mr. Wilson's ultimate problem is lack of vision. He pursues his argument through portentous discussions of Jacob Boehme, Nicholas Ferrar, Pascal, Swedenborg, Kierkegaard, Whitehead, and others, but he never brings it to earth or, for that matter, to Heaven. All his cases in point turn out to be just that: good existentialists and good Outsiders, the archetype of whom, according to Mr. Wilson, was none other than Jesus Christ. The result, of course, is that finally the Outsiders, since they proliferate so vigorously, become Insiders, and the Insiders—if any are still to be found—become the rebels and as such seem, after a few hundred pages of Mr. Wilson, to deserve the world's sympathy. It is not that the idea behind Mr. Wilson's work is not important. On the contrary, the existential concept is one of the most if not the most important idea in the thought of our time, and the most effective challenge to materialistic philosophy yet conceived. But it is not properly served by Mr. Wilson. His book is not a synthesis or an analysis but an exposition, an industriously produced primer on its subject. It testifies, to be sure, to the precocity of his mind and the wide range of his intellectual interests, but one wishes that Mr. Wilson had preserved it in the form of unpublished notes for the work of genuine excellence that he may one day be capable of doing.

[1957]

Philip O'Connor

Philip O'Connor's autobiography, *Memoirs of a Public Baby*, comes to us from England absolutely glittering with critical acclaim. John Lehmann devoted the whole of a recent BBC broadcast to a discussion of its merits; Cyril Connolly wrote a review composed of more superlatives than verbs; Philip Toynbee called the book true, moving, and excellent; a host of other critics clearly consider it almost a masterpiece; a number of exactly the right people have found it outrageous; and Stephen Spender has contributed a deeply respectful introduction. The response has, in fact, struck so shrill a note that, recalling English critics' talent for encomiastic splurge on just about any faintly deserving occasion, one has a strong impulse to give Mr. O'Connor's book a very hard time indeed down at our own critical customs shed.

Unfortunately, however, Mr. O'Connor has nothing whatever to declare: he is precisely as free of all taxable cant, guile, sham, and miscellaneous malarkey as we have been told he is. But he is also one or two things we have rather emphatically not been told he is. For instance, he is something a little bit short of an absolute genius, if only because he writes too brilliantly to be capable of the dullness that frequently distinguishes that order of mind. His prose style is one of the truly remarkable features of his very remarkable book. It has all the sharply epigrammatic wittiness of that special kind of English comic writing that at its best is a sort of lingual snake pit of pun, epithet, and jeer, and it also has a quality, very common to Yeats' prose and undoubtedly passed down to Mr. O'Connor by his Irish forebears, of esoteric Celtic poeticism, the kind that gives the effect Elizabeth Bowen once ascribed to D. H. Lawrence of making every bush, no matter how scrubby, burn. Mr. O'Connor's language fires up the mental and social landscape he is describing to such a high white heat that all the objects in it are refined into brightly glowing essences.

But regardless of the heights he is able to attain as a writer, Mr. O'Connor as a human being is, as he himself makes clear, an unspeakable cad, scoundrel, and snob—in short, a brutally honest man. His book is, in fact, an extremely intimate account of how, from a very early age, he labored against all odds to perfect his caddishness and snobbery, and how in mature life, after a series of near failures, he succeeded in attaining his objective while at the same time learning to conceal the fact from the public. His snobbery he acquired in childhood from his mother who was an aristocrat by upbringing and who exuded an intoxicating air of complete superiority. The child Philip began life by mistaking the loathing of bourgeois society that his snobbery had engendered in him for some innate loathsomeness in society itself. He grew up searching for ways to discharge his disgust, all the while keeping it in trim by vigorously hating his Uncle Haslam for being kind to him, and his working-class guardian for daring to try to understand and love him. Finally, he found the outlet he sought in a series of typically bourgeois political, literary, and amatory enterprises and for a long time was down and out in the London Bohemian underworld. There he tried and failed to become a Communist, tried and succeeded in becoming an unsuccessful surrealist poet, almost managed to become a latent homosexual, and was for a while an illegal inmate of a nerve hospital. At the apex of his underworld career he was able to persuade his upper-class mistress to let him squander her inheritance so that he could live like a member of the upper class, and when there was no more money, he drove her and very nearly himself insane. We last see him seated on a pile of coal in a London air-raid shelter on Christmas Day, 1945, congratulating himself on having finally hit bottom.

Mr. O'Connor suggests in a "Postscript" that he has since achieved humility and a certain measure of autonomy, and that his trouble all along was that he had the social intelligence of a child of four. While one can scarcely dispute this, one could wish that Mr. O'Connor had also been able to find more of the blame for his past in his snobbery and caddishness. But he is so excruciatingly honest in all other respects that one must agree with Mr. Spender who says in his Introduction that the vision with which Mr. O'Connor has been able to dramatize so superbly the nightmare of his youth indeed approaches the angelic, that mysterious and terrible form of vision that "reminds us that we are what we are and that we should not construct views which betray our own being."

[1958]

Alan Sillitoe: The Poor Man's Bore

The more Alan Sillitoe writes, the harder it becomes to account for the high reputation he has enjoyed ever since the appearance in England of his first novel, *Saturday Night and Sunday Morning,* in 1958. That book along with the well-known title story from the collection, *The Loneliness of the Long Distance Runner,* published in the following year, were both undeniably sincere works of some originality and force. But they were ridiculously overpraised by a number of critics whose judgments one had assumed until then to be trustworthy, while his second and third novels, *The General* (1960) and *Key to the Door* (1961), suffered the relative neglect they clearly merited.

Yet Sillitoe somehow remains a young writer for whom one is supposed to have the most extravagant expectations, and it would appear that in some curious way one's expectations are even supposed to increase as he shows less and less evidence of being able to satisfy them. In fact, the mediocrity of his second and third novels seems to be regarded by some people as a positive point in his favor, a sign that he is slowly, if uncertainly, feeling his way toward new themes and displaying a courageous willingness to risk great failure in the attempt. There has, in short, been a disposition to give Sillitoe the benefit of every doubt, to credit him with the very best motives for writing badly.

This seems on the whole to be truer of English responses to Sillitoe than of American, if only because the English tend to be even more naïvely sentimental than we were in the thirties about formally uneducated novelists who write realistically enough to arouse their liberal-democratic sympathies but not radically enough to offend their conservative-aristocratic prejudices. In Sillitoe they appear to have found the perfect blend of irritant and palliative, a proletarian underdog who is at the same time harmless enough to double as a bourgeois lap dog, a genuine working-class writer who not only does not seek to attack or invade the middle-class world, but who seems virtually oblivious to it, apparently having no real interest in or knowledge of any world beyond that of his humble origins.

In this respect, Sillitoe stands as a comforting reminder to the English that the grand old roistering "low life" tradition of Fielding and Dickens may have lost its sting but is not yet dead, and a welcome antidote to writers like John Osborne, Kingsley Amis, and John Braine who have used working-class values and aspirations to bludgeon middle-class hypocrises, and whose characters are always trying to move in social circles for which their family backgrounds clearly unfit them. Sillitoe poses no threat of this kind. Although he does have his grievances, he seems basically content to keep the working man in his place, and as a writer he evidently wants to remain a working man. These attributes combined with the startling fact that he can write at all, and even on occasion write well, considering that he left school at the age of fourteen, give him in English eyes something of the curiosity value of an exceptionally well-mannered circus monkey who can play "God Save the Queen" on a tin horn.

American responses to Sillitoe are apt, on the other hand, to be a bit more complicated. Americans are not likely to find it remarkable that he can write more than his name without having taken a First at Oxford or Cambridge (after all, uneducated novelists are nothing new to us), but they might well find what he writes about rather hard to relate to their own experience. There can be no doubt that working-class life has a reality, a special kind of *presence,* in England that it has not had in America for a very long time. One needs only to drive through some of the industrial cities of the Midlands—or, for that matter, through almost any English city—to be struck by the drab monotony, the nearly uniform shabbiness of the people crowding the streets, the sense that one is moving in some horrible, futuristic Orwellian world where suddenly all men have been socialized into equality, created equal in underprivilege, equal in having the same inalienable rights to life, slavery, and the pursuit of wretchedness. The working-class appearances more and more set the tone of the English social climate. The endless rows of gray-faced, factory-owned tenements inhabited by endless numbers of gray-faced, factory-owned people seen through an endless gray rain—this is the ugly image that remains in the mind.

Yet regardless of how real this life may be to the English, it is something that we have long ago imaginatively *had* in America, something that as literary material we have run through and left behind, and that as social fact we have ceased to sentimentalize or patronize. For better or worse, the working class in America has merged with the middle class to produce a mass society of another kind of grayness and uniformity. And what this society has taught us is that while the material problems of the industrial underprivileged can be solved by the payment of some money and the introduction of certain reforms, the problems of the emotionally and spiritually underprivileged are only worsened by a rise in the material standard of living. The crucial issue for the contemporary writer as well as for Western culture as a whole is not one of people fighting to make a living, but of people fighting to make a life, to learn how to *be,* in a time of physical affluence and psychic impoverishment. The alleviation of physical hunger merely clears the way for the hungers of the mind and heart. Where the struggle for bare animal survival ends, the struggle for meaningful human existence begins. This is the great social and literary drama of the present age; in fact, so far as literature is concerned, it may well be the whole drama. For whether a man lives or dies is not finally important in literature. But the quality and significance of his life and death, these are all-important, because they involve ultimate questions of free will, character, and responsibility that it is the business of literature to engage.

Since literary Englishmen and literary Americans now inhabit an international community of letters, Sillitoe can no more be excused for not knowing this than for not knowing that Norris, Dreiser, and James T. Farrell—to say nothing of Arnold Bennett and Orwell—did all that he has done first and better than he. It might be objected that working-class life is, after all, Sillitoe's material, and that he ought to have a perfect right to use it if he so chooses. But there is little virtue in repeating the discoveries or the mistakes of one's predecessors, or in trying to make literature out of a cultural lag that merely social reform and the payment of some money can rectify, unless, like Faulkner, one can universalize it or wishes, like Norris or Dreiser, to "expose" it —as apparently Sillitoe does not—or, like any really original writer, can penetrate beneath its surface implications and find there new life never before revealed.

Yet this is just what Sillitoe has so far been unable to do, what not only his creative limitations but the limitations of his material prevent him from doing. For to the extent that his people are the victims of their economic situation, they are people without the power of moral freedom. And to the extent that they are unfree, and lack even the opportunity to be enticed to choose freedom and to be damned by it, they are grossly oversimplified as fictional characters, pawns in a chess game in which every move is necessary and therefore none is possible. All that they think and do and want is determined by the exigencies of their class existence, including even their empty gestures of rebellion against that existence; hence, nothing they think is interesting, nothing they do is finally worth doing, and nothing they want will in the end be of any value whatever to them. There can be no doubt that one may be impressed by this and frequently moved to compassion. But one is emphatically not moved to understanding. All one feels like doing is what Virginia Woolf said the novels of Wells, Bennett, and Galsworthy inspired her to do: join a society or write a check. The taking of either of these actions might represent a contribution toward the betterment of mankind, but any fictional dilemma whose solution can conceivably depend on their being taken is clearly a matter for sociology and not literature.

It is for these reasons that there seems little point in "reviewing" Sillitoe's present collection of stories, *The Ragman's Daughter*. Most of the stories are effective enough in their way and within their limits; in fact, Sillitoe continues to seem more impressive as a writer of stories than as a novelist. But one feels that they are successful only to the degree that one is able to put aside most of what one has learned about the complexity of human behavior in the modern age and gear down one's thought processes to accommodate an essentially mechanistic view of life and a story form which one has to strain to recall was once fashionable with certain semi-serious, socially oriented publications in the thirties. It may also be significant that although I read through the collection very carefully, I can at this moment, strain as I will, recall none of the stories except the title piece. Again the reason is not that they are really bad or even really dull, but rather that they seem to say nothing about experience that most people have not already thought and felt, nothing that does not sooner or later end its course in what T. S. Eliot once called "the desert of exact likeness to the reality which is perceived by the most commonplace mind."

Right after *Saturday Night and Sunday Morning* appeared, certain critics expressed the fear that Sillitoe would run through his working-class materials and be left with nothing more to say. The fear now is that he will *not* run through them and go on saying the same thing over and over. He might then become a sort of British James T. Farrell, and the trouble with that is that we have *had* Farrell. Perhaps the fact that we can say this, as we cannot say we have *had* Proust, Joyce, or James, illustrates more clearly than anything else the seriousness of the imaginative impasse that Sillitoe has now reached.

[1964]

P. G. Wodehouse: The Lesson
of the Young Master

SINCE 1902, when he published his first book, *The Pot-hunters*, P. G. Wodehouse has written at least sixty novels and volumes of short stories. For more than a half century he has been the most prolific and original writer of light social comedy in English and very probably in the world. His works have been translated into all the major European languages as well as into Czech, Swedish, Polish, and Chinese, and his following in this country and England alone—to say nothing of the hordes who are probably reading him in Chinese—must number in the millions. Yet it is highly doubtful if any critic, here or abroad, has read him with any diligence; at least I know of no critical discussion of his work that attempts at all seriously to investigate the peculiar quality of his comic gifts or to account for the phenomenally high favor in which they have been held for all these years by the reading public. There is, of course, George Orwell's famous essay in *Dickens, Dali and Others*, defending Wodehouse for his mistaken but apparently quite innocently intended broadcasts over the German radio in the early days of World War II; and John Hayward, in what Orwell calls the only full-length essay on Wodehouse, presents an excellent summary of his career along with a short appreciation of his best-known work. But except for one or two brief and now more or less outdated survey pieces, such as those by Frank Swinnerton and Grant Overton, there has been little else of any importance.

It is of course true that Wodehouse has suffered the effects of the traditional prejudice against the writer of light comedy and of the feeling common among critics that work which merely entertains can have value only to the simple-minded and the very young. There is also a very real problem involved in evaluating work that is intended merely to entertain and that performs that office to perfection. But I suspect that the critical neglect of Wodehouse is in a sense actually a corollary, rather than a condemnation, of his huge popular success, and may even represent the highest tribute that criticism can pay to it. The simple truth very likely is that Wodehouse has never needed the sort of entree into public recognition that criticism normally creates for writers, that there is scarcely anyone around sufficiently like him to enable criticism to exercise its comparative function, and that no serious question has ever arisen concerning his quality or his methods. Besides, it seems to be the case, in this country only slightly less than in England, that a great many people were brought up on Wodehouse, while as many others were brought up on the myth of having been brought up on Wodehouse. The first group are very often the sort who more or less pride themselves on always having had a rather old-fashioned interest in books and who like to look fondly back on one of those contemplative childhoods spent browsing away the long, fly-buzzing summer afternoons in the cool quiet of some ancient relative's library. Wodehouse for them is likely to belong to that shadowy melange of writers—which is just as apt to include Dickens, Swift, and Lewis Carroll as it is the creator of the Bobbsey Twins—whose books they once read and enjoyed but believe they have thoroughly used up and outgrown. The result is that in later life they tend to feel that they know all about Wodehouse without having to read him again, or if they do read him again and become his adult fans, that they neither can nor need get a new impression of him because they already have a perfectly good old one. The people, on the other hand, who were brought up merely on the myth of having been brought up on Wodehouse, tend to feel that they know all about him without having to read him at all. They are usually the sort who react to a casual mention of his name with the most vociferous guffaws and helpless head-waggings. But in either case Wodehouse remains precisely where he was, firmly established in the public domain of a million sincerely and hypocritically adoring hearts, an experience unrehearsed because supposedly so well remembered, as honored and forlorn as a box of old toys locked away in the attic.

I was rather priggish in that insufferable adolescent way about light reading while growing up, and that perhaps accounts for the fact that I did not come upon Wodehouse until relatively late, although when I finally did, the circumstances were undoubtedly very like those in which much younger people read him for the first time.

In 1956 my wife and I were living in Europe. During a trip to Germany I came down with jaundice and was ordered to bed for three weeks. The site we chose for the confinement was a large and ornate old hotel situated on the top of the Schatzalp overlooking Davos, Switzerland, the very sort of place Bertie Wooster, perhaps dragged or pursued by an aunt, would have visited back in the days before the two world wars and the devaluation of the pound. Most of the rooms had balconies that commanded a magnificent view of the town and the surrounding mountains, and there were miles of heavily carpeted halls with domed ceilings, several ballrooms, dining rooms, billiard rooms, and music rooms, as well as an English library, a German library, and a French library. John Addington Symonds and Robert Louis Stevenson had often taken tea there after tobogganing with the children on the slopes outside, and it was said that the place, in one of its earlier incarnations as a sanitarium, had served Thomas Mann as a model for the setting of *The Magic Mountain*. The only drawback was that when we arrived at the top of the funicular—I sweating and straining over our luggage and growing weaker and more brilliantly yellow by the minute—we found the hotel closed for the between-seasons interval. But I must have presented to the manager a sufficiently wretched spectacle, for he was finally persuaded after a good deal of discussion to let us stay on as his only guests. We were given the largest and brightest rooms, and then began the most fantastic and altogether delightful convalescence of my experience.

We were alone in a huge hotel at the top of the world, the only guests of the vast echoing emptiness and the view. Our windows alone, in the banks of windows fronting the valley, shed light out upon the snow; the domed halls, the billiard and music rooms, the libraries, all else was silent and dark, except for the delicate ghosts of faintly ailing English ladies whose skirts sometimes rustled past our door at tea-time, and the gentle knocking-knocking now and again of billiard balls out of the past of some Victorian afternoon. Yet, mysteriously and a little terribly, our single cell of life squarely in the center of nothingness was a switchboard of complicated connections with the external world. Above my bed were five electrical outlets set in a row, each a different size for a different current and function. Beside my bed was a table holding a board of four buttons, each intended to summon a different servant for a different want. Above the table was another row of five electrical outlets, into one of which was plugged the cord of a small palm-sized rubber radio. The receiver was encased in a glove of white hospital cloth so that it could be kept on one's pillow close to one's ear, and attached to it was a rubber-encased wire and thumb-button. One press of the button turned the radio on; two presses selected a station; each subsequent two changed the station. The programs came in over the telephone wire and somehow made their way out through the radio, having been preselected by some unknown central agency. A press of one of the buttons on the board brought the one maid then resident in the hotel, and at appointed hours she would arrive carrying great trays of magnificent food prepared by an absolute genius of a chef who worked alone in the big kitchen somewhere below preparing meals solely for us. Every couple of days Leslie would type up in German the menu we wanted for several meals, and every day exactly on time the meals would be borne in by the desperately willing, smiling, beautifully homely maid, who was always the first to notice and expose her single human failing: "Oh," she would exclaim in a voice full of self-reproach, *"Ich habe etwas vergessen."* Usually it was the salt.

We lived in this way for a little over three weeks, and I recall that it was around the beginning of the second week that I discovered Wodehouse. I had been lying out on the balcony taking the sun and watching through binoculars the movements of some bug-sized members of the Swiss

249

Army engaged in maneuvers on the slopes outside the town below. They would separate into opposing groups and ambush each other, one group making their way over an inch or so of stubbly terrain and then falling flat, the other moving with pathetic slowness toward the spot where I and I alone knew they were about to be slaughtered. I was feeling very godlike when Leslie arrived with an armload of books from the English library, some Conan Doyle, Conrad, Wyndham Lewis, and P. G. Wodehouse. I happened to pick up the Wodehouse first and from that moment on was lost. The book was *My Man Jeeves,* the first collection of stories about that greatest of gentlemen's personal gentlemen, and before we left the hotel I had read all the Jeeves books I could find in the library. It was a perfect setting for both Jeeves and Wodehouse, and I was in exactly the right frame of mind. Like Hans Castrop I was entirely cut off from direct experience of the outside world, literally imprisoned on *der Zauberberg;* life in the lowlands seemed precisely as puny and remote as it had looked through the binoculars. The altitude and the regular routine of my life gave me a very clear head and at the same time a feeling of drowsy timelessness. I felt able without guilt to give myself up completely to a world of warm protection where no struggle or passion or pain ever intruded and where one was looked after with almost superhuman solicitude by a Jeeves, just as I was being looked after by my wife, the maid, and the chef. I had to be ill in order to allow myself to be amused; I had to be invalided out of my own world in order to get into Wodehouse's. But the good thing was that once in I could always get in again, even after we came down from our mountain and back home.

One does have to suspend one's sense of the contemporary world, either through physical isolation or an act of imagination, while reading Wodehouse, for he belongs exclusively to Edwardian times and has apparently chosen to remain unaware of just about every important development that has occurred in the world since those times. All efforts, including his own, to update his work must end in failure; his characters, even when they strike out with brave allusions to Clark Gable and Gatsby, betray in their every gesture, action, and assumption their helpless allegiance to the past. John Hayward has suggested, perhaps a shade too severely, that we shall sooner or later have to estimate just how far "the 'escapism' of Mr. Wodehouse's novels is related to a psychological need to avoid or suppress in his own life the unpleasant realities and obligations of the contemporary world." Certainly when one recalls his broadcasting activities for the German radio during World War II, however innocent or well-intentioned they may have been, one could wish that Wodehouse had had a firmer grasp of those realities and obligations. But the political naïf is not the creative artist (although he may well be the artist's illegitimate offspring), and it must be remembered that Wodehouse as artist acquired his primary assumptions about life from the value system of a world that could scarcely have conceived even of the concept of a Hitler and which, even at that, was so simplified as raw material by the artist's peculiar bias of temperament that it appeared in his work as a perpetual boy's world, pristine of all reality save school and sport. Whether their actual locale is a Shropshire country house, an exclusive London club, or a wealthy bachelor's flat, all of Wodehouse's stories are played out in the moral arena of the public school. The school afforded him his first and last education in the conduct of life, just as it afforded him the setting for the stories with which, in the early years of the century, he began his career and won his first follow-ing—of schoolboys.

Mr. A. P. Ryan has said in this connection that "Jeeves ... is not a valet, a gentleman's gentleman, but the incarnation of our elders who always win in the long run. Scratch Jeeves, and you will find the housemasters of Wodehouse's youth. Nothing ruffles them. They are never shocked. Their culture is such that they are able ... smoothly to patronize their young barbarians. They know the boys rely on them, and cannot do without them." One might add that nearly all the adults in the Jeeves-Wooster world fall typically into two classes clearly identifiable on the scale of public-school values: the helpful and indulgent and the grim, vengeful, and sternly monitory. Jeeves and Bertie's Aunt Dahlia exemplify the first; his Aunt Agatha, Sir Roderick Glossop, and assorted other elderly menaces, the second. It is as if, to the eternally adolescent Bertie, life were a battleground for perpetually warring factions of mother- and father-surrogates, with himself in the middle struggling with the help of Jeeves to preserve his neutrality. But Jeeves is far more than just the diplomatic Secretary of the Wooster State. He is by turns Bertie's big brother, illegal guardian, keeper, intellectual mentor, apollonian censor, undercover agent, hired thug, and knight-at-arms. His most frequent function is to sally forth on the charger of his gigantic brain to the aid of the young master, but he is just as capable, when the occasion arises, of all manner of unchivalrous deceit, trickery, falsehood, forgery, and blackmail. For these services he expects payment, usually in the form of some tactfully suggested change in Bertie's outrageously bad taste in wearing apparel. This Bertie always freely grants because the price demanded by his tormentors is far higher—no less, in fact, than the total abandonment of the boyhood state and the prompt assumption of a deadly adulthood. Not only does Bertie suffer from a cretinous lack of talent for such an enterprise, but he has a good sound sense of the loss to him of psychic income that would be involved in the exchange. With Jeeves to protect him he is free to pursue a way of life exactly suited to his retarded needs and desires. The boyhood world can be preserved intact. There, in an atmosphere blissfully auntless, he can drink and carouse with old school chums at the Drones Club till all hours; he can play the horses, sport in the company of Jeeves on the Riviera, at Monte Carlo, and in New York; waste endless weekends working up backfiring practical jokes at country-house parties; and contract innumerable sexless engagements with bossy girls who (he always learns or has discreetly pointed out to him just in time) are all hard bent on reforming him into at least minimally adult respectability.

Nor is Bertie the only dunce in the Wodehouse classroom; it is a veritable incubator of oafdom. Within the Jeeves stories themselves there are such fluffy-minded personages as Bingo Little, young Tuppy Glossop, Oliver Randolph "Old Sippy" Sipperley, and Freddie Bullivant. All of these have cranial limitations exceeded only by Bertie's, but are always being helped out of scrapes by him upon their appeal to the memory of their school days together. Then there is Ukridge (*Ukridge*, 1924), whom Mr. Hayward calls "the most genial of all Wodehouse's high-grade defectives," but for whom, since he lacks the help of a Jeeves, things nearly always turn out badly. In the *Blandings Castle* series we have, of course, Lord Emsworth and his son, the Hon. Freddie Threepwood—both studies in the miraculous capacity of the human body to operate without the assistance of any mental powers whatever. And in the Mulliner stories there are the hosts of Mr. Mulliner's male relatives who manage—usually with the help of a *deus ex machina* such as "Buck-U-Uppo," a sort of medicinal Jeeves—to blunder their idiotic way through to success. Of all Wodehouse's important characters other than Jeeves only Psmith (*Mike,* 1909; *Psmith in the City,* 1910; *Psmith, Journalist,* 1915; *Leave it to Psmith,* 1923) can be credited with having any real intelligence, although in the best of the books relating to him, *Leave it to Psmith,* his only competition is the nitwit menage of Blandings Castle. It would seem that there is indeed good reason for supposing, therefore, that Wodehouse is, like so many English writers, a case of the romantic permanently arrested at the emotional level of the sixth form. But his saving distinction is that he has been able to turn the handicap into high comic art and, in so doing, to appeal to our delight in the fool and chucklehead, our not so unconscious desire to play the truant in the face of adult authority and responsibility, and our secret yearning to become as a child again, forever under the protection of the ultimate parent.

Of all Wodehouse's stories and novels those relating to Jeeves and Bertie Wooster are, to my mind, the most successful. They are the most complex structurally and the most consistent dramatically; they contain the greatest number of separately developed minor characters and situations; and they give the fullest range to Wodehouse's remarkable gift for creating a genuinely fresh comic diction. But above all they have Jeeves, certainly the greatest of Wodehouse's creations and a permanent member of the cast of great comic fictional characters of all time. In comparison with Jeeves, Ukridge seems pallid and one dimensional, very much as Bertie Wooster would seem if deprived of Jeeves. The formula of his adventures is always the same, as for that matter is the formula of Bertie's, but because this is so, our concern in both is not with the adventures themselves but with the manner of their resolution. We know beforehand that Ukridge will blunder and fail, his outlandish plans will go awry, but about Bertie we can never be entirely sure. There is the unknown quantity of Jeeves to allow for, and who can tell what Jeeves will come up with? The Mulliner stories depend for their impact upon the wild absurdity of their situations rather than upon the ingenuity of their resolutions, and even though Wodehouse achieves in them an occasional effect of high comedy that in its richness is very nearly Dickensian, they seem to me to belong on the whole to a lower order than the Jeeves stories. Psmith, on the other hand, perhaps because he combines in one person the virtues and vices of both Bertie and Jeeves, is a close competitor of Jeeves. *Leave it to Psmith* is an almost perfect book, and as a novel considerably superior to those having to do with Bertie and Jeeves that Wodehouse has written more recently in his career. But Wodehouse's mastery lies in the field of the short story, and there Jeeves is absolutely without a peer.

The genesis of Jeeves is, as perhaps it should be, somewhat obscure; like the supernatural being he clearly is, he should simply have materialized one morning in Wodehouse's typewriter—much in the manner in which he springs out of nowhere into Bertie Wooster's life. But Mr. Hayward tells us that "in an early dramatic sketch entitled *After the Show,* which Mr. Wodehouse wrote in collaboration with Herbert Westbrook some years before Jeeves turned up, there is a slight but suggestive resemblance between Barlow, manservant to the Hon. Aubrey Ford-Rasche of the Albany, and Jeeves, notably in a sharp 'scene' over 'our cravats.' There is some reason to suppose that Mr. Westbrook gave his coauthor the idea for Barlow and that Barlow, if not the archetype of Jeeves, is at least his precursor. At all events *After the Show* is the first piece on record in which a character of a recognizably Jeevesian type figures." Mr. Hayward goes on to say that "Jeeves himself did not make his first discreet bow to the world until 1917. This was on page twenty-five of a collection of thirteen short stories entitled *The Man with Two Left Feet*, and on the opening page of the first recorded chapter of accidents involving Bertie Wooster and his terrific Aunt Agatha—an isolated story called 'Extricating Young Gussie.' He appeared for a moment only to deliver the awful and prophetic message: 'Mrs. Gregson to see you, sir' and then vanish again for another two years."

Wodehouse himself says in his Introduction to *The Jeeves Omnibus* (1931) that "it was only some time later, when I was going into the strange affair which is related under the title of 'The Artistic Career of Young Corky,' that the man's qualities dawned upon me. I still blush to think of the off-hand way I treated him at our first encounter." The story in question—originally called "Leave It to Jeeves"—contextually establishes its direct descent from 'Extricating Young Gussie' by a reference in its opening paragraphs to that embarrassing affair, and is the first of four stories about Bertie and Jeeves that were published in 1919 in the volume entitled *My Man Jeeves*, the original British volume in the Jeeves series. But as if to recompense Jeeves for his initial offhand treatment of him, Wodehouse went on to make him the hero of an entire saga or cycle of episodes, almost as complex, and at its level as satisfying, as those by Balzac, Galsworthy, and Faulkner, and comprising approximately thirty-nine stories and seven novels. As Wodehouse says in the foreword to this book: "Except for the tendency to write articles about the Modern Girl and to allow his side whiskers to grow, there is nothing an author today has to guard himself against more carefully than the Saga habit. The least slackening of vigilance, and the thing has gripped him. He writes a story. Another story dealing with the same characters occurs to him, and he writes that. He feels that just one more won't hurt him, and he writes a third. And before he knows where he is, he is down with a Saga, and no cure in sight."

Nevertheless, the Jeeves saga stands with that of Blandings Castle and the Emsworths as Wodehouse's most brilliant contribution to the art of light comic fiction. Like all sagas it carries a single group of characters through a series of adventures and is liberally reinforced with subplots, parallelisms, and cross references, giving one the sense of moving among intimates in a known world and of sharing with them dramatically the slow accretion of experience. In the stories that form the heart of the Jeeves saga there are about twenty secondary characters who appear at least once, and more than half of these reappear frequently enough to become principals of important subplots. There is, for example, the series of six stories relating to young Bingo Little, his innumerable infatuations, usually with waitresses, his experiences as an impecunious tutor at country houses, his fraudulent activities as a rabble rouser, and finally his marriage to the well-known popular novelist Rosie M. Banks. Then there is the running account of Bertie's misadventures with the famous nerve specialist or "loony doctor," Sir Roderick Glossop; his Amazonian daughter Honoria; his son Oswald, one of the worst of Wodehouse's menagerie of terrible kids; and his other son Tuppy, who once tricked Bertie into dropping fully clothed in evening dress into the Drones Club swimming pool, and upon whom Bertie has not even yet devised sufficiently fiendish vengeance. Other pairs and sequences of stories have to do with the awful Blumenfields, Senior and Junior, the retiring poet Rocky Todd, "Old Sippy" Sipperley,

257

Freddie Bullivant, and Roberta Wickham. Roberta has the distinction of figuring in a minor way in both the Jeeves saga and the Mulliner stories. In the story called "Something Squishy" from *Mr. Mulliner Speaking* (1929) she appears as a beautiful but blackhearted girl who has a penchant for goading her suitors half mad, and in "Jeeves and the Yuletide Spirit" she reappears in the same role, although it is only at the last possible moment, when Bertie is seriously contemplating matrimony with her, that her true nature is revealed. Lord Emsworth of the Blandings Castle stories also appears briefly in the Jeeves saga as one of the respectable old duffers whose youthful exploits are detailed in Bertie's Uncle Willoughby's shocking memoirs.

Wodehouse carries these people skillfully forward along single and multiple lines of narrative exposition, but he never develops them. Unlike more realistic saga characters, they remain entirely unchanged by time and the fluctuations of fortune. We know them very much in the way that we know the principals of a morality play or an early eighteenth-century English novel—by a few fixed traits or humors—and our pleasure in them derives from the dependable recurrence of circumstances calling forth these traits, the satisfying experience of seeing happen what we knew all along was going to happen. Their situations are precisely as stereotyped as everything else in Wodehouse and belong to the large categories of problems and predicaments common to all his characters: the pursuit of matrimony (Bingo Little and the Mulliner nephews), the pursuit of undeserved leisure and success (Ukridge and Psmith), the escape from matrimony, success, and authority into a state of infinite adolescence (Bertie, Rocky Todd, "Old Sippy" Sipperley, etc.), and such general matters as those involving the precariousness of living off one's rich relatives and the various social embarrassments created by the class structure. All these are treated, of course, as burlesques by Wodehouse, but they are burlesques of genuinely human predicaments. The situations they take off are classic both in life and in literature. And in the same sense that the *Decameron* may be said to be a burlesque of conjugal love and *Moll Flanders* of the hypocritical pursuit of moral virtue, Wodehouse's work may be said to be genuine comic literature, less fully and seriously conceived than these, to be sure, but differing from them more in degree than in kind. This is not to suggest, however, that Wodehouse is the social critic or satirist he is so often taken to be, particularly in this country where we tend to mistake almost any comic portrait of the English aristocracy for ridicule. There is nothing in his work to indicate that Wodehouse's attitude is anything but fondly indulgent toward the society he describes. No other attitude could possibly account for the real warmth at the heart of all that he has done, or for his remarkably long life as a popular writer in an age when to be both popular and funny is nearly always synonymous with being in some way petty and cheap.

[1958]

Index

DATE DUE